HOO1!

A Twenty-Five-Year History of the

≡ Greenwich Village ≡
Music Scene

by

ROBBIE WOLIVER

St. Martin's Press
New York

Grateful acknowledgment is made to Straight Arrow
Publishers, Inc. for permission to reprint an excerpt
from the Kurt Loder interview with Bob Dylan by
Kurt Loder from *Rolling Stone*, June 21, 1984.
Copyright © 1984 by Straight Arrow Publishers, Inc.
All rights reserved. Reprinted by permission.

Library of Congress Cataloging-in-Publication Data

Woliver, Robbie.
Hoot! / Robbie Woliver.
p.   cm.
ISBN 0-312-10995-4
1. Popular music—New York (N.Y.)—History and criticism.
2. Folk music—New York (N.Y.)—History and criticism.
3. Greenwich Village (New York, N.Y.)—Popular culture.
I. Title.
ML3477.8.N48W65   1994
781.64'09747'1—dc20   94-20   CIP   MN

First published in the United States as *Bringing It All Back Home* by Pantheon Books

10 9 8 7 6 5 4 3 2 1

This book is dedicated to my family—
my father, Irving, who influenced me to be a writer;
my mother, Shirley, who taught me that we can achieve anything;
my sister, Sheri, whose encouragement comes from her fear of having
to support me; and my wife, Marilyn Lash, who does support
me in every way.

CONTENTS

AUTHOR'S NOTE

. . . .

. . . . *The first voice I recall singing popular music was the magnificent, colorfully textured voice of Odetta. As a child I would sit in front of my parents' record player, staring at Odetta's photograph on the album cover. I was mesmerized by her unique look and sound. I was in love with music because of her, and this was my introduction to folk music.*

My infatuation with Odetta led to exploration of my parents' other albums—Paul Robeson, Josh White, Leadbelly, Woody Guthrie, Pete Seeger, Marais and Miranda, and even the Red Army Chorus. I listened to Indian, African, Israeli, Russian, and Caribbean voodoo (I was afraid of that one) music. Soon all of that music blended in with my parents' politics—a little left of extreme left. Stories of the Rosenbergs, SANE, civil-rights marches, and the Lincoln Brigade formed my ideas and conscience. Whether it was my father telling me about his experience at the Paul Robeson concert at Peekskill or my mother teaching me old union songs, I began to form an impression of the important tie between the life of a people and their music.

I was discovering what the American people and people all over the world were creating—music that described their needs, aspirations, and lives. Through this music I learned about trade unions, farmers, politics, foreign cultures, love, and just about everything else that touches the human experience. I never learned that much in school.

When I was a teenager, I bought my first album. It was Peter, Paul, and Mary's debut album. I was continuing the folk process. I watched Hootenanny every week until I learned there was a boycott against it because it was blacklisting Pete Seeger; I came to Greenwich Village on weekends; I got arrested at antiwar demonstrations; and my record collection grew. Joan Baez, Bob Dylan, Donovan, Judy Collins, Eric Andersen, Odetta, Tom Paxton, were the artists I listened to. Soon I realized that these artists could talk about my experiences, and that there were more—Joni Mitchell, Tim Hardin, Buffy Ste. Marie, Phil Ochs, the Youngbloods, and the Lovin' Spoonful.

Although during the course of time the general public's engagement with folk music changed, mine never did. To me, folk music was always the voice of the people, whether it was accompanied by a guitar, a heavy metal band, or a beat box. If some kid learns how to play a Talking Heads song on his guitar, that is the true folk process.

My tastes broadened and I became even more involved with music. I began to write songs, and through my representative at ASCAP, Eden Cross, I met Leslie Berman, who was looking for someone to help her organize a songwriters' coffee-house with proceeds from the Phil Ochs Memorial Fund. I jumped at the chance. I thought it an honor to be associated with a project keeping Phil's memory alive.

Through a little luck and a lot of wangling ("Mr. Porco, you'll make a fortune") we ended up presenting a weekly Sunday-afternoon songwriters' showcase at the legendary Folk City. Equally unforeseen was the day, a year later, when Folk City's owner, Mike Porco, came up to me and said, " 'Ey, Bobby, how would you like to buy this place?" How could I say no? I immediately called my only friend who had money, Joe Hillesum (I swear I'll pay you back), and tried to tempt him away from his job as a social-work supervisor. Marilyn Lash had just graduated from college and she gave up her social-work aspirations. The three of us undertook an overwhelming job: On May 12, 1980, we bought and began to revitalize the venerable institution called Gerdes Folk City. Marilyn and I were married a few months later and had our reception in the club. At the reception I was able to introduce my parents to my friend Odetta.

For the past five years, Joe, Marilyn, and I have been running the club in what we hope is an exciting, eclectic, and innovative way. We still honor the club's traditions and we try to create some of our own. It's been a lot of hard work and, yes, Joe sometimes yearns to escape and become a social worker again, but it has been an incredible experience crowned by the Twenty-Fifth Anniversary Concert presented on September 14, 1985, at New York City's outdoor Pier 84. The beyond-capacity audience of over eight thousand was treated to performances by Eric Andersen, Frank Christian, the Violent Femmes, Ferron, Arlo Guthrie, Richie Havens, Roger McGuinn, Melanie, Odetta, Tom Paxton, the Roches, Tom Rush, Libby Titus and Dr. John, Suzanne Vega, Peter Yarrow, Joan Baez, and newcomers David Massengill, Lili Anel, Lucy Kaplanski, and Tom Intondi.

Mayor Edward I. Koch opened the show and the City of New York proclaimed September 1985 as Folk City Festival Month. Peter Yarrow paid a tribute to Mike Porco, and generations covering twenty-five years closed the show singing together. That night was followed by other anniversary concerts featuring such disparate acts as David Johansen, Marshall Crenshaw, the Beau Brummels, Lenny Kaye, Ann Magnuson, Peter Stampfel, and George Gerdes.

It was an honor to be a part of the culmination of twenty-five years of American music, and it was an equal honor trying to chronicle those years by speaking to the artists interviewed in this book. Their voices helped shape my life. Whether it was spending an afternoon talking to Joan Baez in the Plaza Hotel, meeting with Bob Dylan and Mike Porco in a TV studio dressing room, having an animated conversation with Joey Ramone, talking to Billy Joel one week after "We Are the World" was recorded, having Kurtis Blow relate his life in rap, or watching Emmylou Harris wistfully remember old Village friends while fans were trying to get her autograph—it has all been a heady and moving experience.

I know as I write this that some kid is sitting in front of a stereo staring at Suzanne Vega's album cover lost in her music, the way I was with Odetta. The voices of all the people in this book shaped our lives in some way. Here's their story, how they helped create a rich, creative, socially aware time in a little nightclub that could barely hold two hundred.

And Odetta, thanks for singing at my wedding.

Writing and researching a book of this magnitude is a massive task. I would not have been able to complete it in the time that I had without the support of many people.

Thank you for the interviews—Dave Alvin, David Amram, Eric Andersen, Hoyt Axton, Joan Baez, Lillian Bailey, Paula Ballan, Louie Bass, Roger Becket, Wendy Becket, Carol Belsky, Leslie Berman, Kurtis Blow, David Blue, Nesya Blue, Anne Bowen, Oscar Brand, Andy Breckman, Marshall Brickman, David Bromberg, Jane Brucker, Paul Butterfield, Dominick Chianese, Charlie Chin, Frank Christian, Judy Collins, Bernadette Contreras, Barbara Dane, Victor DeLorenzo, Gerry Devine, Pat DiNizio, Judy Dlugascz, Alix Dobkin, Peggy Duncan, Marc Eliot, Liz Elkind, Ramblin' Jack Elliott, Larry Ellis, José Feliciano, Ferron, Lorraine Flood, Ellen Foley, Steve Forbert, Erik Frandsen, Rick Frank, Gordon Gano, Herb Gart, Bob Gibson, Allen Ginsberg, Virginia Giordano, Cynthia Gooding, Wavy Gravy, Arlo Guthrie, John Hammond, Jr., John Hammond, Sr., Emmylou Harris, Jerry Harrison, Tim Hauser, Richie Havens, John Herald, Carolyn Hester, Michael Hill, Stephen Holden, John Lee Hooker, Dorene Internicola, Tom Intondi, Jake Jacobs, Jam Master Jay, Billy Joel, David Johansen, Danny Kalb, Ira Kaplan, Lenny Kaye, Fred Kirby, Barry Kornfeld, Marilyn Lash, Harold Leventhal, Buzzy Linhart, Mary Little, Phyllis Lynd, Ed McCurdy, Brownie McGhee, Roger McGuinn, Ellen McIlwaine, Tommy Makem, Steve Mandell, Michael Mann, Vince Martin, Randy Mastronicola, Frank Maya, Ira Mayer, Matt Molloy, Jim Morris, Roland Mousaa, Maria Muldaur, Tracy Nelson, Ralf Nemec, Bobbie Newman, Wendy Newton, Willie Nile, Sonny Ochs, Michael Ochs, Odetta, Tom Pacheco, Tom Pasle, Audrey Pavia, Tom Paxton, Allan Pepper, John Phillips, Poez, Elizabeth Pomada, Mike Porco, J. L. Praeger, Earl Price, Joey Ramone, Brian Ritchie, Jean Ritchie, Suzzy Roche, Terry Roche, Len Rosenfeld, Rosie, Robert Ross, Charlie Rothschild, Susan Rotolo, Buffy Ste. Marie, Lynn Samuels,

Fred Schneider, John Sebastian, Pete Seeger, Robert Shelton, Sam Sherer, Barbara Shutner, Janis Siegel, Irwin Silber, Carly Simon, Lucy Simon, Penny Simon, Pat Sky, Larry Sloman, Betty Smyth, Patty Smyth, Stanley Snadowsky, Phoebe Snow, Jacob Solomon, Linda Solomon, Peter Stampfel, John Stewart, Geoffrey Stokes, Terri Thal, Libby Titus, Peter Tork, Happy Traum, Mary Travers, Dave Van Ronk, Suzanne Vega, Loudon Wainwright, Sammy Walker, Jim Wann, Ilene Weiss, Eric Weissberg, Hedy West, David Wilkes, Wendy Winsted, Jim Wynbrandt, Peter Yarrow, Doug Yeager, Izzy Young, Jesse Colin Young, and Susie Young.

Thank you for the photos, artwork, and memorabilia—Mary Alfieri, Len Kunstadt, Susan Rotolo, Barbara Shutner, Linda Solomon, and Irene Young.

Special thanks go to Jackie Alper for being so generous with Joe Alper's brilliant photographs, to Sonny Ochs for getting out of your deathbed and trekking around in snowdrifts to get me those photographs, and to Paula Ballan and Linda Solomon, whose help and knowledge was much appreciated.

For help in facilitating interviews, thank you to: Gail Gelman and Nancy Lutzow for helping me to coordinate time with Joan Baez; Charlie Rothschild for doing the same with Judy Collins; Phil Kaufman for help with Emmylou Harris; Barbara Bellone for Billy Joel; Vicki for Carly Simon; Andrea Starr for Jerry Harrison, Joey Ramone, and Fred Schneider; Bill Adler for Kurtis Blow and Run-D.M.C.; and Geoff Blumenauer for Buzzy Linhart.

Thank you Pat DiNizio and Leslie Berman for the three interviews you conducted for me. Another thank you to Leslie for introducing me to Folk City. I forgive you for the interview you screwed up.

Lenny Kaye, thanks for all your answers; Harold and Eileen Lash, I appreciate all your support (and the pool); thanks to Nancy Shayne, Susie Schneider, and Sharon Breslau, three talented performers who helped me with typing in their spare time; Randy Mastronicola, thank you for the research. Sorry you smashed your head on the microfilm machine.

Many thanks to Bill Strachan for introducing this project to my editor Wendy Goldwyn. Thank you Tim McGinnis for your editing skills.

Michael Lesser, you have my deep gratitude for all your help, our friendship, and your lawyership.

Deep appreciation goes to Peter Bengtson for retrieving all my erased files and all the other immeasurable help. No matter how hard you try to fight it—you're a great guy.

Beyond-the-call-of-duty thanks goes to Bernadette Contreras, who selflessly gave up her own creative time to assist me with this project. I can't begin to tell you how much you've helped me. I hope your play Sons and Daughters sweeps the Tonys.

Dorene Internicola, thanks for enduring the late-night torture and thanks for stripping my book of all its "glories." Thank God I don't have to listen anymore *to you singing every folk song that you came across while copyediting the manuscript.*

Joe Hillesum, thank you so much for supporting me in this project and passing over my absence from the club. I swear, someday you'll be glad you put all your money into the place.

A very special thank you to Wendy Goldwyn for your faith, enthusiasm, and support. I can't begin to express how impressed I was by your skills, intelligence, and sensitivity. It was a true pleasure working with you.

Marilyn, your faith and all your hard work transcribing, dictating, organizing, and putting up with my grunting every time the word processor screwed up made this much easier for me. I love you.

My warmest acknowledgment goes to Mike Porco—I hope you're happy with this book. You would have been moved by the love everyone expressed for you during the course of my interviews.

And, of course, thank you to all the performers who played the club over the past twenty-five years, employees who put up with strange working conditions, and the patrons who kept the club alive all this years.

I apologize to those performers who were not mentioned in the book but were a part of this history. There was just so little time and space. I hope those I did cover will speak for all of you.

THE
VILLAGE · IN
THE · CITY

Greenwich Village, the town within the city, dates back to an Algonquin Indian settlement called Sapokanickan. The Dutch arrived in 1626, named the territory Bossen Bouwerie (Farm in the Woods), and developed it as a large tobacco plantation. When the British captured Nieuw Amsterdam in 1664, the plantation was purchased by Naval Squadron Commander Sir Peter Warren, who renamed it Greenwich. The settlement became a small town, a northern suburb for the first New Yorkers to escape to after a disastrous fire destroyed the town at the tip of Manhattan Island.

As the Village grew, streets replaced twisting cowpaths and meandering brooks. One stream, Minetta Brook, still flows beneath the block on which the present-day Folk City stands.

In the nineteenth century the Village attracted writers and artists: O. Henry, Mark Twain, Edgar Allan Poe, Henry James, Stephen Crane, Winslow Homer, Edith Wharton, and Augustus Saint-Gaudens. Rents were low in this little Bohemia. In the twentieth century, F. Scott Fitzgerald remembered following Edmund Wilson, his ultra-citified friend from Princeton, through the city and marveling at the streets outside Wilson's Village apartment. The Village continually renewed its charm through a series of cultural invasions of playwrights, socialists, jazz musicians, and Italian and Irish immigrants. In the fifties, one could glimpse Thelonious Monk on his way to a rehearsal at the Five Spot or Lenny Bruce hanging out in front of the Cafe Society Downtown.

For the musicians of the late fifties and early sixties, the chief attraction was Washington Square Park, once the site of a potters' field, as well as dueling grounds and space for public executions. In 1824, the Marquis de Lafayette was the honored guest at the hanging of some twenty highwaymen. In 1831, the grounds became the unofficial campus of the University of the City of New York— now New York University. In 1881 Henry James wrote his novel Washington Square in number 18, across the street. Into this public park, once the site of hangings, grand picnics, and military parades, came the latest brand of musi-

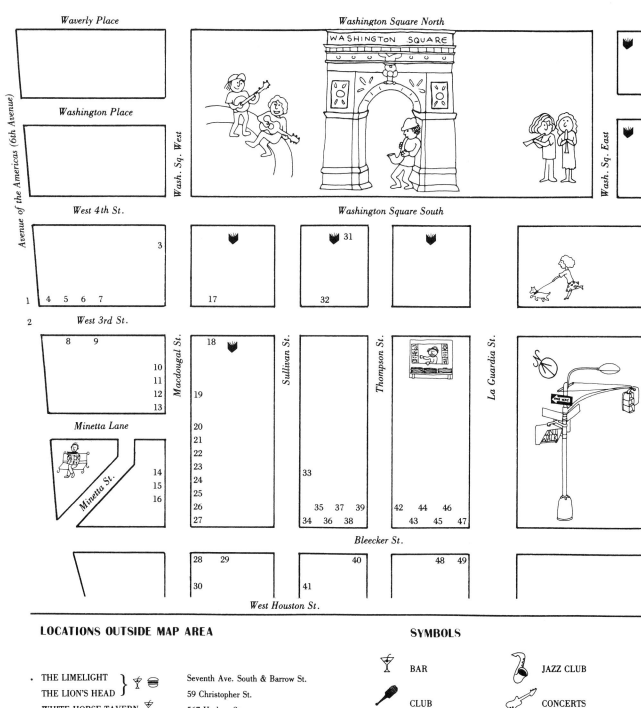

Waverly Place

Washington Square North

WASHINGTON SQUARE

Washington Place

Avenue of the Americas (6th Avenue)

Wash. Sq. West

Wash. Sq. East

West 4th St.

Washington Square South

3

31

1   4   5   6   7

17

32

2

West 3rd St.

8   9

18

Macdougal St.

Sullivan St.

Thompson St.

La Guardia St.

10
11
12
13

19

Minetta Lane

20
21
22
23
24
25
26
27

33

35   37   39

42   44   46

34   36   38

43   45   47

Minetta St.

14
15
16

Bleecker St.

28   29

40

48   49

30

41

West Houston St.

LOCATIONS OUTSIDE MAP AREA

THE LIMELIGHT	Seventh Ave. South & Barrow St.
THE LION'S HEAD	59 Christopher St.
WHITE HORSE TAVERN	567 Hudson St.
VILLAGE VANGUARD	178 7th Ave. South
CIRCLE IN THE SQUARE	7th Ave. South & Grove St.
TRUDE HELLER'S	6th Ave. & 9th St.
MAX'S KANSAS CITY	Park Ave. South between 17th and 18th St.
CBGB'S	315 Bowery
GERDES FOLK CITY	moving to a new location, summer 1986

SYMBOLS

BAR	JAZZ CLUB
CLUB	CONCERTS
STRIP JOINT	MOVIE HOUSE
BASKETHOUSE	NYU
COFFEEHOUSE	PIANO BAR

Waverly Place

Washington Place

Mercer St.

50   51

West 4th St.

52

Broadway

West 3rd St.

53

 RESTAURANT

 THEATRE

A B C   Denotes chronological
          order of occupant at location

•   No longer exists

*   Original location

LEGEND

1		WAVERLY THEATRE
2	.	FOLKLORE CENTER
3		PROVINCETOWN PLAYHOUSE
4	.	PURPLE ONION
5	A .	SAMURAI
	B .	FOUR WINDS
6	A .	JEWEL BOX
	B .	HEAT WAVE
	C	BLUE NOTE
7	A .	ELYSEE
	B .	CYCLOPS
	C .	ZIG ZAG
8	A .	TONY PASTOR'S
	B	GERDES FOLK CITY
9	.	NITE OWL
10		CAFE REGGIO
11	.	PLAYERS THEATRE
12	.	THE UNDERGROUND
13	.	CAFE WHA?
14	.	RIENZI
15	.	FAT BLACK PUSSYCAT
16	.	ALI BABA
17	A .	THIRD SIDE
	B .	PEACE CENTER
18	A	AARON BURR'S COACH HOUSE
	B .	CAFE BIZARRE
19		LOUISA MAY ALCOTT HOUSE
20	A .	THE WHY NOT
	B .	FREUDIAN SLIP
21	.	THE BUTTON STORE
22	.	THE BASEMENT
23	*	FOLKLORE CENTER
24	.	THE GASLIGHT
25	.	KETTLE OF FISH
26	.	THE ID
27		CAFE BORGIA

28		CAFE FIGARO
29	A *	CAFE FLAMENCO
	B .	RENAISSANCE
30	.	HIP BAGEL
31		JUDSON MEMORIAL CHURCH
32		EDGAR ALLAN POE HOUSE
33		GOOGIE'S
34		MILLS TAVERN
35	.	CAFE FLAMENCO
36	.	NOBODY'S
37	*	CIRCLE IN THE SQUARE THEATRE
38		KENNY'S CASTAWAYS
39		BACK FENCE
40		VILLAGE GATE
41		SULLIVAN STREET THEATRE (THE FANTASTICKS)
42	.	THE DELI BOX
43	.	SURF MAID
44	.	THE OTHER END
45		THE BITTER END
46	.	TIN ANGEL
47	A .	PINK FLAMINGO
	B .	THE DUGOUT
	C	PREACHER'S
48	A .	CAFE AU GO GO
	B .	GASLIGHT/AU GO GO
49		BLEECKER STREET CINEMA
50		THE BOTTOM LINE
51	A .	**THE FIFTH PEG**
	B	**GERDES FOLK CITY**
52	*	**GERDES RESTAURANT**
53	A	BROADWAY CENTRAL HOTEL
	B	MERCER ARTS CENTER
	C	NYU LAW SCHOOL DORMITORY

MAP AND DRAWINGS BY SUSAN ROTOLO

cian—the urban folksinger. To the locals, the influx of Beatniks and guitar players meant that their paradise of the past twenty years was about to be lost again. The newcomers signaled weird politics, drugs, and sexual freedom that hadn't been seen in these quaint tree-lined streets since the wide-open twenties.

The Beats turned neighborhood cafes into smoky dens of jazz, folk, and poetry. Jack Kerouac with On the Road *and Allen Ginsberg with* Howl *defined and changed their generations. Berets, the official headgear of the French existentialists, came back in style. Washington Square Park was where all these influences converged.*

A few years earlier, in 1952, a Calabrian immigrant, Mike Porco, had bought a restaurant on West Fourth Street and Mercer. Porco's place became popular, filling with local factory workers who came for the cheap drinks and the good Italian food. Porco, an amiable, self-effacing businessman, fit in comfortably with the Village's large Italian-American working-class community. Porco's place took a few strange turns in the next few years. It was a fluky yet almost predictable evolution. Mike acted on hunches and gut feelings, with one eye cocked toward the rent and license fees. But he could hardly have imagined the impact his simple bar and restaurant would have on the course of American culture.

Down the street, a young, bookish folk-music devotee, Israel (Izzy) G. Young, ran the Folklore Center, an important musical and social center for the "other" Village constituency. It was not long before Izzy and a friend decided that folk music needed a place, a legitimate club, for a professional forum.

These three diverse elements—the quaint Italian neighborhood, the blue-collar bar, and an intellectual entrepreneur—came together to create Gerdes Folk City and the extraordinary music scene that came from its heart. This simple club rather quickly became a main character in the story of popular culture over the past twenty-five years, a phenomenon motivating and defining generations of folk and blues artists, poets, rockers, superstars, and assorted odd characters.

The characters—some talkative, immediately ready to witticize their past; others retiring, uncomfortable with their fleeting pass through fame—all remember the historic moments, the frustrations, the triumphs and the wonderful music they were all a part of.

IN THE
NEW · BOHEMIA

· ·

In 1952, Stevenson was buried in the Eisenhower landslide and the Republicans recaptured the White House. Sid Caesar's Your Show of Shows ruled the airwaves on Saturday nights. Albert Schweitzer was awarded the Nobel Peace Prize and it was the year of Eva Peron's death. B. B. King was performing in Memphis and Charlie Parker was playing the heart of the New York jazz scene, Fifty-Second Street. The Brooklyn Dodgers and the New York Yankees ruled baseball.

In 1952, William Gerdes sold his restaurant on West Third Street to three Italian immigrants. Mike Porco, his brother John, and their cousin Joe Bastone were now the owners of the neighborhood hangout at 11 West Third, where they remained for about four years, until the city ordered that the run-down buildings make way for a couple of highrises. The now fairly popular restaurant, still called Gerdes, moved to 11 West Fourth Street, on the corner of Mercer, where it stayed under Mike and John's management until 1969.

Gerdes was about two thousand square feet, with a bar and a dining room separated by a partition. The building was located in a factory area—dark at night and off limits to middle-class people and even to NYU students just two blocks west. The extended Porco family worked there—sons, brothers, cousins, wives, and girlfriends.

The unassuming Porcos were agreeable restaurant hosts. They sat around with their customers, trading off-color jokes while retaining their trademark aura of gentility. They charmed neighborhood women with their Old-World manners and broken, very broken, English. Mike even knew when pretending complete inadequacy in English would serve his best business interests.

DAVE VAN RONK: Mike was very evasive about business. Every once in a while, someone would put pressure on him for something that would cost money. He immediately brought out these mysterious partners of his that no one had ever seen, who would quash any idea that might cost Mike a few cents. It was also

John Porco (Marilyn Lash)

Mike Porco (Marilyn Lash)

very delightful to watch his English deteriorate when the bargaining got hot. When things were going well, that man could speak English like Churchill.

The Gerdes "family" was gentle with children, tough with troublemakers, businesslike with employees, generous to people in bad times, and always prepared to make a swift business deal. They were successful American businessmen, fully entrenched in the American Dream. They even had a restaurant near Yankee Stadium to fall back on, if the need arose.

Gradually the Porcos brought live incidental music into Gerdes, hiring background musicians, who might even play a favorite old Italian tune for Mike and John. With this, they unwittingly began to turn a local blue-collar bar into a cultural institution.

Mike Porco came to the United States from Italy when he was eighteen. His father died during the trip, so Mike's uncle took him in, treating him as if he were his own son. Though a carpenter by trade, Mike offered to wash dishes in the family restaurant to help support himself, but was immediately rebuffed. Theirs was a tight family, and they did not want him washing dishes. But they were ready to train him in the restaurant business.

MIKE PORCO: I bought Gerdes Restaurant from William Gerdes, who was one of the nicest gentlemen you ever met. He was about eighty-one when we bought it from him. We stayed there something like four years. Business was good until we moved out of there to 11 West Fourth Street.

We used to make a good living with the restaurant on Fourth Street. We'd open at eight in the morning and close at eight at night. Sometimes I even stayed a little later. A couple of people might come in late for a beer, or if I had a customer I figured as long as I had company, I'd stay.

Then the city tore down the nearby buildings. They demolished nine square blocks. Most of it was factories. They lost us all our customers. I was looking around for something to do so we wouldn't have to close.

I thought, maybe it would help business if I put in a piano player. Then I put in a trio for a few days. I used to pay them ten dollars each for about two or three hours' work. But it didn't pick up enough. I knew I would have to try something different.

Elvis Presley entered the Army in late 1957, and if that didn't make the world feel a little safer, perhaps the death of the notorious Joe McCarthy did. Albert Camus won the Nobel Prize for literature, and Buddy Holly and the Crickets were pleasing the public on a less intellectual level. A former black prizefighter named Berry Gordy quit his job on the Ford assembly line to begin writing songs for local

*Detroit singers, creating what would come to be known as the "Motown sound."
In Liverpool, England, another influential sound was in its formative years: George
Harrison, a fifteen-year-old Teddy boy, joined a skiffle-turned-rock band called
the Quarrymen. He and his bandmates, John Lennon and Paul McCartney, were
greatly influenced by American R&B.*

*The late fifties brought us such classics as "The Purple People Eater" and "The
Chipmunk Song," and the cha-cha was the dance craze. Records were suddenly
becoming stereophonic. A folk song, "Tom Dooley," became a chart-topper.*

*In 1960, John F. Kennedy narrowly beat Richard Nixon in the presidential
election and became one of the nation's most popular presidents. Berry Gordy's
Motown label started spewing out hits. The Cold War went into overdrive with the
U-2 incident. On Friday nights a young actor named Clint Eastwood was introduced to the American public on a TV series called* Rawhide. *"Itsy Bitsy Teeny
Weeny Yellow Polka Dot Bikini" is one of the most popular songs of the first year
of one of the most socially and politically conscious decades in our history.*

*The Eisenhower years of the late fifties spawned another literary generation,
an echo of the Lost Generation of the twenties. This time, though, the experience
of Paris was savored on the crowded streets of MacDougal, Bleecker and West
Fourth. The Beats occupied the Village, taking control of the local cafes. Kerouac
introduced poetry to jazz in the Circle-in-the-Square Theater. He got drunk on
Thunderbird and read his work at the Village Vanguard. Coffee shops opened,
and pot smoke and poetry wafted out the dark doorways. At the Cedar Tavern
painters like Larry Rivers and Robert Rauschenberg hung out with poets of what
is now called the New York School—Frank O'Hara, Kenneth Koch, John Ashbery,
Ted Berrigan.*

*Artistic expression in the Village was becoming legitimized by indoor venues.
The Sunday-afternoon hootenannies in Washington Square gave way to formal
concerts. Hanging out was evolving into a fine art. The media gave wide coverage
(most of it negative) to the new Village Philosophy.*

MARIA MULDAUR: The population of Greenwich Village was not nearly as large
as it is now. It was probably the pleasantest place in all of Manhattan to live,
because everything was on a very human scale. It was the city, and a very kind
of busy and culturally intense part of the city, but the streets weren't so crowded.

When the word *Beatnik* got coined in 1958 and droves of people started coming
from the Bronx, that's when the Village developed its Boardwalk-like atmosphere.

When I was a kid I'd go to Washington Square Park and play in the fountain.
The fountain in the middle of Washington Square Park was for children to play
in and not a place where people dealt drugs like it is now. Besides this sort of
artists' community, there were little mini-neighborhoods within Greenwich Village which featured various ethnic groups, like the Italian enclave around Bleecker,

Thompson, Sullivan, and MacDougal streets. There was a more Irish section over by Perry and Charles streets. Up toward Fourteenth Street it was more Spanish and Puerto Rican. It was just a beautiful mixture of people.

Each generation of alternative culture drew the next. Bohemians weren't really blowing their own trumpet. They were happy to be off in their relatively quiet neighborhood pursuing their art and having the freedom to live slightly alternative lifestyles whether that meant living together without being married or whatever. Beatniks had post-atomic angst. Instead of artists being drawn to write and paint and sing about all the joy and beauty in the world, a lot of them got rather bummed out. So it was a sort of negative new-wave artistic expression.

OSCAR BRAND: Around 1945, Pete Seeger came to me and asked if I would help him. He was living in a little house next to the Provincetown Playhouse on MacDougal Street. I had been an editor before and he asked me if I'd like to work with him on a new idea he had. He wanted to put out a magazine in which we'd put out the new songs which we were writing, rather than depending on the old collections of antique songs that everyone seemed to be depending on.

I said all right, and I began working on the first issue of what became *People's Songs*, a bulletin concerned with promoting progressive causes through music. This was around 1946. I wasn't crazy about all the songs and I asked to be taken off the board. By this time, they had also become a booking group, called People's Artists.

At this time, the people that were hanging around the Village included Cisco Houston, Leadbelly, Josh White, Will Geer, and Woody Guthrie. It was a free, easy attitude. Coffeehouses started to be formed, but nobody sang in them. The atmosphere was very warm, and the fact that Pete had a house there where we could all meet was very important.

Harry Belafonte was singing jazz; Sammy Levenson was still a teacher; Jack Gilford was doing stand-up comedy routines. There were so many people around. Mrs. Roosevelt had a place south of Washington Square Park, so we would meet at her house for political rallies. That was also a center. Everything revolved around the Village.

The Weavers had just gotten together and were learning their trade. They got together in Pete's basement and they were called the No Name Quartet. Then one day they decided they would be called the Weavers.

RICHIE HAVENS: I discovered the Village in the newspapers with a friend of mine. There was an article in the Sunday section on the poetry and Beatniks in the Village. So we went over to the Village because we wrote poetry and we thought maybe we could fit in there somewhere, because we sure didn't fit into Bedford-Stuy writing poetry. I was about nineteen and this was in 1958.

Woody Guthrie, Jackie (Gibson) Alper, Cisco Houston (Collection of Joe Alper)

I spent about a year and a half going back and forth, reading poetry and listening to poetry and traditional folk music. They also had a lot of improvisational mime going on then. I was really lucky, I just caught the tail end of that.

There were a lot of poetry clubs. Ferlinghetti and Jack Kerouac used to read. They were all coffeehouses back then—no liquor. Allen Ginsberg and Ted Jones—people like that used to read. It was a nice time. The music was traditional folk music. That scene started to die around 1960. The poets were more or less leaving town. The artists were leaving town, so you were left more or less with the commercial artists who did portraits on the street. Movies were made that told the Beatnik story in very weird, strange ways. Right after that, the Village had about five or six years of the most incredible assault of tourists, and it was great.

DAVE VAN RONK: The whole Beatnik thing had become a mass-media preoccupation. The Beatniks *hated* folk music. The real Beats liked cool jazz, beebop, and hard drugs, and the folkniks would sit around on the floor and sing songs of the oppressed masses.

When a folk singer would take the stage between two Beat poets, all the finger-poppin' mamas and daddies would do everything but hold their noses. And when the Beat poet would get up and begin to rant, all the folk fans in the house would do likewise. But in the eye of the media, folk music and Beatniks were

The Weavers at Carnegie Hall Reunion, 1963 (Joe Alper)

one and the same. So a lot of people came to the Village to see the Beatniks and they ended up seeing folk music.

RICHIE HAVENS: There were a few restaurants that had bus tours and if you ate there they'd ride you around the Village. And it got to the point where even the Beatniks themselves, or so-called Beatniks, would stand on the side of the street and when the buses would go by they'd point at the tourists. It became a game.

CHARLIE CHIN: I was born and raised in New York City. I was living in Queens and I started drifting down to the Village while I was in high school. In those days, the heavy thing was jazz and poetry. There was a lot of poetry in Greenwich Village. I decided I'd graduate and come to Greenwich Village and be a Beatnik. Unfortunately, it was 1962 by the time I got there, and most of the Beatniks had already left for San Francisco. But there was a big scene going on, anyway.

As time progressed, more and more of these folk musicians started to take over from the Beat poets. Some were doing very esoteric Anglo ballads or flamenco guitar. There wasn't a specific popular folk music then. Most of the people were academicians or musicologists. They enjoyed playing. It was split up between them and old-time lefties from the thirties who were into Pete Seeger and union stuff. There wasn't any kind of counterculture, really. It was just turning away from what was popular at the time like Tin Pan Alley.

Being "hip" meant being partly an egghead. Wandering around with a Penguin edition in your hip pocket and being knowledgeable about Sartre and existentialism. Going to rent parties in Greenwich Village, drinking cheap wine, and personally knowing a woman who was a dancer. They were interesting days.

MARIA MULDAUR: Instead of artists celebrating life, a lot of them got in a more kind of cynical nihilistic what's-the-use-we're-all-gonna-blow-up-anyway state of mind. After Kerouac's *On the Road*, the Beatniks started blowing their own horns, and it started attracting a lot of people from the other boroughs who were closet renegades anyway. These were the public Beatniks. They started having poetry readings and bongo drums and this spilled into Washington Square Park. A lot of people from other neighborhoods were attracted by the promise of "free love." This was around '58.

The neighborhood became a place where people flocked because they heard that Beatnik chicks put out easy. Also, dope began to be an attractive social factor—mostly marijuana. There were a lot of wild parties involving bongos, jazz, poetry readings, loose women, horny men, and lots of cheap Italian wine usually drunk out of one of those wineskins; and the surreptitious passing around of a few joints. The Beatnik clubs which had poetry readings and bongo drums were now turning into folk clubs.

Whether the young kid was Mary Travers growing up in the forties just blocks away from Folk City's future sites or the writer and filmmaker Marshall Brickman visiting from Brooklyn in the fifties, the Village was an intoxicating blend of the Old World and the new Bohemia.

MARSHALL BRICKMAN: The Village had a lot of character. We'd go in on Sunday and we'd play and then we'd go to a little pizza place where you could order a Coke special. That was a Coca-Cola bottle filled with red wine with a straw in it. That was during the height of decadence and sophistication. I guess we were fourteen then.

ERIC WEISSBERG: I went to school at the Little Red Schoolhouse in the Village. Our music teacher was Charity Bailey. We learned folk songs from all around the world. So I was exposed to folk music at a very early age.

To raise extra money on Saturday mornings, Pete Seeger, who used to live on MacDougal Street, ran a "wing-ding" for kids under twelve. He, Cisco Houston, Woody Guthrie, and Leadbelly would just sit around and sing to us, and we'd sing along and they'd tell us stories. It was a real children's kind of thing. It was an unbelievable experience then, and it's even more unbelievable to think about now.

MARSHALL BRICKMAN: Going to the Village was the thing to do. Nowadays, kids go to the mall, but we used to go down to the Village. The food was better, the environment was a little more stimulating, and the crosscurrents were a little more interesting. It was an adolescent kind of endeavor, but it also had an overlay of something a little more worthwhile, because we were singing and we were playing. A lot of us were trying to be excellent and were succeeding at what we did.

VINCE MARTIN: The Village was very different in the early sixties. When Lorraine Hansberry, the black woman who wrote *Raisin in the Sun*, her husband Bob— a white Jew—and I used to walk in the Village, Sidney Poitier came along as her beard, as her cover. In those days the Village wasn't so liberal. You had problems if you were an interracial couple then.

MARY TRAVERS: I grew up in Greenwich Village, and it was the most wonderful experience. I moved into the Village in 1938 when I was about two. The Village then was about eighty-five percent Italian and the rest were artists, Bohemians, and counterculturists. It was a good balance. Italians have a tendency, from a cultural position, to view artists as sort of benign idiots blessed by God. Their idiosyncratic behavior was of no particular threat to them as long as the artists were in the minority.

It was a very community-oriented neighborhood. People sat on stoops and watched out for other people's children. There were real traditional Italian folk musicians wandering in the park playing Italian folk music.

It was a terribly safe neighborhood to grow up in. When I got to about high-school age, there was a tremendous cultural explosion in the Village of rural American folk music being sung in Washington Square Park. Banjo players from as far as New Jersey would come and sing in the park, along with fiddlers and guitar players and devotees of Woody Guthrie, if not Woody Guthrie himself.

MARSHALL BRICKMAN: The Village was a very fertile atmosphere—just the coffeehouses and the social intercourse and the sexual intercourse. All kinds of intercourse were going on. It was a marketplace, in the best sense.

There were so many creative, interesting people around at that time. Those people later moved on to different careers, or persisted at what they were doing and eventually excelled. Joan Rivers was in a comedy-music trio called Jim, Jake, and Joan. Richard Pryor, Lenny Bruce, and Bill Cosby all learned their craft on the Village stages. I met Woody Allen when he was working at the Bitter End. The Simon Sisters—Lucy and Carly—made the rounds of the Village clubs. From what I recall, they were singing mostly ballads in a maidenlike presentation—totally unlike what they ended up doing.

ERIC WEISSBERG: Before 1959, when I'd walk around the streets carrying my guitar, people would call me Elvis—it was that uncommon to see someone with a guitar. People started picking up the guitar, because it wasn't too difficult to play. It was difficult to play *well*, but anybody could just *play* it.

Washington Square Park was the meeting place for the folk musicians of the late fifties and early sixties. A melting pot of musical personalities and styles, the park came to symbolize what folk music was all about. It was the place where traditions were learned and passed around, where new traditions were created. It was the place where old friends met once a week, new friends were made, and friends of friends were brought together. The local Italian residents brought their children to the park to play, spent the day with friends, and played their own folk songs. Important musical alliances were sealed in the park on Sunday afternoons.

PAULA BALLAN: I picked up bluegrass in the park. It was so easy. If you knew six chords you could play nine hundred songs. If you could sing harmony—Jesus, you could be part of a million groups. I'd go over to all these different groups and sing with them. But at six o'clock the police came, and they were nasty.

There was this old Italian man, very Old World. He played an Italian-style mandolin. The Italian residents would be out in the square and he would play for them. And when six o'clock came along, the cops would tell *him* to stop playing, too. He was adamant, and one night they arrested him. After that he went to the Italian cappuccino places to play and sing.

ARLO GUTHRIE: There was a lot of good folk music going on outside in the park. It was just as much for ending up and playing in the park that we came down to the Village. There were all kinds of people—Dylan, Bill Monroe. Anybody, you could hear anybody. It was a good time. We would just hang around, and when things would start cooling off, we'd just go down the block and hang out at Gerdes.

DANNY KALB: The park was a place where you could learn how to get along with music. There was a lot of bluegrass there—John Herald, Marshall Brickman, Eric Weissberg, Lionel Kilberg, and even Pete Seeger would be there sometimes.

It was a very open and wondrous place, like a Middle Eastern fair. You could choose which music you wanted to get involved with. There were easily ten or fifteen groups around there. Blues and bluegrass predominated, even though people were interested in all kinds of music.

JOHN SEBASTIAN: I was born in Greenwich Village and raised from Bank Street to Washington Square. I was able to penetrate the club scene earlier than most of the other people. I was about two years younger than everybody else. Everyone else had to either be eighteen years old, leave home, or reject their parents. All I had to do was say, "Mom, I'm gonna be down at a new club four blocks down the street." My parents knew where I was all the time, because they lived where I was all the time.

My career in that scene began with spending Sundays in Washington Square Park. I was living on Washington Square West at the time. I was about thirteen years old. The only restriction at that time was on bongo drums. I played with people like Mike Mann, Bob Dylan, and a number of people whose names I didn't know, but who I saw every week.

ERIC WEISSBERG: Washington Square Park was a good seventy-five percent of helping me hone my technique. I would practice all week, and then on Sundays I would go to the park and see if I could do it in front of people. I'd go there for hours and hours and do the same things over and over all day, because the crowds would constantly change.

THE
FIFTH · PEG

If the Village was folk singer's heaven, then Izzy Young was certainly its god.

Izzy Young was born in New York in 1928. He grew up in the various boroughs, but was soon drawn to Greenwich Village. He sold and published mail-order folklore and began doing well, but was not completely satisfied. He needed a more concrete outlet for his passion for folklore and folk music. In March 1957, he bought a storefront at 110 MacDougal Street and opened the Folklore Center.

The Folklore Center became a clearinghouse for folk singers. They could find everything from guitar picks to emotional support. All types of folk singers and folklorists passed time there exchanging songs, political theories, gossip, and musical tips. Musicians came from all over the world to find out where the places were to play and who the key players were.

DAVE VAN RONK: I guess Izzy was in his mid twenties when he opened the place. The first thing you remember about Izzy Young is his ears. They looked like mug handles.

He was extraordinarily energetic. He was constantly organizing. Anybody who came into town that couldn't find work, he'd organize a concert for them.

His private passion was harness dancing. Every once in a while, he'd put on his harness and bells and take off down MacDougal Street. It was a wonderful sight and he was actually pretty good at it.

Folk music was definitely on its way in, Izzy Young or no Izzy Young. But it's quite possible that Folk City would not have happened if it hadn't been for him.

By the middle to late sixties, every city of over a couple of hundred thousand had a folklore center, and almost every single one was inspired by Izzy Young.

He wasn't really a good organizer. He had great enthusiasm and he had good ideas, but he was too diffuse. He was the kind of man who was great for a one-shot thing. It was only at sustaining things that he had difficulty. The Folklore

Izzy Young at Folklore Center

Center was always in trouble financially. No matter how it seemed to be prospering, Izzy was always on the verge of bankruptcy.

CHARLIE CHIN: The first time I met Izzy Young, I walked into his Folklore Center on MacDougal Street. As I was walking in, some guy was walking out and asked me, "Are you going to be here for a minute?" I said, "Yeah," so he said, "Do you want to watch the store?" It was Izzy Young. So I just walked around, looked at things, and he came back about twenty minutes later and said, "Thanks. Can I help you?"

Like Mike Porco a couple of blocks away, Izzy saw the American Dream come true. He was running a small business, supporting a group of talented people, and involved in work that he loved. There was only one step to take, and that was to expand.

Izzy began to promote concerts. His first was in conjunction with a Chicago club owner named Albert Grossman. They presented Peggy Seeger. After that success, other concerts followed in quick succession—Sonny Terry and Brownie

McGhee, Oscar Brand, Rev. Gary Davis, the New Lost City Ramblers, Happy Traum, Dave Van Ronk, Jack Elliott, and, as Young refers to them, "all the other saints of folk music."

In addition to the Center and concert promotions, Young also began writing columns which he recalls as "historical-gossipy" for the popular folk music magazine Sing Out! *and ran radio programs for New York's Pacifica station, WBAI. He was always there to lend money if someone needed it, although he was by no means rich. Young remembers himself as being "very happy, if broke most of the time."*

Soon after the 1960 New Year, Izzy was approached by the man who would broker the marriage between Mike Porco's Gerdes and Izzy Young's Folklore Center.

IZZY YOUNG: A dapper, well-dressed advertising man, Tom Prendergast, walked into my store and convinced me to take a look at a dilapidated bar on West Fourth Street near Broadway where we might open up a folk music club. Why not? We walked over to the bar and met Mike Porco, who was serving the entire clientele of two or three regular customers. We quickly came to an agreement and made the following disastrous (for us) deal with Mike: We would pay all the publicity; we would pay all the singers; and we would keep the gate. He would sell drinks and food. He couldn't lose. We couldn't win.

MIKE PORCO: At the time I just had bongo players which were drawing pretty good. I tried a few things before like guitar players and accordion players. I had [the jazz pianist] Cecil Taylor in there with a group of jazz musicians. When I had the bongo players a couple of cops came in and said, "Mike, you know, you have people over here who smoke marijuana."

So I said, "What is that?" I didn't know. I never heard of it before. We're talking about twenty-five years ago. He took me in the corner and said, "Do you smell anything in here?"

I said, "It's smoke from a cigarette." He said, "It's a different kind of cigarette. If you keep up having those people here, you're gonna get in trouble, because they're a bunch of junkies. We know you are running a clean place, but I warn you."

So a couple of days later Izzy and another guy, Tom Prendergast, come in. They look like two investigators. That week they were supposed to run music at a luncheonette but they saw it wasn't fixed right. So they came into Gerdes and figured it was better than nothing, although it was not set up for entertainment.

They ordered a bottle of beer and I see them looking and looking. They finally asked me, "Do you have entertainment here?" I said, "Yes, certain days I do." "Oh," they say, "do you have a cabaret license?" "Yes. I have every license which is necessary." He says, "Tell me, would you like to put folk music here?"

So I said, "Tell me what is that." So he says, "Those people who play guitar." I said, "Well, a lot of people play guitar. But the type of music you talk about don't ring no bells with me." So he says, "Have you heard of Pete Seeger?" I said, "Yes." He said, "Have you heard of Burl Ives?" I said, "Yes." He said, "Well those are all folk singers." "Oh," I said, "those are people who sing songs, who try to deliver messages through their songs." He said, "You've got it! I would like to offer you something. Do you have microphones?" I said, "No; if I have a piano player, you can hear him. I don't want anything too loud." He said, "Well, you've got to have microphones. I'll tell you what I want to do. If you want to get together, we'll give you an offer. We will take care of the music. We'll bring in some lights. I guarantee we'll bring some people in here. This way you can do more business at the bar." I said, "Yeah, but how are you going to pay the entertainers?" He said, "We're gonna charge at the door. Whatever we charge at the door, we'll keep. Whatever food or drinks you sell, you keep." I said, "I have friends who come in at night. How am I going to charge them at the door?" "If you have a few friends," he said, "just give me the signal, we'll let them come in."

So I said it would be okay. We didn't do anything in writing. I just said, "Okay, when do you want to start?"

So the alliance had been made. Izzy and Tom were now running their folk music club at Gerdes Restaurant.

MIKE PORCO: He put up a sign and called it the Fifth Peg. If he could bring in some people, that's all I was looking for at the time. They opened up with Ed McCurdy and Molly Scott. They brought in their folk music and brought in a few people.

I wasn't making out that good. They were not doing great business or filling up the house. They were bringing in about thirty, forty, fifty people. I was even paying half the advertising because I figured it was worth something, because they were advertising the name of the place and the address.

The Fifth Peg, named for the fifth tuning peg of a banjo, was the answer to a lot of people's prayers. To some, it was a real home for the music they loved to play and hear. To others, it was finally a place to socialize where liquor was sold. To most, however, it was a legitimation of a career. A club was finally going to pay for an artist's talent.

There were many hotbeds of folk music around the country—Chicago and Cambridge being two of the hottest—but New York was where it was all happening. Within a few months, Izzy had the cream of the folk music circuit playing his club: Ed McCurdy, Brother John Sellars, Cynthia Gooding, Tommy Makem and the Clancy Brothers, Memphis Slim, Billy Faier, the Tarriers, Charlotte Daniels, Brownie McGhee and Sonny Terry, Hedy West, Carolyn Hester, Cisco Houston, and Theodore Bikel. From Young's journal: "The first of March, Theo Bikel showed up to do a set. There were only three people there but he sang for two hours—a house record!"

BROWNIE McGHEE: In 1960, I helped open up the Fifth Peg. I was doing practically what I'm doing now—folk and blues. Things like "John Henry" and "Betty and Dupree," train songs, and cotton songs and songs about my life and my environment.

Even on a good night Izzy still didn't make much money, but he cared more

Brother John Sellars

for the music and the movement than he did for his personal needs. For example, one night Izzy felt he had done well, so he donated $10 to the Pete Seeger Fund, even though he didn't make much more than that.

On January 26, 1960, the Fifth Peg officially opened with Brother John Sellars and Ed McCurdy, and they were paid about $150 for that first week. The first night was a wild event and musicians and music lovers hoped for a long association with this seedy little out-of-the-way bar.

On opening night the club was filled beyond its capacity. Some people were coming to hear the music while others were checking out the scene. The walls were gaudily wallpapered with tacky red-flocked designs, and the folkies found themselves mixing with the working class, the people they sang about. The chemistry did not always work. Territories were being threatened. There were often fights breaking out, either because the workers at the bar were disrupting the show (which was taking place on stage in the adjoining room), or because some unsuspecting folk singer was interrupting a heated discussion at the bar by wailing some plaintive ballad.

RAMBLIN' JACK ELLIOTT: One of my favorite memories of Folk City is the night I brought in and introduced a cowboy singer who was better known as an artist. He's a very famous artist now, living in Wyoming. His name is Harry Jackson, a very excellent western artist and sculptor. He was also a very accomplished cowboy singer. I brought Harry on stage one evening and the audience was into their usual high murmur, and Harry wanted their attention before he started to sing. The audience quieted down momentarily and Harry seized the moment and started his cowboy song. Well, he got about two thirds of the way through and the murmur started up again. He said, "Well . . . ar . . . ar . . . ah . . . I ah . . . shucks . . . you know . . . I mean . . . doggone it . . . what I mean is . . . a fella gets up to sing a song, he's got something to say and it's good. A lot of you are just drinkin' and talkin' and it's kinda hard to hear, and a fella wants to sing and ah . . . doggone it, *shut up!*"

That shut them up. There was a dead silence in Gerdes like you never heard before. After a couple of songs the crowd started up again. You couldn't keep those drunks quiet. It was one of the finest moments in the annals of Folk City performances. Harry never went out professionally on stage after that.

The Fifth Peg closed for a couple of weeks after Mike announced that he had to straighten out some permit and licensing problems. Izzy didn't believe him, he felt that Mike was trying to ease him out. When the Fifth Peg reopened it could not maintain its original momentum. It was just not drawing the crowds it attracted when it first opened. The friction between Mike and Izzy was becoming evident and people were uncomfortable having to choose sides. Izzy began to suspect that guest sets by folksinger Logan English and visits by another young enthusiast, Charlie Rothschild, were merely to "case the joint."

His suspicions were not unfounded. By the end of April, Mike asked Tom and Izzy to take a brief vacation from the club and "see what happens." Since Izzy had no more money to continue running the Fifth Peg he felt he was coerced into agreeing to leave. He knew the brief vacation would turn into a permanent one. His arguments with Mike over money were too much for Mike to deal with. The final straw was when Izzy asked Mike for a portion of the bar receipts, since the door receipts alone could no longer support Izzy's operation.

Izzy took an ad out in the May 12, 1960 Village Voice *that read, "I FEEL BAD. Everything I do turns out to be successful—artistically only. Now THE FIFTH PEG is added to the list; but I'll be back on the active folk scene soon, and so will my marvelous partner, Tom Prendergast."*

Three weeks later, Izzy read an advertisement in the Voice *which he took as an answer to his, but in reality it was a tribute to what he started and, more importantly, was the next building block upon which the great folk boom would grow. On June 1, 1960, the ad for the first official performance at Gerdes Folk City appeared, listing Carolyn Hester and Logan English. The new regime consisted of Charlie Rothschild as manager and Logan English as MC.*

IZZY YOUNG: I was furious that no one had spoken to me. I set up a large sign in the store window on MacDougal Street stating that Charles and Logan had stolen the club from me without ever once asking for the time of day. They, in turn, got furious and said that I had to "understand—that's how it is." They even threatened to sue me. My friends convinced me to take the sign down. Tom Prendergast disappeared.

LIZ ELKIND: I remember someone who I always thought of as a very young kid named Charlie took over. My recollection is that Charlie did not try to weasel Izzy out. I think Tom did. I know that Tom and Izzy had a very bad falling out. Izzy just got fed up with the way he was treated. He was very difficult and very hard to get along with. When things were going well, everybody could have whatever he had. When things weren't going very well, it was awful. He'd think everybody was to blame. He'd curse everyone publicly.

Izzy's hard work in laying the groundwork for what was to become Gerdes Folk City did not go unappreciated. Almost everyone connected with the club at that time feels that Izzy was one of the most influential forces in what eventually became the folk phenomenon, and many hold him directly responsible for their successful careers. However, most agree that his organizational abilities did not match his creativity and imagination. Many of his associates felt that Izzy ran his businesses from his heart and not his head and that he probably reached the limit of how far he could bring the Fifth Peg. Mike realized that Charlie was a better businessman than Izzy and that he would bring more revenue into the bar.

The Fifth Peg was a popular social center but it was not making money. Izzy forced regulars—the same people he lent money to at the Folklore Center—to pay, and that infuriated many of them. His concern at the Peg was to pay the performers and satisfy Porco. He didn't have the luxury of "no overhead" that he had at the Folklore Center. The Fifth Peg's admission charge was $1.50—free on Mondays—and Izzy admits, "We were really hurting."

Izzy continued with his radio programs, the Folklore Center, and his Folklore Center Folk Festivals. He produced first concerts for Joni Mitchell, Bob Dylan, the Fugs, and the Even Dozen Jug Band. He presented concerts in simple setups so that the audience could be close to the artist.

He is presently running the Folklore Center in Sweden and is producing American folk music concerts there. He says, "I still love American folk music, and will continue to do my part to keep it alive."

AMERICAN FOLK MUSIC
FINDS · A · HOME

..........**M**ike *was now on his own and he wasted no time setting up the next incarnation of Gerdes.*

MIKE PORCO: I fixed up the club after Izzy and Tom left, but I didn't have anybody to work with. I spoke to the Clancy Brothers, and Tommy Makem said, "Look here, Mike. We happen to like you. I'll send you a young fellow. He knows everybody. His name is Charlie." That was Charlie Rothschild. I called him in and paid him about $25 a week to help me out. He was happy, but he got mad sometimes because he had to pay for his drinks. Well, I wasn't making much and I didn't know if he was a drinker.

Izzy started calling Charlie "a skunk" and he didn't want Charlie to come into Gerdes. Izzy was trying to start a boycott. Charlie got scared and said, "I can't get anybody to play.'" So the only person that I knew was Vince Martin. The first act that I booked myself was Vince Martin and Laurie Holland.

After that, Charlie finally took over. Charlie was telling all the musicians that the newspapers and everybody was at the club to review people. That's how he got them in to play. Robert Shelton from the *New York Times* used to come in during the Fifth Peg, but when he first came in I didn't know who he was. He started to boycott me because Izzy was telling everybody stories, like that I was in the Mafia.

DAVE VAN RONK: Out of loyalty to Izzy, I more or less disassociated myself from Gerdes for a period of time, but the offer of hard cash was difficult to turn down. It became obvious that you could have your cake and eat it too. You could work at Folk City and still walk into the Folklore Center without violence being done to you.

I suspect Izzy was not all that happy with the Fifth Peg anyway. He was happy with his Folklore Center, and he might even have been a little relieved that the Fifth Peg ended.

Once Mike took over, he quickly became a popular figure on the folk scene. Although he was unfamiliar with folk music, his basic good sense and shrewd business acumen enabled him to book some of the finest talent around; and he also prided himself on being a charmer with the women.

A former female folk singer remembers Mike: "He would try to get a good kiss on the lips every time I'd come in. The trick was to turn at the last instant so that he wouldn't get your lips. You'd also learn to swing to one side because he was awfully tricky about it. He knew what he was doing. The success rate was about fifty-fifty."

OSCAR BRAND: Mike Porco was a little scrunchy man—a troglodyte who obviously was not interested in anything good or class, you'd say. But that crazy man got himself the best people to play his club.

He kept calling on people who were damn good. I don't know how Mike Porco managed to show such good taste. Better than anybody I know. Better than me. How many times we sang and worked there and had great times!

STEVE MANDELL: When I would get up with my bluegrass band, Mike would let us do a little guest set. At the end he would say, " 'Ey, thatsa very nice, but do you know 'O Sole Mio'?"

MIKE PORCO: I didn't know the business too well, but I knew I wanted to keep running a folk-music club. I kept advertising the club as the Fifth Peg. The name was known for the music. About a month later I received a letter from a lawyer who said we couldn't use that name because Izzy had it copyrighted. So I talked to Marty Lorin, who was a waiter there, and Marty said, "I've got a good name for you. Call it Folk City." So we made it Gerdes Folk City—New York Center of Folk Music.

JOSÉ FELICIANO: Mike really helped me out because he gave me a job so I could earn some money. I just left my parents' house. I didn't have a winter coat, so Mike bought me one.

Mike is a good man. We've always been very close. Of all the artists that Mike had at Gerdes, I think that he and I were the closest. Mike was like a father to me. He made it possible for me to become an entertainer. Mike had me play really often. He paid me well. The first money I got from Gerdes was about $150 a week. Something like that. I want to be sure because if I get it wrong Mike will be saying to me, " 'Ey, whatsa matter witha you, man. I used to paya you good an you tella everybod I didna pay you good. Ey, José, come on."

BROWNIE McGHEE: I was the one who started hanging the pictures on the walls. I thought it was a great idea and they seemed to follow through with it. It was just a naked wall and I thought it would be a good idea to stick people's pictures up there to see who was there, and who had been there. Soon the wall became

Sonny Terry and Brownie McGhee (Collection of Douglas A. Yeager Productions)

full of pictures—of people who are still around and people who have been gone for a long time.

MIKE PORCO: A friend of mine asked me if I wanted to manage a girl he was working with. I told him I had a kid, Bob Dylan, I wanted to work with. He said, "Let's work with both of them." I said, "Does your girl sing folk songs?" He said, "No, but she'll learn some." I said, "If she doesn't sing folk songs,

ANDY BRECKMAN: I always got the highest number, so I realized that if I got four bums from Washington Square Park to come in and sign up for me, I'd have a much better chance. And that's just what I did. I got four bums and I paid them thirty cents each and they signed up for me. They had no idea where they were or what they were doing, but I did get my choice of numbers and I was finally on in prime time!

RICHIE HAVENS: A lot of people would sign up on a list. It was really well-run. Everyone would go to the basement, so there wouldn't be a lot of singers standing around at the bar. We'd all hang out in the basement and they'd come down and call us when they wanted us to go up and play. We'd have fun waiting down there for our turn.

ERIC ANDERSEN: The good thing about hoot nights was that if anyone had a new song they wanted to sing, they'd sing it then. The bad thing was all these bluegrass groups from NYU.

DAVID AMRAM: One night I brought Steve Goodman to check out some of the great underground geniuses who were playing hoot night. He got so excited, he went up and played a new song. No one flipped out. They thought it was just normal. That was hoot night for you—anything could happen.

DOUG YEAGER: Many nights after Josh White and Louis Armstrong were working uptown, they would come down to the hootenannies at Folk City. They would come in with four or five women in mink stoles and diamond rings and they'd come up and jam. Josh White and Louis Armstrong, together at a Folk City hootenanny!

The hoots were the social center of Greenwich Village's week. For most of the time it was on Mondays, but for a while it switched to Tuesdays—two historically slow nights when most of the established artists weren't working anyway. It was a perfect night to gather and exchange the past week's adventures as well as new songs. So for no admission (a drink minimum or a dollar towards a drink) people were encouraged to spend their free night there. The public knew that they would see a show of high quality and great potential—for free.

Some other acts who have played hoots over the years include Janis Joplin, Pat Benatar, Joe Piscopo, Mary Kay Place, Steve Forbert, Melissa Manchester, Phoebe Snow, Lou Gossett, Jr., Hoyt Axton, Arlo Guthrie, Stephen Bishop, the Roches, Loudon Wainwright, and Paul Simon.

MARIA MULDAUR: One night I was down in the basement warming up for my turn and Dylan was down there warming up. Down the stairs bounds this enormous black guy wearing overalls and toting a banjo. He was so nervous. The sweat was popping off his forehead. He was practically shaking, saying, "Oh man, I'm so nervous. I'm going on next." We said, "Just relax, it'll be okay." It was Taj Mahal.

He pulls out his banjo, tunes it up and just kind of starts warming up, singing and playing. We took one listen to that and we said, "You have nothing to worry about." He had real serious musicality coming out of every pore.

The club was packed with amateur and professional listeners. People would attend to see who was up-and-coming. Other performers would attend to perform, check out the competition, and support their friends. The factory regulars soon gave way to record moguls, concert promoters, top managers and agents, TV and radio scouts, and journalists. Folk City became the place where Albert Grossman, Harold Leventhal, John Hammond, Moe Asch, Maynard Solomon, Jac Holzman, and Herb Gart began to look for new talent.

HOYT AXTON: Albert Grossman asked me if I wanted him to manage me. Like an idiot I said, "No, I don't think so. That sounds too permanent."

Mike adjusted quickly. He was enjoying his role of star-maker and friend to the influential. And in his way, he was as influential as any record company executive that came in the club. The execs needed Mike for talent and a place to showcase that talent.

He flourished in this atmosphere, holding court in his powerful little kingdom in a most populist way. If a musician needed money, food, clothing, shelter, or advice, he could get it at Gerdes. His love for the musicians and his fair treatment of them made Mike Porco an extremely popular figure on the folk music scene. Some artists, like Jean Ritchie and Barbara Dane, who wouldn't ordinarily play a club, would play Gerdes because of their fondness for Mike.

EARLY
INFLUENCES

. . . .

. . . . *T*he years 1959 through 1961 were formative years on the Village *music scene. The personalities who came through the neighborhood during those years constituted the backbone of American contemporary music. Some of these performers achieved fame and still retain it; others have attained more modest goals. There were many others behind the scenes—industry types—managers, agents, and writers—as well as fans, employees of the music clubs, and Village residents. They all took part in the foundation of the commercial folk revival.*

OSCAR BRAND: The blacklist hit us all very badly in the fifties. I was called by the House Un-American Activities Committee, and I had also been blacklisted by the left wing. It seemed that my dropping out of *People's Songs*, and the feelings that I had expressed on occasion about the very rigorous dictatorship of the Communists, had me blacklisted by People's Artists. So I became persona non grata in the world in which I had just been rising.

IRWIN SILBER: *Sing Out!* started in 1950. It was founded to continue the work of *People's Songs*. In 1950, a lot of people were afraid to be associated with *Sing Out!* because of its identification with the politics of *People's Songs*. It was a changed atmosphere. There was the Korean War, McCarthy, and the Cold War. *Sing Out!* was associated with left politics during a time when everyone was running scared. So when we first started, we couldn't start *Sing Out!* with the same aura of respectability.

The purpose of *Sing Out!* was to provide a practical vehicle for the rapid communication of new political songs and to keep singers and songwriters of the same ideological views and commitment in touch with each other. The first year, the number of political songs was overwhelming. The second year, more traditional songs were increasing. They were inherently progressive, in and of themselves. Their background and their social and cultural history were dominated by the left politics of the period.

Barbara Dane and Irwin Silber, 1964 (Dave Gahr)

The leading force of the Left at this time was the Communist Party, so the natural position to take was usually the same position the Communist Party took.

In 1959, the modern folk-song revival had begun and the first civil-rights songs were coming out. As time went on, *Sing Out!* couldn't keep up with the flow of political music during the period when everybody was writing topical songs. *Sing Out!* was focusing on songs by movements, instead of individual songwriters. *Sing Out!* was a folk-song magazine. *Broadside* started becoming popular as a topical-song magazine, featuring the new breed of political song-writers.

I couldn't pursue serious politics through the new music. The concept of valuing traditional songs as being important in their own right, when traditions were falling apart, I just couldn't be a part of. It was incongruous. So, I left *Sing Out!* to pursue serious politics. I was the editor of *Sing Out!* from 1951 through 1967.

OSCAR BRAND: I was blacklisted by the right wing first. It was quite a special list. I never testified against anybody. People like Burl Ives did. He said that he had been taken into all these causes by his good friend Richard Dyer-Bennet. I never thought of Richard as political. His songs certainly weren't. That was the end of Dyer-Bennet.

Ives went in front of the committee and gave them a list of about a hundred names. They absolved him of any kind of guilt. Woody went out to Hollywood about a year later, and when he came back he said, "Lord, that Ives is God's angry man. He hates everybody, especially himself." But . . . that may have been Woody's perception.

The pall and the atmosphere were gray and dismal. It was like a rainy day up at the top of Katmandu. You just lived in a fog. Everybody felt it. There was fear and worry, and the creative aspects of our work just seemed to disappear for a while.

It wasn't until the sixties that all this started to change. A lot of people were asking questions about the American Dream, and that kind of questioning also questioned the validity of blacklists.

Starting in '59, there was a lot of ferment. It was a very, very busy time, and the Village itself was a symbol of folk music all over the world.

It was becoming a business for us. It was becoming big business, and people started selling major records. The Weavers were the first group that really encompassed country music and the popular music fields, and that was unusual, because those two had always been disparate. Right-wing people considered the Weavers' songs as being American, and left-wingers liked them as being American. So in a way, we were coming together then as a country, and it was quite interesting and very exciting.

You could walk from the East coast to West coast, from coffeehouse to coffeehouse, without putting your foot on the ground. They were being set up all over, and people were coming to them. Young people were learning their trade and making a couple of bucks a week, enough to live on.

We were all friends; we all knew each other; we understood each other; we traded songs; we borrowed from each other. You had to make it in New York first. Every place else was the provinces.

One hometown boy who enhanced the reputation of the New York music scene was Dave Van Ronk.

JOHN HAMMOND, JR.: Dave Van Ronk was the veteran guy who began playing long before I started playing. He was from the Village and was established. The great Dave Van Ronk. He wasn't exactly "the father," but he was the big guy nobody messed with. He was politically aware. He was a great guitar player and a rough, tough singer-personality. It was as much who you were as a person as it was the music you played. Personality had a lot to do with it.

TOM INTONDI: Van Ronk was always legendary, even before anyone knew who he was. He was a blues assimilator. He is one of the few people from that early era who has taken an active interest in the new stuff that's happened since. He has been encouraging to no end.

TERRI THAL: David was being courted by Albert Grossman, who wanted him to change his name and become a part of Peter, Paul, and Mary when he was putting the group together. David thought it was a devastatingly horrible idea. He wanted him to change his name to Blind Boy Raunch or something like that.

Albert had Mary and Peter, and was looking for a third. He offered it to Logan English and David and a few others. He finally found Noel Stookey, who was perfect. David would have been a total bomb. David was obviously not the right person for a pop-folk group. It was going to be white music and a pop-folk group. It would have been a horror all around.

TOM PASLE: David was enchanted with the idea that you could be a one-man band by using a six-string guitar and most of the fingers on the right hand when

Terri Thal and Dave Van Ronk, August 1963 (Ann Charters)

you play. It was astounding that a non-black, political intellectual was interested in something as obscure as an acoustic guitar and mostly twelve and nine bar blues. I would pay money to hear Dave Van Ronk sing.

DAVE VAN RONK: Essentially I'm a blues and jazz singer. I'd rather listen to Dinah Washington sing than anybody I can think of. At first I was trying to make a living playing jazz guitar with small jazz groups, but that didn't work out very well. That scene pretty much withered away.

I had been fooling around with folk music for a long time, so when folk music began to loom large in the Village, I was in the right place at the right time, for once in my life.

I started to do shows with the Folksingers' Guild around 1957. We used to rent the Sullivan Street Playhouse and some of the other local theaters on their dark nights, and we'd do concerts. Mostly, we'd introduce ourselves or, sometimes, we'd get some luminary like Paul Clayton or Logan English.

It evolved into a co-op concert and workshop. It lasted for about two years. We would never do solo concerts. There were always about three or four people on a bill. Somebody would be up there for about fifteen or twenty minutes and we'd yank them off just before everybody left and then hit them with the next screecher.

There were also concerts happening. People like Susan Reed and Cynthia Gooding. Jazz and legit clubs would bring in folk music occasionally, but in 1959, I had to leave New York to get work.

It was when I was in Oklahoma City that the riot squad was called out and essentially panicked and attacked the mob of folk singers in Washington Square Park. Lionel Kilberg and Izzy Young worked in tandem on that demonstration. It was the only time I was ever happy to be in Oklahoma City.

The New York music scene began to flourish and artists with varied musical interests and backgrounds soon found a home in Greenwich Village.

PHYLLIS LYND: When Ed McCurdy was in his prime, he was very dynamic, warm, giving and helpful. He was a very sweet man. He did a lot of bawdy songs, but coming from him, they sounded very beautiful. He really knew how to sing a song. He was a purist. He was really true to the art form. He was a true disseminator of the art form. He had a wonderful voice and he often delved into classical technique.

ED McCURDY: I was the first person singing folk songs at Gerdes Folk City. I once had a marvelous experience with someone in the audience. I was accusing someone of being blind-drunk and after the show, this man came up to me and said, "You're right. I'm both blind and drunk." It was Judy Collins's father.

Ed McCurdy (collection of Douglas A. Yeager Productions)

LOUIS BASS: I used to wait tables at Folk City when José Feliciano would play there. I usually paid more attention to my customers than the people on stage, but I did pay attention to José Feliciano. He was a really good guitar player. He would always come in with his seeing-eye dog, and his dog would sit by the stage, next to a table where customers sat. Whenever I served the people at that table I always stepped on the dog's leg, at least five times a night. But the dog was good, it never once let out a whimper or a bark.

You could always fool around with José. My brother would take out pictures and say, "José, look at these pretty girls." José would look at the pictures and say, "Oh, they're ugly." He was barely nineteen, and he was great.

HERB GART: There was a man named Harold Waters who used to work with

José. He would announce a song and José would sing it. Harold would sit there with a mike and say, "Now José will sing . . ." and announce a song, and José would sing it. I thought José was wonderful, but I had to find out why he did his show that way. Harold told me, "José knows over two thousand songs, and that's how I keep him on his toes. He doesn't know what he's gonna sing next." José was a great kid. Every minute he was telling another bad joke.

DAVE VAN RONK: When I first heard José Feliciano he blew me away. I said, "My God, you can't do that with a guitar." He was a pretty good singer, too. People were saying, "You've got to come down and hear this guy, he's fantastic." So I went down and heard this guy, and he really was fantastic.

I had the impression when I first met him that he was just a shy kid who was a little bit withdrawn. I subsequently discovered that he has one of the most vicious wits of anyone I have ever met. He is hilariously funny, and you don't want to cross swords with this man unless you're in the top of your form.

JOSÉ FELICIANO: I was the only guy who used to deviate from folk at that time. I used to play "Flight of the Bumblebee." And I played "Dueling Banjos" on one guitar. People used to freak out because a folk musician wasn't supposed to play that good. The more traditional people didn't like me too much because I wasn't playing that old folk bullshit. I wasn't a folk guitarist. In other words, I played more than three chords. It kind of got to them a bit.

DAVE VAN RONK: If you were new and hot, the audience would be quiet and attentive, like when Ian and Sylvia were on for the first time. You always got one free ride. From then on, you were just another one of the bums that gets in the way of the conversation.

It was all around me. There I was in the midst of the songwriting explosion. I practically did no songwriting of my own at that time. The grapevine would keep you informed of who were the good songwriters and what were the good songs. The grapevine reached all around the country.

ERIC WEISSBERG: I met John Herald at a freshman mixer at the University of Wisconsin. He liked to sing but he didn't play anything. He asked me to show him things on the mandolin and we started to play together. We hooked up again later in Washington Square with Bob Yellin. After the square, we'd go to the American Youth Hostel and sing there. And then we decided to do it on a slightly more escalated scale, and maybe even get paid for it. We actually even rehearsed a lot.

There were a lot of people who knew us from the square, and they'd follow us. This was the beginning of the Greenbriar Boys. We started it in 1958. We'd

José Feliciano

tour in my father's Rambler. It was funny, because the New Lost City Ramblers, which was also a big group then, were touring in an old Greenbriar, an early Chevy version of a Volkswagen van. We picked our name from the song, "The Girl on the Greenbriar Shore." I don't know why.

MARSHALL BRICKMAN: There used to be hootenannies when I was in high school, and I used to go to meet girls. If it was good weather, then we'd go to Washington Square Park which was given over to a loosely organized informal hootenanny. I used to come in from Brooklyn, which was a long, long trip, schlepping five instruments around. I'd get there about one o'clock and leave about six o'clock. I was a Brooklyn cowboy. I played bluegrass.

When I was around thirteen, I heard Eric Weissberg play. He was entertaining at somebody's birthday party. I never heard anything like that before and it was

It was very important to sing songs of social significance. Almost everybody had some political songs. One half of the songs by the New World Singers were political. The New World Singers were one of the few integrated groups.

VINCE MARTIN: I dropped out of college and began singing. I didn't want to do anything. I was completely devoid of ambition. My father taught me music as an avocation.

One drunken night, a buddy of mine and I went to a bar in Coney Island, a very sleazy joint. There was a girl on stage with false teeth, wearing a long shabby dress. She was jaded and tired and was singing "Smoke Gets in Your Eyes" very badly. My friend said, "You can sing better than that."

I got up on stage and I sang "Casey Jones" and "John Henry." I knew about three or four tunes. I got my first job, ninety dollars a week plus tips. The bar owner changed my name from Vincent Marcellino to Vince Martin. I came back and there was a billboard that said "Vince Martin, the singing cowboy."

I worked there for about four months and then I packed up my guitar and came to the city. I knocked on doors, because I wanted to be a star, whatever that meant.

A guy on the subway saw me carrying my guitar. I had all of no experience— four months in a bar in Coney Island. He said, "Do you play the guitar?" I knew seven or eight chords and I said, "Yes." He gave me a card to go to Glory Records. I went to Glory Records and they told me to come back, because they wanted me to meet some people. I came back two days later and I walked into the office and there were three barefoot guys. They were Erik Darling, Bob Carey, and Alan Arkin. They were called the Tarriers.

They handed me a song called "Cindy, Oh Cindy," which they had rewritten from some other song. I sang it with the Tarriers, and they said it sounded good and that we should go into the studio to do it. The Tarriers had a song called "The Banana Boat Song," a version of "Day-O," which they were recording also. We recorded "Cindy, Oh Cindy" in nine takes and two tracks with the Tarriers. Panama Francis played drums.

They released "Cindy, Oh Cindy" first, before "The Banana Boat Song." That pissed Alan off tremendously. It was a thorn in the Tarriers' side. I was not part of the politics. Here I was, twenty years old. It was ridiculous. I was a kid.

One day, I turned on the *Make Believe Ballroom* on the radio and I heard, "And now a new hit song by a new artist, Vince Martin." I was in the car and I almost drove off the fucking road.

It was a wonderful feeling. I got all the girls. I was the only guy in the Village with a car. I had a hit record, and it ruined me. It got up to number two or three on the charts. I don't think it ever beat out "Doggie in the Window."

Ramblin' Jack Elliott

DAVE VAN RONK: New people were coming into the city constantly, and I think the change in quality reflected that more than anything else. There were a lot of good performers around, suddenly.

Richard Fariña was a good performer. I saw him with Carolyn Hester. I saw Carolyn for the first time at Gerdes. My God, she tore the place apart. Richard Fariña was doing a lot of dulcimer in those days. It was so funny to see Dick, a hipster—I mean a real hipster—on stage with the shades, the motorcycle jacket, and this delicate dulcimer. He did southern mountain tunes. He didn't have a big voice, but he was a wonderful performer.

Everyone who was performing in the Village at this time seemed to be unique. Ramblin' Jack Elliott was no exception.

JOHN HERALD: I've seen Jack Elliott fall asleep on stage. There were no people in the audience and he would be singing, and it would get quieter and quieter, and he'd literally fall asleep, wake up in the twilight zone, and then do it again. He's great, a real character.

DAVE VAN RONK: I was at Gerdes for Jack Elliott's New York debut. He had just put out an album on Vanguard for which he wrote the notes. In the notes, he admitted his real name was Elliot Adnopoz and that he was from Brooklyn. Consequently, this brought him back into favor with his mother and father.

They were very prominent people in Brooklyn. His father was chief of surgeons in a hospital, and the family had been in medicine for several generations—and that Jack had turned into such a bum and, furthermore, changed his name, was a great source of grief.

So when he wrote this thing and more or less acknowledged his background, a great reconciliation was struck, and Dr. and Mrs. Adnopoz came down to see the kid.

I was sitting at the table with the artist Harry Jackson, Bobby Dylan, and Dr. and Mrs. Adnopoz. Jack was on stage having some trouble tuning his guitar and the audience was utterly hushed, a very rare occurrence in that room. Mrs. Adnopoz, sitting about two chairs from me, was just staring at him, raptly, and she lets out with a stage whisper, "Look at those fingers—such a surgeon he could have been!"

DOUG YEAGER: Jack left home at the age of eleven to run off and join the rodeo. When he left, he changed his name to Buck Elliott. In 1950, Woody Guthrie suggested he changed his name to Jack Elliott. Jack and Odetta claim that it was Odetta's mother who gave him the "Ramblin'."

Jack went out to visit Odetta in California and Odetta was in the bathroom, taking a bath. So for forty-five minutes Jack talked away at Odetta's mother, and when he left, she said to Odetta, "My goodness, that's the ramblinest boy I ever heard."

Now, Woody Guthrie had this rebel, hobo type of spirit, and Jack Elliott was the one able to make that image famous and make it commercial. He was inspired by what he observed in Woody, but it could never have been commercial in Woody's time; and then Dylan took it one step further from Jack. Jack was really responsible for forming the new image of what folk music was going to be.

RAMBLIN' JACK ELLIOTT: The very first person I met when I came back from Europe was Bob Dylan. I met him while we were visiting Woody in the hospital. I didn't know who the kid was, but there he was with his little black corduroy cap and round oval face. He had this peach fuzz. He looked kinda country and kinda cute. This was in 1961. He had only been in New York a short while. He told me about Gerdes. He said that Cisco Houston was hanging out there. He told me that it was a nice bar and we ought to have a look at it. He wasn't big enough or good enough to play there yet. He played the hoots, though.

Back in 1962, I was going around thinking that I was the king of folk music;

and I probably was, sort of, at the time, because Bob hadn't overshadowed me yet. He was still following me around.

ARLO GUTHRIE: My Dad met up with Cisco Houston probably sometime in the late thirties or early forties, and they palled around until my father got sick and went into the hospital, which was 1952. They shipped out together in the merchant marines.

I met Cisco in the fifties when my Dad was in the hospital. Cisco did real simple folk songs. He used to do a lot of old cowboy songs, old ballads. He had a real simple style. There were a lot of friends of mine who really loved his particular way of doing things. He was a very handsome man. Very forthright. He looked like Errol Flynn. He was just a wonderful guy.

I remember the last time I saw him play because it was the first time I ever played, in 1961. I found out later that he was sick with cancer, and had been for some time. He refused any treatment or medication, and went home after that show, and died in California shortly after.

HAROLD LEVENTHAL: One dramatic night at Folk City was the last performance of Cisco Houston. He could literally hardly stand on his feet, but he wanted to go on with his engagement.

A whole bunch of us came down for that show—the Weavers, the Tarriers, Pete Seeger, Arlo, and Bobby Dylan were there.

Cisco was one of the greatest guys I ever met. He was tall and handsome. He rejected a Hollywood actor's career. He was very political and very close to Woody. During the war, they went to sea together and were sunk two or three times. He could have been a popular country singer. He worked in a copper mine outside of Denver, and that's where Woody met him.

MIKE PORCO: Cisco was my favorite. He would come in and be a pleasure to talk with. He would sit at the bar and we'd have a drink. If nobody was there we would talk. He was friendly and serious. He got to like me and I got to like him, also. So every three months I tried to book him.

The last time he came in and took the gig he said to me, "You should make money on this gig." I said, "Well, let's hope so." He said, "No, no. If you listen to me, you will—if you put it in the papers as 'The Last Appearance of Cisco Houston.' Because, Mike, after this I'm not gonna perform anymore."

Following Cisco was a whole group of disparate success stories. Tom Pasle came in through the side door and fell into folk music. Bob Gibson became a great influence proving that commercial folk music could be high quality. Peter,

Paul, and Mary came under the management of the influential and controversial Albert Grossman. Grossman would soon be managing Dylan, and then American music would have a full-fledged "scene" on its hands.

In the early sixties, the New York–identified songwriting teams were becoming as well known as their songs. Lieber and Stoller, Doc Pomus and Mort Shuman, Barry Mann and Cynthia Weill, Carole King and Gerry Goffin, and Ellie Greenwich and Jeff Barry were writing classics like "Save the Last Dance for Me," "Will You Still Love Me Tomorrow?" and "Chapel of Love." The girl groups were becoming the rage, and in 1963 they had twenty-six songs on the Billboard chart. The teenagers couldn't get enough do-wah-diddies and doo-langs.

The songwriters in the Village were operating on a more "adult" plane. Their music was being enjoyed by an older crowd—mostly college students. Different issues were being addressed. The girl groups gave us "Soldier Boy," and the Village offered "The Universal Soldier." The Brill Building writers defined popular rock music throughout the early sixties. The Village writers were not yet as influential as their more commercial counterparts who were cranking out the hits at 1619 Broadway, but their impact was beginning to be felt. In 1963, folk music was represented on the charts by "Walk Right In," "Puff," "Blowin' in the Wind," "Washington Square," and "If I Had a Hammer." New voices, styles, and myths were being created. Gerdes was becoming folk music's Brill Building. A wide variety of styles prevailed.

VINCE MARTIN: Tom Pasle would stop singing a song to light a girl's cigarette. Unrelenting schmaltz. He was great. I'd yell, "Tom, sing the song!" and he'd calmly say, "In a minute, Vince."

TOM PASLE: I started out singing in neighborhood bars in Brooklyn. Little by little, I kind of edged my way into being a performer. When I found I couldn't get anybody to accompany me for free, I thought it would be neat to accompany myself. So I learned how to play the guitar.

I was an insurance claims investigator and I was following a guy who was supposed to be disabled, and I followed him up to the racetrack at Yonkers. Then I followed him to a place near the track where he did a lot of mambo dancing, which was very big at the time. So I was catching all this action and this guy doesn't know me, I'm just an insurance investigator. I'm having a good time, and there's this guy playing the piano.

I went out to my car and I got my guitar and I came in and I played, and to my amazement everybody bought me free drinks. I met a couple of ladies who wanted to leap on my bones and I made about fifty dollars. You've got to understand that I was being paid eighty dollars a week by this insurance company.

The manager of the place said "Hey listen, you've really got to come back on a weekend when we're doing business." And I did, and I then turned my back on the law and pursued a tawdry career in gin mills.

BARRY KORNFELD: Bob Gibson was part of the Midwest, somewhat slicker school of traditional folk music, but he was writing his own songs. He was rewriting a lot of songs. Extensive rewriting particularly in harmonies and melodies.

Most of us credit Bob Dylan with having changed the course of lyrics in popular music, and I have always felt that it was Bob Gibson who changed the course of harmony in popular music. You can hear a lot of things that Gibson

Bob Gibson (Ron Gordon)

was doing even in the Beatles. Not that they necessarily heard Bob Gibson, but it filtered through. I thought Bob Gibson and Hamilton Camp were electrifying when they performed as a duo.

VINCE MARTIN: Bob Gibson brought the twelve-string guitar to more prominence than Pete Seeger did. Nobody knew about the twelve-string until Gibson. Gibson was instrumental in my, in Fred Neil's, and everyone else's playing twelve-string. He'd play ragtime on that twelve-string and everyone wanted one.

RICHIE HAVENS: Bob Gibson was a survivor of the Beatnik era into the contemporary folk-hippie era. He crossed that line.

He inspired me, in the sense of singing songs about injustices and justice. He was singing songs like "Let Freedom Ring." Songs that really inspired you about your contemporary surroundings. He was one of those inspirational guys.

DOUG YEAGER: Bob Gibson was a major influence and idol to many people. He brought Joan Baez to Chicago and she started opening shows for him and Hamilton, and then she'd sing with them. They were a trio for a little bit. Bob took her to the first Newport Folk Festival and he wanted to bring her up and sing a few songs, and he was told he couldn't. He brought her up anyway. They sang four songs together and brought the house down. She was signed to Vanguard Records the next week.

Joni Mitchell was another Bob Gibson discovery, and he's greatly influenced Roger McGuinn, Tom Paxton—everybody. Everybody in folk music loves him, and he changed the look and sound of folk music.

BOB GIBSON: In the early Village days I was hanging out at the Bitter End and Folk City, which I used to go to with Albert Grossman. I liked Grossman's vision. He knew that folk music would become a good, prestigious thing to do. Everyone moved from club to club during that time. We moved wherever there was energy.

SONNY OCHS: The first time I came to the Village, I wanted to see what was happening there. I just happened to catch Peter, Paul and Mary. They did a set of the songs that eventually came out on the first album. Wow! I thought, this is fun, coming down here. I thought everything was like that.

A lot of people put them down for being "too perfect" musically. If it weren't for groups like them I wouldn't have gotten interested in folk music. You need your Kingston Trios and you need your Peter, Paul, and Marys. You need that bridge. Those transitional people are super-important.

ERIC WEISSBERG: Peter, Paul, and Mary's first show was at Folk City, before their first official public appearance. Albert Grossman was standing right next to me and asked me what I thought after they finished. I didn't really like what they were doing. It wasn't my cup of tea; it didn't satisfy my listening desires. He may have asked me what I thought, but he didn't really care, because he said to me, "Well, they're going to be huge." And he was right.

DAVE VAN RONK: Paul Stookey was a good single, a damn good single. He was a stand-up comic, poor man. He used to use the mike a lot. He did imitations. He did Hitler at the Nuremberg rally in Sid Caesar German—in a high falsetto voice that sounded nothing like Adolf Hitler. It was hilarious. Also, he had this very convincing imitation of an old-timey flush toilet. The Cafe Wha? had a big sign up when he was working there that said, "Noel Stookey, the Toilet Man."

I've always liked his solo singing a lot. He used to do straight ballads, and very convincingly.

ED McCURDY: Paul Stookey was a marvelous stand-up comic, and he did a marvelous parody of Little Richard. It was very funny. I didn't like Peter, Paul,

Peter, Paul, and Mary, 1965 (Joe Alper)

and Mary when they started because she sang out of tune. They got too slick for me.

MIKE PORCO: Peter Yarrow used to play Folk City all the time. He was a very, very nice boy. I was very friendly with him. I also became friendly with his mother.

People used to play for two weeks at a time then. One time when he was playing for his two weeks, Albert Grossman came to me and said, "Mike, would you do me a favor? I just put together a trio with Paul Stookey, Peter, and Mary Travers." I knew them all. Grossman said, "They're going to be very big, but if they don't get a gig, Peter is going to go to Chicago and the whole thing will fall apart. Will you hire them?" I said, "Well, I have to hear them, and I'm not going to hire them if I have to pay extra money. I can't afford all three." He said, "Don't worry about the money. We'll just pay them twenty dollars extra and I'll cover it myself." So I hired Peter for another two weeks so he could work with the group and try it out.

Peter used to sing two songs, the most three, alone, and then he would say, "I want to introduce my future group." And he introduced Stookey and Mary Travers, and they'd do the rest of the show together.

I didn't pay for the trio. I paid for Peter Yarrow. It wasn't billed as Peter, Paul, and Mary, because they were just trying it out. They didn't know if they would stay together. It was a rehearsal for them.

After the second two weeks finished, Grossman approached me and said, "Mike, how did you like them?" I said, "I liked them very much." He said, "Listen, being that you did me a favor before anybody else, do you want to keep it another two weeks here? Because otherwise, I could put them at the Bitter End." I said, "Go ahead and do it, because as you know, Peter has been here for four weeks. If I put them on another two weeks, I'm pretty sure I won't draw anything." Grossman said, "In a way I don't blame you, Mike."

I didn't book anybody for more than two weeks, and Peter was already doing four. He would have been there six weeks altogether. I figured, if people saw the same name for six weeks, they wouldn't come anymore.

Grossman still owes me the twenty dollars.

MARY TRAVERS: Peter, Paul, and Mary began while Peter was producing a couple of folk concerts at Cornell. I was interested in folk music and living in the neighborhood, right across the street from the Gaslight. When he got out of college he decided to take a year's sabbatical and maybe play around a little bit before he went back to school. Paul had gone to Michigan State for three years and decided, a scholar he wasn't gonna be. He came to New York and worked in a chemical photo company during the day and was singing and being a stand-up at night.

The Simon Sisters

men with cigars. Downtown it was much warmer. It's too bad there isn't really a life for a performer today unless they're very successful. That's what was so good about the Village in the sixties. It was a start on a small scale. It gave you a sense of bearings. It taught you how to relate to an audience. So many big performers who were Village artists learned how to prepare themselves for big amphitheaters by working in the Village. If you can get back somebody you lost at the far table in a Village club, you'll be a success.

You were also lucky to learn from all the legends who were playing in the Village. These were people whose albums you learned from. In the Village you could see them first hand, front row.

John Phillips was another new face in the early sixties who went on to national fame. With the Mamas and the Papas, who were products of the New York folk scene, Phillips had six top-five hits in 1966 and 1967.

JOHN PHILLIPS: Although I was around for years before, the late mid-sixties was really my time. But the early days were important for experience. In 1961, I used to play with the Journeymen—Dick Weissman, Scott MacKenzie, and myself. Scott is a good friend, and he later went on to record "If You're Going to San Francisco (Wear Flowers in Your Hair)."

One night we were playing and it was about 110 degrees, and there we were in our Kingston Trio sweaters. The sweat was just pouring off us. We had to suffer for style. We went over very well, considering that we were thought of as pop singers.

Albert Grossman saw us at a hoot and wanted to manage us. Soon after that, we went to Colorado; and one night we went to dinner with Grossman, who was also there, and we talked to him about managing us. He said, "I'll tell you something. I think I'm gonna take Dylan instead of you." We said, "You must be kidding." He said, "Dylan will sell more records off his first album than you'll sell in your whole lifetime." It was totally uncalled for.

GEOFFREY STOKES: Bob Dylan, a woman known only as Fat Sybil, and I briefly, extremely briefly, formed a group called the White Horse Singers. We formed this group chiefly because I had my guitar with me and he didn't have his. We were truly terrible. We just played in Folk City's kitchen, totally one-shot.

I think, to some degree, the folkie movement was nostalgia oriented. It represented a pretty shitty time—the McCarthy era and the Eisenhower era—and there was a tendency to romanticize the Depression and the radical movement that came out of it.

It was a very sharing time. Performers would always come to see other performers. They came to pay their respects and learn from and rip off. But, it was a time of real generosity and sharing. There was none of this holding the handkerchief over the left hand so no one could see the changes. There was a lot of trading songs and teaching going back and forth.

The competition came in when the money came in. When folk music was a self-consciously minority taste, everyone was on the same side versus the big, bad, commercial tastelessness. When big, bad, commercial tastelessness reached out and embraced these artists, the competition increased as well. And people who were marginally talented had to face the fact of their marginality—because if folk music doesn't sell, then there's no problem with not having a record contract. If it does sell, the problem becomes not the medium, but the performer.

The big thing then was a record company releasing singles, not albums. All the folkies had albums. I can remember just being thrilled when Phil Ochs had his single released.

BOB DYLAN:
MAKING·THE
DREAM·POSSIBLE

.... **O**ne of the first performers of the new crowd to get a record deal was Bob Dylan. It was interesting that he would be the one, because he not only personified the clash between tradition and innovation, but also typified the almost desperate need these new performers had to be recognized. He absorbed the styles of his idols and he twisted his observations into his own unique persona.

New York was ready for a new spokesman. The new music was coming out of New York, and the scene needed an interpreter for this jittery new generation. Dylan was a fighter in his own quiet way. He fought against tradition, although he was steeped in it. He was referred to as "the new Woody Guthrie" and "the son of Jack Elliott." He was sarcastic yet tender. He was a loner, but he wrote some powerful love songs. He was despairing, but still he could offer a glimmer of hope. He was a user but he remained true to some life-long friends. He was what the public and press wanted—an Everyman. He spoke for the nonconformist, but he had a record deal with Columbia Records. He was all sides of every question and he was what his circle of musician friends needed. With his initial cult following and his charisma, he changed his generation.

In a 1984 Rolling Stone interview, Kurt Loder asked him, "Do you notice that you've influenced a lot of singers over the years?"

BOB DYLAN: It's phrasing. I think I've phrased everything in a new way that it's never been phrased before. I'm not tryin' to brag or anything—or maybe I am. But yeah, I hear stuff on the radio, doesn't matter what kinda stuff it is, and I know that if you go back far enough, you'll find somebody listened to Bob Dylan somewhere, because of the phrasing. Even the content of the tunes. Up until I started doin' that stuff, nobody was talkin' about that sort of thing. For music to succeed on any level . . . Well, you're always gonna have your pop-radio stuff, but the only people who are gonna succeed, really, are the people who are sayin' somethin' that is given to them to say. I mean, you can only carry "Tutti Frutti" so far.

There is no way to document popular music's twenty-five-year history without chronicling the career of Bob Dylan; and without question, Dylan, Gerdes Folk City, and popular music are linked forever. Each was essential to the growth of the other two. Moreover, Dylan affected the lives of all the personalities of the

Bob Dylan

early era—and still does today. He is as important an influence to the young kids coming to today's hoots as he was to his contemporaries in 1961.

The bare facts are familiar: Robert Allen Zimmerman was a quiet young man who purposefully cloaked himself in myth and mystery. He made his way from

Minnesota—where he played rock-and-roll at Hibbing high school, and folk music at the University of Minnesota—to New York to become a star, bringing with him tall tales, an invented past, and a dream of his future. His skills included self-taught piano, harmonica, and guitar. His obsession, to transform himself from a small-town, small-time amateur into the idol of sophisticated New York audiences, might have seemed overwhelming, but Zimmerman's drive was stronger than most.

He was secretive and uptight about his privacy. His head was occupied by musical demons—country and western, rhythm and blues, and rock-and-roll. The flashy, nonconformist accessories of the fifties were appealing to him—rebellion, leather jackets, motorcycles. He was often depressed and alienated. He was a loner looking for a way to fit in.

One way was to create a colorful past. Another was to join the legions of the disenfranchised. He tried college, but it didn't hold his interest. He became drawn to folk music, and the left-wing, artistic Beatnik types that folk music attracted. He picked up the name Dylan, and after floating around Minneapolis for a while, he became enamored of the hobo legend and its greatest spokesman, Woody Guthrie. Dylan assumed the hobo myth completely. Determined to come to New York and meet Woody, he told many people along the way that he already had.

MARSHALL BRICKMAN: When I was going to school in Wisconsin, Eric Weissberg and I roomed together. Our apartment was the place where all the folksingers wound up. We were the underground railroad. One day this guy, Bob Zimmerman, came through town on his way from Minnesota. He had a brown suit and tie and he played this sort of blues on the piano the way Dustin Hoffman plays the piano in *Tootsie*—not great. He was on his way to New York.

DAVE VAN RONK: I remember when Big Joe Williams was coming into town. Bobby had been telling stories for months about how the first time he ran away from home he jumped on a box car and who did he meet but Big Joe Williams, who began to teach him old blues. They went all the way down to Mexico together. Bobby was thirteen or something like that. Nobody believed him. But nobody held his tall stories against him, either.

What Bobby never really understood was that nobody really cared. It just wasn't very important who you had been before you hit town. So Bobby was telling these stories about Big Joe Williams and people were listening politely. When Big Joe Williams showed up it was just something nobody wanted to miss.

So a bunch of us came down with Bobby, and Joe saw him and came over and said, "Hey, I haven't seen you since the boxcar down to Mexico!" I still think he must have gotten a hold of Joe first, but it really did blow us away.

Dylan was making himself known to all the right people. He hung out at all the coffeehouses, playing with any musician who would let him. He was regularly visiting Woody. He was one of the few performers who was actually doing his homework. Through his regular visits with Woody he began to associate with Cisco Houston, Ramblin' Jack Elliott, and Pete Seeger. Ramblin' Jack remembers how Dylan very rarely played in front of his idols—"He just sat there listening, absorbing everything he could."

Dylan's relationship to Ramblin' Jack was critical to Dylan's future. Ramblin' Jack became his guide. Here was Woody's best friend, a cowboy-storyteller who took Bob under his wing and taught him about the ramblin' life. Jack Elliott himself was busy learning—he was modeling his own style after Woody Guthrie.

Once again, the folk process was intertwining a number of lives, creating hybrids—Jack who was emulating Woody, and Bob who was emulating Jack emulating Woody. In the early days, Dylan was even introduced as "the son of Jack Elliott."

Many of Jack's friends were furious at Dylan's outright imitation of Jack. Jack was much more understanding, and tried to maintain his relationship with Dylan. Arlo Guthrie sees both sides: "Ramblin' Jack knew Dylan real well, and I'd hear stories about Dylan from Jack who would relay these stories in detail. Beyond belief—in detail! It's not a reciprocal kind of friendship. Although Bobby may have liked what Jack did at one time, or learned from it, he hasn't maintained that kind of respect for him. I think that hurt Jack a bit. But Jack can get on your case, and maybe Bobby was scared off by him."

Woody Guthrie grew fond of Dylan, and appreciated both his talent and his reverence. Although Dylan was shy, he couldn't help bragging to everyone. Woody became one of the few verifiable connections in Dylan's past.

BARRY KORNFELD: Woody was in very bad shape. His mind was functioning, but his body wasn't. He kept having Bob sing his [Woody's] songs. "Sing this one. Sing that one." Woody couldn't sing them and he couldn't play them, so he had a surrogate. It meant a lot to Woody. Here he was, locked away from the world, and here is somebody who comes out every other week and is obviously enamored, a fan who knows every one of your songs, exactly the way you play it on guitar.

ARLO GUTHRIE: The first time I went to the Newport Folk Festival, my mother just sort of dropped me off with Dylan and said, "Here, take care of him," and I trailed behind him. But the first time I met Dylan was in '61. He had come out to our house in Queens looking for my father. We were sitting around, a bunch of us kids, and there was an older girl there watching us, a baby-sitter type who was kind of straight and nice and went to parochial school.

Arlo Guthrie and Bob Dylan (Armen Kachaturian, copyright © 1974)

This sort of ragamuffin-type human with weird shoes and crazy sort of hair—he looked like he just got off a freight train—was banging at the door. She opened it up and she was so nervous, she had two cigarettes in her hand at once, forgetting that she had just lit one.

My mother wasn't home, but eventually he talked his way into the house, and I guess my brother and sister were scared, but I took to him. I thought he had sort of neat shoes. They were like hiking boots. I figured, he can't be a crook—not wearing hiking boots. So I invited him in. He showed me something on the harmonica. Didn't last probably more than ten or fifteen minutes. The girl finally got the nerve to ask him to leave and come back sometime when my mother would be there.

I remember visiting my Dad. It was around the same time I kept hearing stories about Dylan showing up there and hanging out with him. He obviously made a big impression in New York, but when I was old enough to come down a year or two later, I didn't see what was so great about it. He sounded terrible to me. But eventually I got to like what Dylan was doing, because it was so terrible that it was really unique and kind of different.

I came back to New York from going to school in Massachusetts, and it was like the whole Village was walking around trying to find Bob Dylan. Like "He was just there—was that Bob Dylan?—I think he's over at. . . ." And people were just sort of herding around looking for him. Other singers too. It always seemed to me to be a little bit absurd, but he created quite a stir down there.

"Positively 4th Street" was a song I heard when I was going to college in Billings, Montana. I heard it on the radio out there and I said, "My God. That's incredible that they're playing this song on the radio." It was enough to make me leave college, although it wasn't the only thing. I left college just to go to the Village and see what was going on.

OSCAR BRAND: I went with Dave Van Ronk to see Dylan's early performances at Folk City. I thought they were terrible, even though Bob had more musical ability than us. He could play the piano and read and write music and do all the things we couldn't do.

I thought Bob was pretty crummy. He was a pale version of Woody, and I thought some of his songs were maladroit. However, he was right there when the audience needed him.

Once in a while, he would hit the right element of poetry. He was like Woody, in that he wrote bad and he wrote good. When he wrote good, he was a genius.

He was a performer of some considerable fire; and that makes you overlook a lot of things. Also, for people who didn't know Woody Guthrie, it was very exciting.

Dylan didn't get to see Woody Guthrie until he was in the hospital and sick. Logan English always said the reason Bob Dylan sang the way he did was because he was copying Woody Guthrie when he was sick.

Bob was siphoning off from everyone, but that came with the true folk tradition, so it really didn't upset anyone. He was sleeping on friends' living room couches, and eating meals made by girlfriends' mothers. He was working on his craft, and just waiting for the right time and place.

The place was Gerdes Folk City, and for a while he just blended in with the crowd.

Initially, Mike Porco wasn't impressed by Dylan. Mike listened to many new performers, but, as he was relatively unfamiliar with the folk scene, each new unknown act sounded like the last. Still, Mike was open to the overwhelming suggestion that he hire the kid. At least four people take, or are given, credit for getting Dylan hired—Dave Van Ronk, Dave's wife Terri Thal, Charlie Rothschild, and Robert Shelton. Mike says that it was Mell and Lillian Bailey's persistence that was truly the catalyst—but, in any event, Mike finally decided to hire him, and a bond was formed between the two men which remains as strong today as it was back in 1961.

MIKE PORCO: Dylan came in and said he was from out of town. He said, "Can I go on and play?" He looked too young and I asked him for proof of age. There was a Youth Squad checking all the time, so the first time Dylan came in I didn't let him play.

The following week he came in with proof of age. I don't remember if it was a birth certificate. He was called Dylan from the beginning, but Zimmerman was on his papers.

Bob Dylan, December 1961 (Joe Alper)

He came in on the Monday hoot a few times and he would perform. The first couple of times I didn't pay much attention. He sang a couple of his own songs and a couple Woody Guthrie songs. He didn't sound bad, and a couple of people would say, "Mike, that kid is very good. Did you pay any attention to him?" Mell Bailey and his wife Lillian were very good friends of mine and Bobby's. They would say, "Mike, you know he wrote that song." So, when Dylan got through one night, I went to him and said, "You wrote that song?" He said, "Yes, that's my song, 'Don't Think Twice,' " so I started paying attention. The songs, they sounded pretty good.

Then he started to go out with Suze Rotolo, and she used to come in with him or I would go to their apartment for dinner; or some nights Suze would come in and make the circulars for the club. She used to draw for me. She was pretty good. So we became a little more friendly. He came in every week to play for a couple of months.

One day I said "I've got to give this kid a break. I like him." He was very shy. If he didn't have anything to eat, he wouldn't ask you. But you could see that he would like to grab a piece of bread or something. Once he gave me an address on Sixth Street, all the way on the East Side. I found out that maybe he was sleeping in a doorway.

There was a woman named Miss Adams who took care of him. When I gave him money for a haircut, he didn't get a haircut. This woman cut his hair. I gave him shoes, but they didn't fit him. This woman gave him a pair of shoes. She dressed him up and cleaned him up. People did this for him because they felt sorry. He was very good natured. He was a young kid, but he wrote very good.

I couldn't tell you a hundred percent that he was the best singer or the best songwriter, but when you put everything together, he was very good. He was a nice kid. He didn't look wild. He didn't argue with anybody. He would stand on the side like a little orphan. I sympathized with his manners, the way he handled himself. Then I heard the songs and I liked them.

When he got through singing one night I called him into the kitchen, which was my office. I said, "You did a nice set, Bobby. Tell me, you would like to work a couple weeks?" He said, "With who?" I said, "With John Lee Hooker." "Ooo yeah," he said. "Ooo Mike," he said, "great, great, oh man, great." So I told him, "The only thing is you've got to join the union. Otherwise the union comes in and won't let you play. You come in tomorrow and we'll go to the union. I know some people up there, so I'll go up there with you." "Oh," he said, "great, Mike."

I called up my friend Mike, the head of Local 802. "I have a young kid who one of these days you're gonna read about. He's gonna be a big star," I said to him.

We went up to the union. The man says, "Robert, Mike told me you're going to be a future star, you're gonna be great. Tell me the truth—what will you do when you become big? Mike has a lot of faith in you." So Bobby looked at him and he was very shy—even now he's shy—and he hunched his shoulders as if to say "I don't know." Then he filled out the application. Mike told him to come the next day with his mother because he was only twenty. Bobby said, "I ain't got no mother." The man said, "That's all right. Come with your father." Bobby said, "I ain't got no father, either." The man looks on the application and looked at me and whispered, "What is he, a bastard?"

So the man said, "I can't give you the contract because you have to be twenty-one—unless some legal guardian wants to sign." He said to me, "Mike, do you want to sign it as his guardian?" I said, "Bobby, do you want me to sign it?" Bobby said "Oh, sure Mike. I would appreciate it." So I signed his contract as his guardian.

So he played that show. He did the same as anybody else. They didn't break the doors down to come in. John Lee Hooker was the headliner, and Bobby didn't get the applause John Lee Hooker got. But he built up a following from the show.

I told Bob Shelton I was booking him again, and Shelton told me to remind him when so he could do an article. I almost forgot. I called him just the day before and told him Bobby was starting his gig the next day.

By the second show, people were telling other people, "You know, there's a good kid, Bob Dylan." So the word spread; but the write-up in the *New York Times* broke him through.

JOHN LEE HOOKER: I met Bob in Gerdes. He wasn't playing then. He would come to me for advice and to watch me. He would hang around me and come home with me at night. Finally he got up on stage and began playing.

In those days we would sit around and play guitar with no bands, and you could do what you wanted to. I liked what he was doing. He had such good lyrics. He was a good writer. He learned stage presence. He might have learned a few tips from me but he never picked up my style, because he had his own thing. He was strictly a folk singer.

Bob Dylan was a very funny guy. After work we'd sit there and drink white wine. He was kind of a fun person to be around. His talk was real funny, his conversation. He wasn't trying to make jokes, it was just there. He said he wanted to become a star—and a good star.

He loved his music. He loved music in general. It happened to him so quick. He didn't know it was going to happen to him that fast. He was the toast of the country. It went on for a long time.

Dylan went into seclusion before his crucial first Gerdes gig. He knew his whole career rested on that one night. His cronies were starting to rumble because one of their own was finally heading for the big time. Dylan had a paying gig in one of the most important clubs in the country, and he was opening for the legendary performer John Lee Hooker. Along with the arrival of a new breed of performer came a new breed of jealousy.

On April 11, 1961, Dylan brought all of his brilliance and intensity into the professional world. He was now legitimate. He had built up a devout following of fans who went wild with every word. Now those fans were joined by a larger crowd, totally unfamiliar with the young, scruffy kid on stage. The audience had no idea what to expect, nor did Dylan's friends.

DAVE VAN RONK: It was one of the most electrifying performances I have ever seen in my life. I had seen Bobby on stage before and I always thought he was a good performer, but I'd never seen him like that before; and I've never seen him like that since. He did "Letter to Woody" with a long set of harmonica breaks consisting of one note at a time spaced so as to be so totally unpredictable that you could never tell when he was going to hit that one chord on the harmonica. He had the audience in stitches. He also did his version of "Hava Nagilah"—you know, "Hava nagilah, have two nagilahs . . ."—"Talking Hava Nagilah Blues."

It was all in the performance. It was all in the delivery. There was lot of stage business. He would make a whole production out of tuning the guitar. Also, he was much given to chatting back and forth with the audience. He was very funny. "Talking Bear Mountain Picnic Massacre Disaster Blues" was one of his funniest songs.

You know what a nervous guy he is. Very jumpy. But he'd work that nervousness into the show. He was even more nervous than ever for his first show. Afterwards, it took him a couple of beers to calm down, but he had torn the house apart.

There was something positively Chaplinesque about him. He was one of the best natural performers I have ever seen. He could do a funny thing. He could do a pathos thing. You would have thought that we invented him, we were so pleased and proud. I didn't expect anything that dynamic on stage. All the stage business—little bits here and there, things with his cap and guitar—were used to their best possibilities. That first show was just incredible.

TERRI THAL: We made a tape of Bob and I took it up to Springfield, Massachusetts, where Carolyn Hester and Richard Fariña were playing. The guy who ran that club flipped. We really did a selling job. We went to Boston and I tried

Bob Dylan

to get Manny Greenhill to do a concert with Dave and Bobby, and he turned me down. I went to Cambridge's top folk club, Club 47, and a couple of other places, and they all turned me down. Nobody wanted him.

DAVE VAN RONK: Terri signed Bobby early. Nobody wanted to touch him with a ten-foot pole. He was too raw. We were just coming out of a period when people's idea of folk music was Harry Belafonte.

His friends and followers may have responded ecstatically to his Folk City debut, but commercially, nothing happened. Dylan was bitter, and he expressed it in his music and his lifestyle. Instead of writing paeans to Woody, he was writing diatribes in Woody's style. "Talkin' New York" was typical of his hard feelings toward the New York music establishment.

Dylan picked up and left New York for a time. But he was a different man now, a far cry from Robert Zimmerman. He was seasoned and he sounded like the real thing. He looked and talked like Woody. He performed like Woody. He lived like Woody. However, it all had the Bob Dylan signature of mystery and arrogance. He was beginning to form the protective cocoon which would soon become his trademark and solace. His patience was shorter and his drive was greater. His reputation was starting to spread. It was time to come back and conquer New York.

Meanwhile, his "sort of" manager, Terri Thal, was carrying his informal demo tape all over the east coast, and failing miserably with it.

BOB GIBSON: My first thought was, what does this guy have going? And the answer was nothing, by all contemporary standards of the time. He couldn't play real good. He couldn't sing real good. And he had funny songs. But, you were drawn back. You wanted to go back again to see what this guy had. Dylan was not an overnight sensation with everybody saying, "Wow, that was something." Dylan took a year and a half to happen.

TERRI THAL: I came home from a booking trip in Boston and found all the dishes in the sink. Bobby had been staying at our house. Bob said that Albert Grossman offered to sign him. Being incredibly stupid and young, and not being in business to make money, I said, "That's great. Go ahead." I couldn't do much with him anyway; but what I had done for him was get him his first gig. I had screamed at Mike and insisted that he book him.

It's more than coincidence that Dylan's genius emerged during his years with girlfriend Susan Rotolo, who may be forever known as the woman walking arm in arm with Dylan down Jones Street on the cover of the Freewheelin' album.

Former Greenbriar Boy John Herald reflects on that historic cover: "It really captured the mood of the time. We all had girlfriends. We all felt that spirit." Songwriter Carol Belsky describes the effect the cover had on her: "Suze was the epitome of everything that was hip. I wanted to recreate the essence of that album cover. I wanted to dress like her and look like her. I wanted to be Susan Rotolo. That cover was a symbol of my generation, the free-spirited freedom."

Susan was a seventeen-year-old product of a cultured, left-wing, political family. She was well-liked and very familiar with the Village scene, because she had been hanging around there since her early teens. Susan was living in the Village with her older sister, Carla, when she began dating Dylan.

The years they spent together were highly creative ones, and the bulk of his early original material was written during this fertile time. Many songs were written about Susan, or were inspired by her—"Boots of Spanish Leather," "Tomorrow is a Long Time," "Restless Farewell," "Ballad in Plain D" (a very bitter song towards her family, who were not too fond of the relationship), "Honey, Just Allow Me One More Chance," "All I Really Want to Do," "Down the Highway." Susan modestly agrees that " 'Tomorrow is a Long Time' is a beautiful song. I'm proud of that one."

They were in love and embarking on an adventure which few people experience. They were soon to be on top of the world. John Herald remembers that "Dylan was head-over-heels in love with her."

Lillian Bailey, Mike Porco, and Susan Rotolo (Thom Wolke, copyright © 1985)

She is credited by many for having politicized and intellectualized Dylan. Susan has a more modest theory: "It was a very political time. Politics was in the air in those years. Most of the people I knew were socially conscious, so I don't know if I really politicized Bob or not. I'm not sure. When you grow up with that social awareness, it's surprising to think that someone else might not be that aware."

The political atmosphere of the country was starting to heat up, and Dylan decided to make his material a little more topical. As the civil-rights and anti-nuclear protesters began to voice their discontent, Dylan became their early spokesman. He wrote protest songs and, once again, unknowingly started an unprecedented trend. He made political music fashionable.

Although he was not the first of the contemporary protest singers, he was the most influential. Bob Dylan was suddenly America's white conscience. "The Ballad of Emmett Till," for example, was written for a young black boy who was murdered in the South for whistling at a white woman. His murderers were never brought to justice. Ironically, Dylan claims he "stole" the melody from a young black folk singer, Len Chandler. Joan Baez recalls the impact "Emmett Till" had on her. "I was basically a traditional folksinger. I was not a 'political' at that time. When I heard 'Emmitt Till' I was knocked out. It was my first political song. That song turned me into a political folk singer." Judy Collins remembers her introduction to Dylan: " 'Blowing in the Wind' was printed in Sing Out!, *and I remember I wrote Dylan a fan letter. I loved the song, and I learned it; and I believe that was my first fan letter."*

Bob and Susan were having their own personal political problems. Dylan was living through a whirlwind of achievement and success, and Susan wasn't willing to go along for the ride. She didn't feel the impact of his impressive Gerdes performances, his record deal with Columbia, or his success as a songwriter. It wasn't until he played Carnegie Hall, when she got out of the car and saw the blow-up of the Freewheelin' *album cover in front of the hall, that she realized she was a part of something phenomenal.*

The album cover immortalized her. She was now part of the mythic cult which has always surrounded Dylan. Gerdes became a sort of safe haven for Susan—it was a place where most people remembered and accepted her as Suze Rotolo, not Bob Dylan's girlfriend.

SUSAN ROTOLO: It was very hard to talk to anybody because of all the prying. I was very vulnerable to this clinging "tell me about it" business, as if I was one step closer to God. I could never stand it.

Although Susan was Dylan's companion during his initial creative period, she still shies away from taking credit as a great influence.

SUSAN ROTOLO: People say I was an influence on him, but we influenced each other. His interests were filtered through me and my interests, like the books I had, were filtered through him. There was a book of satirical cartoons from the

Depression by Art Young that I showed him. It was during the time he was beginning to write his songs. It was wonderful satire.

My interest in Brecht was certainly an influence on him. I was working for the Circle in the Square Theatre and he came to listen all the time. He was very affected by the song that Lotte Lenya's known for, "Pirate Jenny."

It was always sincere on his part. He saw something. The guy saw things. He was definitely way, way ahead. His radar was flying. He had an incredible ability to see and sponge—there was a genius in that. The ability to create out of everything that's flying around. To synthesize it. To put it in words and music. It was not an intellectual approach that he had to research something—he did it on his own.

Outside the sphere of Folk City and the Village, Dylan was not yet the universal hero he would become. His fame was spreading mainly through the support of other performers—some of them performed his songs, while others taught and groomed him, and still others continued to feed and clothe him.

One artist instrumental in Dylan's emergence was Victoria Spivey, a flamboyant black blues singer who encouraged Dylan, immersed him in the blues, and recorded him for her blues label. Although his first recording experience, playing back-up harp for Harry Belafonte, was an unpleasant one (because of endless retakes), Bob was happy to go back into the studio for Spivey Records and record with his idol, Big Joe Williams.

On the album Three Kings and the Queen, *featuring Victoria Spivey, Roosevelt Sykes, and Lonnie Johnson, Dylan steals the spotlight with a passionate display of harmonica playing in "Sitting on Top of the World." He also plays on "Wichita," in which Big Joe at one point says, "This is Big Joe, and Little Junior's blowing his harp," later calling out to Dylan, "Play it for me, Junior."*

Things were beginning to happen quickly for him. Carolyn Hester, the rage of the New York folk scene, a singer as much admired for her beauty as for her soaring, country-tinged voice, asked Dylan to accompany her on her Columbia album. Through the recording session with Carolyn, Dylan made one of the most important connections of his life. He met one of the best-respected men in the record business, John Hammond, Sr.

CAROLYN HESTER: We were arranging to do my first Columbia album. We were discussing what instruments to use. On my very first album, I had used my Dad to play harmonica. I also had bass, and I played guitar. And that's what we wanted for this one. At Folk City, I had just met Bob Dylan and we all went up to Club 47 in Cambridge and Dylan played with us. We went to the beach the next day and we were sitting around and we said, "Gee, we had so much fun last night . . ." and one thing led to another and so Dylan came with us to the taping at Columbia.

Dylan taught me three of the songs we used on that LP. One of them was "Come Back Baby." We went to the studio one day and at that point, Dylan had played Folk City and Bob Shelton wrote a beautiful review, the very famous review of Bob Dylan. And right there in the studio, Hammond starts talking about taking Dylan on his own.

As a record company representative and director of talent acquisition, Hammond was responsible for the careers of such unique talents as Count Basie, Leonard Cohen, Donovan, Duke Ellington, Aretha Franklin, Billie Holiday, Pete Seeger, Bessie Smith and, later, Bruce Springsteen. He was known for his integrity in a business where there was precious little. He would fight hard to sign a controversial artist like Pete Seeger, regardless of the repercussions. With this sensibility, he was the perfect man to sign this new peculiar entity on the music scene, Bob Dylan. Hammond liked Dylan from the start. And Hammond was one of those rare record executives who was able to turn quality artists into commercial successes.

JUDY COLLINS: John Hammond, Sr., is a genius. He has a spirit about him and an understanding of the process of making music that I think is very rare in somebody connected with musical development and recording. He's a very special man.

CAROLYN HESTER: He used to see the seeds of someone's talent and the talent would blossom under his auspices.

JOHN HAMMOND, SR.: I lived in the Village from 1932 to 1953. I lived on Sullivan Street first, then on MacDougal Street. I got to know the Village awfully well.

My first experience at Folk City was under a previous incarnation when it was a real low, rough joint. When I was in the Army I felt that this was the ideal place to do a documentary on a Greenwich Village club. I came out of the Army and I started hanging out there, and by this time I had a son who was interested in singing. After he got out of college, he started at the hoots down there.

When I first saw Dylan at Folk City, he had just come in from Minneapolis. I heard Dylan when I was recording a girl called Carolyn Hester. She had him playing harmonica and guitar on her session. It was at a rehearsal on West Tenth Street. I was so delighted with what I heard I suggested he come up to the studio. I asked him if he could sing and he said, "Yeah." I asked him if he could write and he said, "Yeah." And that's how I signed Bob Dylan in 1961. Dylan was

John Hammond, Sr., and John Hammond, Jr. (Armen Kachaturian, copyright © 1980)

a rebel and I wanted to record protest. This was when we were getting involved in Vietnam, and so I started at the right time. When I first saw Dylan at Folk City he was rough, but the crowd just loved him. This was before the Shelton review.

The Shelton review came out the day after I signed Dylan for CBS. They all thought I was crazy. Dylan thought I was crazy. He had been turned down by Folkways and every other label there was at the time. But I thought he had something. By the time we did the second album, he had written "Blowing in the Wind," which Peter, Paul, and Mary made a hit of, and suddenly Dylan became an absolute star.

During that time he was playing "Talking New York," "Talking Bear Mountain," and he did a lot of Jesse Fuller's blues. The only two things he wrote were the talking numbers, but he was recording about seventy sides. It didn't cost anything for studio time in those days. My first album with Dylan cost $402, because all it was, was union scale for him as an artist.

At one point I began working at Vanguard Records. I got Vanguard into folk. I started them recording the Newport Folk Festival. I was on the Board of Newport.

Out of that they got Joan Baez. I went back to Columbia in 1958 and signed Pete Seeger, who was blacklisted by CBS at the time. I signed Dylan, Malvina Reynolds, Len Chandler, and all sorts of folk artists. But it was Dylan who started it all.

On September 26, 1961, Mike Porco booked Dylan into the club one more time. For this engagement, he was to open for the extremely popular bluegrass group the Greenbriar Boys. That group, which was then compromised of John Herald, Bob Yellin, and Ralph Rinzler, was winning over all sorts of audiences and breaking all stereotypes with their brand of urban bluegrass, even winning top honors at a prestigious, often chauvinistic southern fiddlers' convention. They were local heroes and were highly respected by other musicians. They were big time, and Dylan was the new kid on the block—a friend, no threat.

Dylan was ready. He was determined to have this Gerdes gig produce better results than the last. He was ready for his leap into big time, and he was certainly ready for his long-awaited review in the New York Times. *Shelton, too, was gearing up for this moment, but no one knew what a dramatic effect it would actually have. It was this review of Bob Dylan's September 26, 1961, performance, written by Robert Shelton, that turned Dylan's career around:*

Friday, September 29, 1961

BOB DYLAN: A DISTINCTIVE FOLK-SONG STYLIST

20-Year-Old Singer Is Bright New Face at Gerdes Club

by Robert Shelton

A bright new face in folk music is appearing at Gerdes Folk City. Although only twenty years old, Bob Dylan is one of the most distinctive stylists to play in a Manhattan cabaret in months.

Resembling a cross between a choir boy and a Beatnik, Mr. Dylan has a cherubic look and a mop of tousled hair he partly covers with a Huck Finn black corduroy cap. His clothes may need a bit of tailoring but when he works his guitar, harmonica, or piano, and composes new songs faster than he can remember them, there is no doubt that he is bursting at the seams with talent. . . .

JOHN HERALD: Dylan took us by storm when he opened for us that gig. He was getting a bigger hand than we were. I was getting a little envious. He was a friend of mine, but I really didn't understand what he was doing. We were supposed to be the main act, and he just won the place over. I couldn't get the gist of why he was so popular. I told a friend, "If this guy makes it, I'll eat my hat." They're trying to hold me to it. He really tore the house down, though.

Greenbriar Boys (Irwin Gooen)

DAVE VAN RONK: He had the audience in the palm of his hand. Of course, they were pre-sold. The word had gotten out, so he wasn't working to a hostile group, far from it. It was an unbelievable performance.

The Times *review was an unprecedented rave for a newcomer. It was also unprecedented in its effect.*

SUSAN ROTOLO: Robert Shelton's review, without a doubt, made Dylan's career, because that brought the establishment. He couldn't have gotten the Columbia thing, in a way, without that. That review was unprecedented. Shelton had not given a review like that for anybody.

It not only created a heretofore unheard-of level of success for Dylan, it also generated an emotional reaction from Dylan's peers and the public. Many of Dylan's fans were now evolving into devoted cultists in awe of a new hero, and many of his peers were reduced to petty jealousies and bitterness.

RAMBLIN' JACK ELLIOTT: When I first came back to America from England, I got a very good publicity story in the *New York Times* by Robert Shelton. He later came and heard Bob Dylan and got real excited about Bob, and wrote a much more glowing story. I felt kind of pissed about that. But I have no right to be pissed other than the right to be jealous, which we all have. I was a little hurt that he wrote this fantastically glowing account about the talented young new Bob Dylan. But what he wrote was absolutely correct.

On a less charitable note, one bitter contemporary who was never reviewed favorably by Sheldon claims that he witnessed the decision-making process that led to the writing of the review: "One night at Gerdes, Dave Van Ronk, Robert Shelton, and a number of other musician friends and I were sitting around the bar. I think it might have been a hoot night. Shelton asked David who he thought was the spokesperson for the new generation. David, who by this time was tired of having Bobby sleeping on his couch and mooching off everyone, slyly looked up in that way that he has, and lifted an inebriated finger at a sloppy little kid on stage and said, 'Him!' Everyone laughed because it was Bobby Dylan, who none of us took seriously. Everyone thought that David's joke was quite funny, except Shelton, who took it seriously and made him a star."

Terri Thal denies the incident vehemently: "First of all, if we had a problem with Bobby sleeping on our couch, it would never have been made public. But the truth is if we didn't want Bobby sleeping on our couch, he wouldn't have been sleeping on our couch. Dave and I loved Bobby. We had a lot of people staying over. Dave loved Bobby's music and he hardly liked anyone else's—even our good friends'. He always, privately and publicly, felt that Bobby was the spokesman for us all."

Dave laughs the alleged incident off—"Maybe it did happen. We were probably all drunk."

Dylan was the first of the new breed to be recognized on a massive scale, and the Village began to boil with anticipation. Everyone thought that their turn was next, and many of them were correct. As word about Dylan spread, Folk City became more crowded with aspiring folk singers.

Dylan had been safely buffered until now. He had been secure with his friends and fans at Folk City. But now that he was becoming bigger, he had to play different venues. A concert produced by Izzy Young at Carnegie Recital Hall was poorly attended, and showed Dylan he was not yet the star that Greenwich Village led him to believe he was. But there was no question that Dylan was on his way to stardom.

JEAN RITCHIE: Izzy Young ran a concert for Bob Dylan at Carnegie Recital Hall.

My husband and I were taking a walk and had just come into the Folklore Center. Izzy said to us, "Hey, I'm running a concert with Bob Dylan—why don't you come as my guests?"

We went along and there were about six girls in the place. That was the complete audience. He made us sit in the front row. About forty minutes late

Jean Ritchie

Bob Dylan walks up on stage and talked about what a little country boy he was and how he got lost on the subway. Then he started tuning his instruments. We thought, "Poor thing."

He had a table with about twenty harmonicas on it and he was blowing into each one. After about fifteen minutes of experimenting he said, "I think I won't sing that song." The whole concert was like that. At the end, he rushed off the stage and came up to me and said, "I'm so glad you came." It wasn't long after that when he became very well known.

Dylan began to gain national prominence and as his fame began to soar out

of control in 1962, so did his personal life. He and Susan were fighting and their fights were becoming more public.

Dylan would hang around Folk City, because there he would have the best of both worlds. People would recognize him, and he could hold court. A musician friend remembers: "He was a very nervous person, and to be around him was strange. He was full of himself. He had a lot of power. He'd come down to Gerdes and buy people drinks. I was always intimidated by him. It wasn't like having an easy conversation with somebody. Everyone wanted a piece of him, and I think he felt that, so he was very guarded and self-protective. He'd be nervous and you'd never get a straight answer. He'd make people uncomfortable. He was also a showoff. He would like holding court. He liked to play headgames with people. He was very paranoid. But, there were times when I had great times talking to him. He's very interesting when you get a chance to talk to him."

Lillian Bailey reacts, "Everybody was paranoid during that time. Everybody was on the brink of something."

Although Dylan was the center of attention at Gerdes, it wasn't bothersome like it was on the streets. He still felt comfortable enough to play hoots and try out his new songs; and, like everyone else, he could be sloppy. It was hoot night and nothing more than working on your craft was expected. The audiences at Gerdes were lucky. They could hear the premiere of many Dylan songs while they were still being honed.

DAVID BLUE: The night Bob Dylan's "Blowin' in the Wind" was first heard by an audience, Dylan and I had been killing the latter part of a Monday afternoon drinking coffee and bullshitting. About five o'clock, Bob pulled out his guitar and a paper and pencil. He began to strum some chords and fool with some lines he had written for a new song. Time passed and he asked me to play the guitar for him so he could figure out the rhymes with greater ease. We did this for an hour or so until he was satisfied. The song was "Blowin' in the Wind."

We decided to bring it over to Gil Turner who was hosting the Monday-night hoots at Gerdes, and we arrived about nine thirty or ten. Gerdes was packed with the regular Monday night jam of intense young folk singers and guitar pickers. We fought our way through the crowd down the stairs to the basement where you waited and practiced until your turn to play was called. It was a scene as usual.

Gil Turner finally took a break and came down to the basement to organize the next half of the show. Bob was nervous and he was doing his Chaplin shuffle as he caught Gil's attention. "I got a song you should hear, man," Bob said, grinning from ear to ear. "Sure thing, Bob," Gil said. He moved closer to hear better. A crowd sort of circled the two of them. Bob sang it out with great passion. When he finished there was silence all around. Gil Turner was stunned. "I've got to do that song myself," he said. "Now!" "Sure, Gil, that's great. You want to do it tonight?" "Yes," said Turner, picking up his guitar, "teach it to me now."

Bob showed him the chords and Gil roughly learned the words. He took the copy Bob made for him and went upstairs. We followed, excited by the magic that was beginning to spread. Gil mounted the stage and taped the words on to the mike stand. "Ladies and gentlemen," he said, "I'd like to sing a new song by one of our great songwriters. It's hot off the pencil and here it goes."

He sang the song, sometimes straining to read the words off the paper. When he was through, the entire audience stood on its feet and cheered. Bob was leaning against the bar near the back smiling and laughing. Mike Porco bought us a drink. Later in the evening Bob went home with Suze, and I split with some friends. Another moment in time ticked off.

In 1962, Dylan's great influence as a songwriter was becoming obvious. His obsession with Susan was becoming overwhelming. The two parts of his life were having difficulty resolving themselves separately, but they made for a rich creative period. Many of his best songs were written during this time. When Susan left Dylan and the spotlight for Europe, he eventually followed her. Lillian Bailey recalls, "He was devastated when she went away."

In January 1963, Susan returned, ready to try to make it work with Dylan, but there was more pressure on her now than ever before. She was the envy of everyone around, and therefore was in the public eye—but not for her own work.

A close friend during that time has her own theory: "I always felt that Bob was trying to show Suze what it was like on the top. Trying to have her realize what it's like in the spotlight. A lot of us thought that was the reason why he put her on the album cover; that maybe she would understand his needs better if she, also, was a star."

SUSAN ROTOLO: Later on Dylan began talking about being a "thing"—you were no longer who you were—and how devastating that was. He was becoming two people—this public persona and the person I knew. He was a true paranoid. That song "Positively 4th Street"—that was a kind of nasty song, but it was understandable. I remember at the time he wrote it, I was on his side. I could understand why his friends Mark [Spoelstra] and Dave [Van Ronk] would feel bad about that song, because he was pushing them off. But you have to have some kind of growth and you have to have some space for yourself to become what you're becoming. He was becoming famous. That was part of our problem as a couple.

His popularity was originally in a small circle. There was no way to know how huge that circle would become.

domain song but he got the copyright on it, and then when he got crazy he sold his shares.

Paul had a copyright on a song called "Who's Gonna Buy Your Ribbons When I'm Gone." The lyrics are "Ain't no use to sit and sigh; ain't no use to sit and wonder why . . . tell me who's gonna buy your ribbons when I'm gone."

I was with Paul one day, and Dylan wanders by and says, "Hey, man, that's a great song. I'm going to use that song." And he wrote a far better song, a much more interesting song—"Don't Think Twice."

When it became a legal question, the song was actually traced down to a song that was exactly the same as Paul's called, "Who's Gonna Buy Your Chickens When I'm Gone." So, in effect, everything that Dylan took was actually public domain. They remained friends but their publishing companies were suing each other.

RALF NEMEC: Bob Dylan waltzed into Folk City one night with his wife. This was just prior to his comeback and his tour with the Band. I was working the door and he came in, gave me a funny look, and walked right past me. I looked up to check with the bartender if it was really Dylan. From the look on her face I knew I didn't make a mistake.

He walked right into the back and started talking to Mike. He came back up front to get a pack of cigarettes and he was fumbling for his change. I walked up to him and asked him if he needed change, and I bought him a pack of Kools. When I reached out to get the matches, I was shaking so much it was like I was having an epileptic seizure.

I was always cool around well-known people, but Bob Dylan was Bob Dylan. It was all that legend and history right there in front of me. I lit his cigarette for him and then asked him for one. He said, "Sure, you bought 'em." He lit mine for me and we sat at the bar and smoked a cigarette together.

I still have his cigarette butt in a plastic bag. The bartender took home his brandy glass. I said to Dylan, "I work here, you know," and he said, "I used to work here a lot myself."

JOAN BAEZ: I came to Gerdes one night with my boyfriend and someone grabbed me and said, "You've got to meet this guy. You've got to meet this guy." Everybody was dragging me saying, "You've got to meet this guy."

Someone came to Bob and said, "You've got to meet Joan. You've got to meet Joan." So we were sort of forced to meet each other. We both said, "Okay" and there he was "His Scruffiness" himself, Bob Dylan.

We both made incredibly sixties-ish, introductions like, "far out" or "like wow, man" and meanwhile I totally forgot about my boyfriend. But Bob was only nice to me because he liked my sister, Mimi.

Bob Dylan and Joan Baez at Folk City, 1964 (Norman Vershay)

I watched his performance and I was completely knocked out by it. There was something so gut-attractive about it.

After we became friends we sang together a couple of times, in fact one night at Gerdes we were up on stage making up a song together, "Troubled and I Don't Know Why." We had good times at Gerdes. I just loved being in the Village and that was Bobby's home turf.

He was so mesmerizing and attractive, he immediately drew the audience into what he was doing. I thought about his music way after I left that first night and I came back many more times to see him, but by then we were friends. There was something so magnetizing about him and you could certainly sense genius. He just looked so peculiar with that weird little hat on.

He was a magnetic, charismatic performer and he made that room his whenever he performed.

DAVID AMRAM: A lot of music people would always say "This is the new Bob Dylan" about somebody. But, of course, Bob Dylan became the new Bob Dylan every two years himself.

The thing that endears me to him is that he's still out there, searching and trying to get a deeper understanding of life, and he's still not content with what he's doing.

That's what I think most good artists are like. They're always trying to improve, to advance, to go into other areas that they haven't worked in before, and to take the thing that they did before and do it even better.

GEOFFREY STOKES: The Dylan song I remember best was "Talking Picnic Blues." There was a big church picnic from one of the Harlem churches going up the Hudson River on a chartered boat, and someone had sold a batch of counterfeit tickets. So there were about twice as many people as the boat could hold—but they loaded them all on anyway. And it turned out to be a disaster, with the boat almost sinking and all these fights breaking out.

Dylan did a talking blues about it—"I almost lost my picnic spirit." I was floored by that song. It was so cranky and so wonderful. I always thought of his talent as being a writer's talent, and this proved it out. If he didn't exist, I wonder if we would have had to invent him.

WOMEN

....

BARBARA DANE: If you were going to discuss all the artists in this era, you'd have to really reach and knock yourself out to find out who are the women.

Folk music was a man's world in many ways, and the few women who made it there were giants. They stood alone, on the stage at Newport or in front of a packed house at Folk City. Nineteen-sixty-three may have been the year of ascendancy for Joan Baez, Judy Collins, Carolyn Hester, and Buffy Ste. Marie, but mainstream America was listening to the sound of breaking hearts as sung by the Shirelles, Chiffons, Marvelettes, Crystals, Ronnettes, and Shangrilas. American pop culture accommodates the wildest juxtapositions. As Joan Baez began to sing protest songs, and the civil-rights movement was heating up, the Angels hit number one with "My Boyfriend's Back."

While the men were trying to keep up with Bob Dylan, the women folk singers had their own battles. The press was intent on promoting a war between the Queens of Folk Music, and the record companies felt their quota was full if they had one woman folk singer signed up. If a label had Judy Collins or Joan Baez in their catalog, then others need not apply. As in the jazz and blues worlds, women had a tough time maintaining their own identities, getting past comments like "She plays almost as good as a man," and "she's okay for a chick." This, moreover, is a problem that doesn't appear to have gone away entirely. When one of the men I interviewed was asked to comment on a well-known female folk singer, he referred to her in sexual terms: "She used to ball everybody. Put her on spin cycle and let her go. This is in no way to degrade her. I wanted to ball her." But when a lesser-known, peripheral male singer's name came up later on, the man said: "He worked hard on his songs. He didn't always do a good job, but he was working."

The Four Queens, as they were called then, were Joan Baez, Judy Collins, Carolyn Hester and Buffy Ste. Marie. Whether there was a true rivalry or not, as a gimmick it sold papers and brought attention to the folk scene. Whether it was divisive, is another question. Some genuinely believed it was. The wife of an early sixties folksinger recalls that "Judy Collins swallowed green tears every time Joan did something or got noted for something. She absolutely whipped herself to get up there with Joan."

ALIX DOBKIN: I don't know about the rest of show business, but in folk music, you never put two "chicks" back to back. This was common knowledge. It was too much to have two women—"chicks"—singing right after each other. You could have fifteen men, but two "chicks" back to back was verboten.

I felt equal then, but looking back I could see that there were certain things I took for granted that reflected a lack of male privilege. But at the time I felt very much a peer in the group. I just didn't allow any space for feeling inferior, although there was all this male bonding. I would watch their poker games but I could never play. I used to sit around and bring them coffee. It never occurred to me that I had a right to be playing with them.

MARIA MULDAUR: I was always tuned in to some sort of alternative music. Early fifties pop music was pretty nowhere. In junior high school I had a group called the Cameos—three Puerto Rican girls and myself. We did Everly Brothers tunes. In high school I had a group called the Cashmeres. We wore tight white sweaters and tight black skirts and we would go to the Brill Building every afternoon after school and work our way through all the music offices. We landed a record deal but my mother wouldn't let me sign. She thought they were going to make a white slave out of me. To this day I don't know what a white slave is. So that abruptly ended my rock-and-roll career.

Rock and roll began to get whitewashed. You'd have Pat Boone singing "Ain't That a Shame" instead of Fats Domino. I naturally lost some of the verve I had for rock music. I then got very interested in jazz, and started hanging out in the Village. I realized that right at my doorstep there was something just as exciting and more interesting musically. Then I heard an Odetta record, and some friends had a Josh White record. I soon got turned on to very risqué old blues.

BARBARA DANE: I had a Midwesterner's attitude about New York. I thought New York was too easy. I thought that everyone who was rushing to the Village with their folk songs should be back at their home base making music and interacting with their own people. The Village was too commercial.

JOAN BAEZ: I was the only Mexican around and I was basically a loner when I was a kid. I spent a lot of time with myself. It gave me the opportunity to learn about myself and certainly gave me the time to get totally involved in folk music.

One of my greatest musical influences was Odetta. I learned everything she did. Her passion moved me. In Harvard Square all these places were opening up where you could hear real people singing real songs. That soon became my life.

The Club 47 was a little jazz club and they hired me to work a weekday night for something like ten dollars. The first few times I played, the place was nearly

Joan Baez

empty—just friends and family. Soon people began talking about what I was doing, and the crowds started coming.

The more I got into folk music, the more I got interested in the real thing, the traditional music. I was becoming well-known in Cambridge, and when I ventured out I was a little leery. Bob Gibson introduced me at the 1959 Newport Folk Festival and we sang a couple of songs together, and the audience really liked it. After that I was already "the madonna." It's tough being the madonna.

I recorded my first album for Vanguard. You've got to remember how confused and young I was at that point. Here I was, this lonely Mexican kid with no self-confidence, and suddenly I'm the madonna, queen of folk music. I was very mixed up.

Gerdes Folk City was the heart of it all. It was the ultimate of hip. It was the pure thing. And it could still be if the record business didn't have so much control over the everyday business of making music. Back in the sixties at Gerdes everyone was performing for the love of the song. There's still beautiful music being made, but it doesn't always get out to the people.

JUDY COLLINS: Albert Grossman brought me a tape of Joanie's which I still think is one of the real beacon lights of folk music. It was a tape of her first album, and her voice was impeccable. The kinds of things that were on the record were real special. I thought she was fabulous.

CAROLYN HESTER: I loved Joan Baez. I'm one of her great fans. Her voice was from the gods.

Joan quickly became the toast of the folk music world. Her dark Hispanic looks and dramatic voice became a perfect foil for Colorado's blond, blue-eyed Judy Collins and the beautiful singing sensation from Texas, Carolyn Hester.

JOAN BAEZ: There was no rivalry between us. We were all working hard at what we were doing, and we all were doing different things. For a record company to say, "Sorry, we already have our Judy Collins" or "We already have our Joan Baez"—well, that would only work against the company. They would be losing out on a lot of new talent. We weren't trying to outdo each other, we were trying to do the best we could for ourselves and our audience. People could appreciate what we were all doing. They didn't have to select one. They didn't have to select one *male* folksinger. I guess that kind of controversy sells records.

MARSHALL BRICKMAN: Joan was always very amazing looking and she had enormous charisma. She was real good and had a real wonderful, natural, clear voice, and an amazing sort of charisma. She always seemed more mature than I thought I was.

There was something very clear about her presentation. As a film director, I can see that her quality is what you look for in a film actor—enormous economy.

There's nothing superfluous about her. Everything's working and facing in the same direction.

CHARLIE CHIN: At the time, she used to do something we thought was totally outrageous. She used to take her shoes off on stage. I remember thinking it was kind of sexy, but it wasn't sexy—it was really intense. There was something about her that was really magical. Today I would say, "Get off it, girl; get off that stool and get real." But at the time, it was really magical. It was like she was from another place. She would sing in this high voice and play simple guitar technique. It was just ethereal.

Joan Baez, fall 1961 (Joe Alper)

JOAN BAEZ: I had some pretty wild times, but I also had some serious times. In fact, some people think I'm too serious. I've worked for a lot of causes—non-violence, civil rights and international human rights. In your life, you've got to do what you can to make life better for everyone on the planet. I do it through my work which is singing, raising money, or raising consciousness. That's what music is at its best, a force for social change and a force for good. That's why the music of the sixties is so important. It was good, it made a statement, and it did its part in moving society. There are different kinds of music and all good music makes some sort of impact or statement. Lionel Richie's "Hello" makes an impact. Tina Turner's "Private Dancer" makes a statement. Good music is good music no matter what decade we're in.

CYNTHIA GOODING: There was one time I heard Judy Collins on the car radio. They were playing the song that she does with the whales. It was so beautiful I had to drive to the side of the road. I couldn't drive anymore. There were tears in my eyes.

ERIC WEISSBERG: Judy Collins was a good guitar player, which was unusual. It was unusual for the female folk singers to be good instrumentalists. I thought Judy was the most advanced of the women, although Joan had a truer voice and Joan was more exciting. Judy got into your brain more, and stayed there.

DAVE VAN RONK: Judy's stock-in-trade was magic on the stage. She had a really pure delivery. I think one of the most important things about her show, which many people didn't realize, was her posture. She stood straight with her head back, and she could really belt. People would just drop their teeth. They'd never seen anything like that before. Cynthia Gooding used to do that, too, and I wondered if Judy had ever caught Cynthia.

JUDY COLLINS: I had no illusions about a career in music or about my own possibilities as a recording artist. My reason for working, frankly, was to pay the bills. I love to sing. I was totally devoted to my work. I wasn't told or questioned about what I was going to do as a career when I was younger. We came up in a different generation and I was singing because that's what I do. I loved the singing. I loved the work that I did.

I was putting my husband through school at that point. When we came to Connecticut I was a college wife who was on the road, whereas other college wives worked in the library or worked as secretaries, or whatever. My job as a college wife was to go to these places and sing.

After the initial intimidation I found New York to be my natural home. A sort of zeal came over me and I saw there was something I had to communicate. I didn't think of myself as a singer so much as a storyteller anyway.

Judy Collins (Irene Young)

When Jac Holzman, who started Elektra Records, came to see me in 1961, he said to me, "I want you to make a record. You're ready to make a record." I said to him, "You've got to be out of your mind. This is the farthest thing from my talent." One just had no idea. I have been with Elektra for twenty-five years.

CHARLIE ROTHSCHILD: They were all friends. I once threw a party, and I had Joni Mitchell, Mimi Farina, and Judy Collins all at the same table; and, you know, they were all friendly. But if you put them on stage, sparks would fly. It was competitive. They were all friends until they got on stage. They would all hang out and they would each perform for each other and they would all be

Note: Judy Collins left Elektra in the fall of 1985.—Ed.

friends socially afterwards at parties, but when it became time for the big concert, it was competitive.

JUDY COLLINS: The rivalry was nonsense. It was silly. There was never a rivalry. The press was always looking for something sensational to say. They have to get that paper out every day and say something. There's always room for people who work, no matter what field it is.

Judy Collins

CHARLIE CHIN: In the early sixties Judy Collins had short cropped hair and she used to wear clothes like the Carnaby Street look. She was kind of sexy. She had a very good voice and a very wistful nature. There was something about her that was otherworldly. In the beginning, she had a light jazz-folk feel. She did a lot of popular tunes, too. It wasn't really strictly folk in the beginning. She had a broad repertoire.

GEOFFREY STOKES: Judy Collins was very well respected by her peers. I'm sure she was treated with greater respect as an individual on the folk circuit than at faculty parties in Connecticut, because there she was a faculty wife and not Professor Collins. In the music world, she was a talented star in her own right.

CHARLIE ROTHSCHILD: Carolyn Hester was a big star. She was equal to Joan Baez, but Joan was happening in Boston. They came on the scene at the same time and they overlapped. Carolyn was happening in New York. She was the big favorite.

Carolyn Hester was a very pretty lady. When you took away the presence and you put her on to a record, some of the edge was lost. When she was performing, you would look at her and be overwhelmed by her beauty and her presence and her singing.

GEOFFREY STOKES: Carolyn was brilliant, a very good performer. And she was beautiful, which was clearly a plus. She was a New York version of Joan Baez.

She was in the group the Song Spinners. They were a locally performing, Weaver-ish kind of group with a little more country to it. When she left, Judy Collins took her place and the group was not as good without her.

CAROLYN HESTER: When the press and radio started picking up on folk music, then the uptown people came. I remember playing at the Gaslight and the owner, Clarence Hood, would say, "When Carolyn comes, I tell ya, I can count ten fur coats a night."

After appearing at Newport in 1966, Irwin Silber wrote something about how demeaning it was to see the battle of the Folk Queens. He was talking about Joan, Judy, Buffy, and myself.

Harold Leventhal, Judy's agent, once sat down with me and said, "Well, you know, the kids only have so much money. They can only buy a few of the women's records every year." That kind of made me sad, because I felt that was the source of our problem.

About 1962, Joan appeared on the cover of *Time*, and it was one of the most important moments for women in folk music. They had a whole article about her and I was one of the little blurbs. I felt like my life was either changed or over. I wasn't sure.

Then, in 1964, I got on the cover of the *Saturday Evening Post*, and that was just earthshaking. I understood that the Judy Collins people were very upset. In fact, it turned out that a lot of people were upset about it. There was always room for all of us, and I thought the competition thing was dangerous for the movement.

Carolyn's husband, David Bloom, felt that the record companies were a large part of the problem.

DAVID BLOOM: I would bring her tape to a record company and they would say things like, "Gee, this is terrific, but she sounds too much like Joan Baez" or "we already have our Judy Collins." She sounds as much like Joan Baez as I do. I was an A&R man for a while, and I know there was more room on the records roster for men.

Carolyn was more than professionally affected by the competitive situation she found herself in. It crept its way into her personal life.

CAROLYN HESTER: Richard Fariña and I met in January of '60. He was in the audience at Folk City. It was one of those weeks when I was playing a full week, and he was sitting at a table right in front of me and he followed me when I left after the first set. And that was it—we were stuck together like glue. We got married in two weeks. Now, if you want to talk about mistakes! I couldn't get rid of the guy. He was going to follow me everywhere. It would be more convenient if we got married, I decided.

He was a copywriter at J. Walter Thompson. At this point, he was about to give up his job, because he wanted to start his book. He loved folk music very much and he would sing at the drop of a hat.

A fellow named George Emerson made me a dulcimer, so I gave the dulcimer to Richard and he started playing. We started playing together.

I went to England in 1962. At this point, we were singing together a lot more and he began writing a lot more. He started to write songs and he was well into his book.

We just had a lot of irreconcilable differences, I guess. We were very different. We were crazy about each other, but couldn't live together.

His career hadn't really taken off at that point and it was a strain on me because I earned all the money. It was a good time for me professionally.

I tried to encourage him to go ahead and keep on with the book and at the same time, I was upset by the insecurity of it. It was very hard to earn your living in the entertainment field, anyway. So, probably my being our total support wasn't good for either one of us and our relationship

In the end, I typed the first ninety pages of his book. I was getting calls to come back to the States. There were a lot of jobs waiting. Richard was very mad

In "Cod'ine" her voice was just what being strung out on codeine was all about. The voice made the message very, very heavy.

TOM PASLE: Buffy did an extremely dramatic thing for the socially aware sixties. She opened up with a tune that was mostly Indian cries, that utilized that great contralto voice of hers and that profound vibrato that could shake the ceiling. It had tremendous impact. She was an immediate success.

BUFFY STE. MARIE: When I first came to the Village, I played at Gerdes; and I met Bob Dylan there and he told me about the other places to play, like the Gaslight. So I began playing the different clubs. I used to like to come to Gerdes and see the hoot. I liked to hear the things that the new people were writing. During those first few weeks in New York I was approached by lots of managers and agents. I was overwhelmed by all the success I was having. Being approached by all these people, Robert Shelton reviewing me in the *New York Times*, and

Buffy Ste. Marie at Folk City, summer 1981 (Liz DeMayo)

Odetta and Joan Baez at the Pier Concert, 1985 (Thom Wolke, copyright © 1985)

ODETTA: I grew up with an incredibly wide span of music. I'm a radio baby for sure. We had rhythm-and-blues, classical, pop ballads, Grand Ole Opry, Metropolitan Opera, and the church. I was a snob of a kid, 'cause there was a time if it wasn't classical I wasn't interested.

When I was around ten years old, a neighbor friend and I were waiting for the piano teacher to come. While we were waiting, we were seeing how high we could sing, and the piano teacher got there and tested both of our voices and became a voice teacher on the spot and started teaching me voice. Mine was a coloratura voice. I would sing a lot of churches and sing all that stuff.

One night in San Francisco, where I was playing the Tin Angel, there's a knock at the door and this man said, "Hello, Odetta, I'm Herbert Jacobi from the Blue Angel in New York." I said, "Oh, that's nice." He said, "I would very much like you to someday come to the Village." I said, "Thank you very much." I knew not what the Blue Angel was. I did not know that the people in show business killed to get to the Blue Angel. It was like your reputation was made once you got to the Blue Angel. What did I know? I had sung at Yugoslav Hall and somebody's dining room.

Jacobi called me and told me that someone couldn't get back from Europe for her date and he booked me into the Blue Angel. I'd been in show business two weeks by the time I got to the Blue Angel in New York.

In those days if somebody played a good lick in New York we heard about it in Los Angeles the next day. I remember hearing from Albert Grossman out of Chicago when I was in San Francisco. He heard about me and asked if I would like to come to the Gate of Horn. So there were grapevines all over the country. But the Village was the place—not only as far as folk music was concerned, but as far as writers and artists were concerned. It's an area of renegades, people with imagination, or just goof-offs.

JOHN LEE HOOKER: Big Mama Thorton was a great lady. She and I used to hang out together all around New York. We'd go to all sorts of places. Willie Mae was a warmhearted lady, and a tough, tough lady. She didn't back up off nobody like club owners or record company people.

She was very close to me and had been for a very, very long time over the years. She was a really good entertainer. I don't think any woman could sing the blues as well as she could.

Unfortunately, like a large number of other blues artists of her time, Big Mama died in poverty, panhandling in West Coast bars. Her last appearance at Folk City was in 1984, and when she arrived for the show, the doorman stopped her, mistaking her for a bag woman.

Her "Big Mama" frame had dwindled down to a shell of its former size. Apparently suffering from bad ulcers, the heavy-drinking Willie Mae had glasses of milk—mixed with gin—continuously brought to her on stage. She put on one of her best shows and tore the house down with a laid-back set of blues. Although a sad figure, sitting frailly on a stool, she wailed away. Big Mama was in complete control. The last thing she said to me was, "Here's my number. Call me, don't call my agent. I'll make more money if you just call me."

A few months later she died.

ROBERT ROSS: Victoria Spivey was one of the first black woman singers to make her mark on the world. Her big hit was "Black Snake Blues," and she used to wear this white gown with all these plastic snakes attached to it. It would have been gaudy even without the snakes.

She was one of the greatest people I ever knew. She was beautiful. She was kind to everybody. Not just those who played the blues. She helped with encouragement, gigs, and her record company. She put out my first professional record.

She also had another side to her. She would drink a lot and she could get rowdy. She was no pushover. If she had to say no, it was no!

She had a heart as soft as cotton and as beautiful as gold. It was a great loss when she died. Even Dylan sent a wreath to the funeral home when she died.

In her early days she had a very sweet voice. She wasn't in the Bessie Smith or Ma Rainey mode. She wasn't a bellowing blues singer. She had a much softer, sweeter sound, and her lyrics were very hip and touching.

In the mid-seventies she was a leader. Everybody would come to her for help, because there wasn't much of a blues scene going on in New York. None of the local cats were playing. She was there plugging away for everybody. She gave

Bob Dylan, Victoria Spivey, A&R Len Kunstadt, Big Joe Williams, Spivey Records session, Cue recording studio, March 1962 (Spivey Records archives, courtesy Len Kunstadt)

people a chance to record, get gigs, get reviews, and look professional. What she did for Dylan, she did for so many others. She saw something in him. She had an eye for talent.

PAULA BALLAN: When I heard Hedy West's phrasing and her style—that was it! That's what I wanted to sound like. Hedy West was the real thing. She was the one who everyone went out and learned how to do. Probably Mary Travers got her phrasing and some of her thing from Hedy. Hedy was one of the few younger "real" people. There was a special quality to her, and she's as spectacular today as she was then. In fact, she's even better because now she's the mistress of what she started out doing—her heritage.

HEDY WEST: I arrived in New York in 1958. I went to Washington Square, where the New Yorkers were making folk music. I was introduced as, "This is Hedy West—she comes from the South and she learned her music from her family, so I guess we're going to have to accept her whether we like her or not."

BARBARA SHUTNER: I was raised in Oklahoma and I got tired of listening to hillbilly music so I came to the only place where I knew I didn't have relatives— Greenwich Village. I moved in with a girl who worked at NBC, and the next thing I knew, I was at the White Horse Tavern where I met the Clancys, Tommy Makem, and Logan English. And I learned to like hillbilly music much more than I ever did in Oklahoma.

PHYLLIS LYND: The singer-songwriters who came along were wonderful writers, but the singing was god-awful. They were great guitarists but not such great singers. I think one reason the movement died out was that it is hard to keep a trend going unless it's rooted in excellence.

Their songwriting was rooted in excellence and there were about six or eight wonderful voices. But, that's not enough to make the folk music last. The people who lasted were good singers—Judy Collins had pure beauty of tone and Joan Baez had a thrilling voice.

I was never really accepted in the milieu. They never really accepted me because I was a classical artist performing folk music.

Elizabeth Cotten truly embodies the strength of the women in folk music. While some artists were learning, artists like Cotten were teaching. She is as respected for her unique fingerpicking guitar and banjo style as she is for her songwriting. She wrote her classic song, "Freight Train," when she was just twelve years old.

Born in 1893, "Libba" is self-taught on guitar, and her "Cotten Picking" or "Cotten Style" is a left-handed, upside-down, two-finger, broken rhythm guitar

Elizabeth Cotten (Armen Kachaturian, copyright © 1969)

style. She demonstrates it as clearly and powerfully today as she did seventy years ago.

While working in a department store in Washington, D.C., she once helped a woman find her lost child, and as Libba recalls, "The woman asked me if she could do anything to pay me back, and I thought about it and said, 'Yes, maybe I should come work for you so your children don't get lost no more,' and she hired me to work for her. She was a very nice woman."

That woman turned out to be Ruth Crawford Seeger, composer and author and wife of Charles Seeger, a well-respected ethnomusicologist. The lost child was Peggy Seeger, sister of Mike and Pete, and later to become an influential folk singer-songwriter on her own.

SINGER-SONGWRITERS

···

········· **I**n 1963 America's conscience came to the Capitol. Over two hundred thousand freedom marchers descended on Washington, D.C. In South Vietnam a Buddhist-led military coup overthrew the government and the U.S. immediately sent "aid." President Kennedy was assassinated on November 22 and Lyndon Johnson was sworn in as President. Dr. Strangelove wowed audiences at the box office and Edith Piaf died at the age of forty-seven.

The Beatles stole the hearts of the American youth and at 1:20 p.m. Friday, February 8, 1964, they arrived in the U.S. The Nobel Peace Prize was awarded to Martin Luther King, Jr., while the younger generation concentrated on more frivolous things like dancing the Watusi, the Frug, the Monkey, and the Funky Chicken. Cassius Clay became the World Heavyweight Champion and soon changed his name to Muhammad Ali.

The Beatles had eight songs in the 1964 year-end top one hundred—a year that produced such classics as Roy Orbison's "Pretty Woman," the Supremes' "Baby Love" and "Where Did Our Love Go?" the Kingsmen's "Louie Louie," Mary Wells's "My Guy," and hits by the Beach Boys, Manfred Mann, the Kinks, Dixie Cups, Zombies, and Four Seasons.

But, if measured by standards other than sales, the upper echelon of songwriters during the years 1962 to 1966 were those who were not only providing the world with songs to sing, but were also making statements that served social and political purposes. They were the new voices which spoke for a restless, socially conscious generation.

The civil-rights, anti-war, and hippie-drug movements were all flourishing. There were many causes, ranging from banning the bomb to legalizing marijuana, and there was always room for more spokespeople. They found their natural home in Greenwich Village.

There were also some singer-songwriters who dealt with more personal issues. They were all part of a snowballing movement that was soon to turn into a multi-million-dollar industry.

As Dylan began to have his first successes, he was followed by singer-songwriters like Eric Andersen, John Sebastian, Jesse Colin Young, and others. Tom Paxton, a seasoned vet by 1964, would keep his music acoustic and simple; and he was an outstanding writer. Michael Mann was a perennial Village face, with connections to just about everyone. He would remain on the streets after the folkies-turned-rockers like McGuinn and Colin Young had taken the trip to the more commercially prosperous West Coast. What became folk-rock came from Dylan-imitations or brilliant steps forward by the Byrds, whom Lillian Roxon called "Beatlized Dylans."

ERIC ANDERSEN: Leonard Cohen came up to me once and said, "I'm a poet and I never thought of writing songs; but then I heard 'Violets of Dawn' and I began

Eric Andersen (Norman Vershay)

to write songs." Also, Kris Kristofferson liked my sexy songs, my love songs. It helped him to write the kinds of things he did in Nashville, like "Help Me Make It Through the Night." He said that my song "Come to My Bedside" was an inspiration for him to take a chance to write a different kind of tune like that.

I learned guitar off old rockabilly albums. Between that, reading Jack Kerouac and having fantasies about hitting the road, I finally decided to hitch out to California. I worked in a place where Janis Joplin and Howard Hesseman were also working. Dino Valenti, who wrote "Come On People, Let's Get Together," was playing there some nights, and I started playing there once a week. One night, Tom Paxton came in, heard me sing, and told me he thought I wrote good songs. He suggested that I come to New York. I came to New York and he introduced me to Robert Shelton.

Shelton liked me and he placed a couple of calls. One was to Elektra Records, but the owner was out of town. Then he called Vanguard Records and the owner was in town, so I ended up on Vanguard Records. It was just caprice.

He introduced me to Milt Okun, who was a producer who agreed to publish my songs. Then, Shelton got me my very first gig, which was at Folk City and he wrote a real nice review. I opened for John Lee Hooker. It was in 1964. I was so nervous I could hardly stand up. I was just shaking all over. I think I sang my songs too fast. I did a forty-five-minute set in twenty minutes. I did "Come to My Bedside" and a lot of rambling songs. I was really into rambling.

I was scared. There was all this hoopla. I was this new kid in town. You know, "All right, let's see what he can do." There had been Dylan, Phil Ochs, Paxton—I was the new young punk. Everybody was checking me out. I was very excited and elated, but I was very nervous at the same time.

JOHN STEWART: It was very intimidating for me at that time. I grew a lot just from doing little solo sets at the club. Folk City was the most petrifying place I'd ever played in my life; absolutely scared me to death. It was a real trial by fire. But I was drawn to it. I was living way up on 122nd Street and collecting Coke bottles to get the subway down there.

When the Kingston Trio played at Folk City I'm sure we had a few cocktails before we got on stage, because it terrified us. These were the people who thought we were bullshit and in many cases were right. So to play in front of our peers was terrifying. I was a fan of the trio when I joined in 1961, so I can speak from within it and without it.

On the other end of folk music there were people who really got their start from the Kingston Trio. Bob Dylan in a recent *Rolling Stone* said, "Yeah, it was the trio who got me started." He took it from there and put it in a more serious form. Peter, Paul, and Mary were the real serious group.

The Kingston Trio, 1963: Bob Shane, Nick Reynolds, and John Stewart (Maureen Wilson)

There was always a rivalry of us defending "good time" folk music and them defending serious folk music, and me being a songwriter really yearning to be a serious folk musician but really not having the courage at that time to step out and be one of the guys on the block.

VINCE MARTIN: Fred Neil and I were walking down the street in the Village and this crewcut kid with an overcoat on and a holster full of harps comes up to us. We needed a harp player and we asked brashly, "Can you play, kid?" He said, "Yes, I think so." That night he got up and blew our asses off. John Sebastian worked with us for years.

STEVE MANDELL: John Sebastian was the unofficial accompanist to everybody.

He never went anywhere without his belt full of harps. At a moment's notice he could play in any key because he had his beltful of harps and a glass of water to dip into.

JOHN SEBASTIAN: The scene that birthed the next generation of American rockers. It was a hybrid of folk and electric music. In 1963–64 there was a whole scene which revolved around Bleecker, MacDougal, and Third streets. It was all these coffeehouses where you could play for the passing of a basket. It was in these coffeehouses where I first established myself as a solo.

When I played the baskethouses, my only trick was to try to avoid playing right after Richie Havens. He would empty everybody's pockets. Not only was he incredibly good, he would sweat a lot and people would think they were getting their money's worth. Richie was a tremendous performer.

Lines were starting to be drawn. Gerdes was non-electric whereas the coffeehouses were more catch-as-catch-can.

I used to play with Felix Pappilardi [producer and bass player for Mountain] a lot. A number of performers used us to get their scene a little rockier sounding.

Richie Havens Trio

The Lovin' Spoonful: (top) Joe Butler, Steve Boone; (bottom) John Sebastian, Zal Yanovsky

Felix and I were moving towards an R&B area more than the other artists. We were anxious to contribute to the context of this whole new group of young white blues artists like Fred Neil, John Hammond, Jr., and Timmy Hardin.

I met Cass Elliot and the Big Three and we began a friendship. She invited me to her house to watch the Beatles on TV and said, "By the way, Ringo will be there." They tried to pass Zal Yanovsky off as Ringo—he bore a striking resemblence to Ringo. Cass always felt that Zal and I would be a perfect combination.

After the Mugwumps broke up, Zal and I heard of a guy whose brother was in the Sell-Outs, the first rock-and-roll group in the Village. They were from Long Island. The guitarist was Skip Boone; his brother Steven played a great bass. Steven was coming back from a motorcycle trip in Europe. We figure he couldn't be that bad if he had a motorcycle.

Joe Butler was the drummer with the Sell-Outs and we auditioned him at the

Albert Hotel. Rehearsing right before us was the Paul Butterfield Blues Band who had one of the greatest, most fantastic drummers alive, Sam Lay. Poor Joe Butler had to do an audition after this. He was so adamant about playing loud that during the course of one song he lost both sticks and started playing the drums with his hands. He cut his hands on the cymbals and was bleeding all over the drums. We said, "You can't beat this," and hired him.

Our first night at the Night Owl we were fired and told, "You guys are no fucking good."

Our original premise was to create a hybrid between traditional bluesy style and the electric music which was very sterile at this time. At this time rock-and-roll was very uninspiring.

The Village was really exploding. It had always been a changing environment. When I was growing up it was classical. It was an artistic community. A lot of European artists, writers, and painters. By the time the Lovin' Spoonful left the Village, rock-and-roll became more common.

JESSE COLIN YOUNG: In the Spring of '62 I made the album *Soul of a City Boy*, which wasn't released by Capitol until about nine months later. It was delayed because the Beatles were just happening.

The Youngbloods evolved out of the folk scene. Most of the solo musicians might have liked to jam but there were a lot of funny, introverted musicians like myself who just played solo, who didn't play with other musicians. We didn't fit in. The big thing was to develop your own style and practice guitar four or five hours a day.

SUSIE YOUNG: I was very interested in folk music as a social tool. There was a little fear then about rock-and-roll—that it would go back to the old days. But then the Beatles came out and everybody was falling in love with rock-and-roll again. So I was very excited about it. I was rooting so much for that new music that was happening around '64 and '65.

JESSE COLIN YOUNG: The audiences in general were somewhat mixed. We were playing folk clubs that were just turning to bands. Some of them hated it and some of them liked it. This was in '65. Ours was one of the first bands to come into Gerdes. The sound system was designed for folk music. I don't think there were any monitors. Although we had little dinky amps, just bringing in the drum set was the end of the PA.

Herb Gart, our manager, kept saying the sound isn't good so we went and bought new microphones and speakers for the gig at Gerdes. But what we were doing was basically fighting the fact that we had to sing over a set of drums through a hundred-watt amplifier, which is basically impossible.

SUSIE YOUNG: The folk-rock scene was just coming about. The Lovin' Spoonful were just getting together and I remember McGuinn saying "This is what's happening. I'm going to California to get together a band."

WAVY GRAVY: When Tom Paxton first showed up from Fort Dix, John Mitchell of the Gaslight was positive he was a cop. So everybody was nice to Tom until it was time to get stoned; then it was "Well, we have an appointment."

Tom thought he had leprosy. Finally a friend and I got Tom so loaded he couldn't stand up. We said, "If you're a cop, arrest us." Tom was crawling on the floor saying, "I am not a cop!"

ED McCURDY: Tom Paxton went through a period when I called him the Young Narcissus. If he had three hands, one would be up by his ear, listening to himself. I love the man and I think he's certainly one of our best writers.

TOM PAXTON: There was a period when I played nine months solid at the Gaslight. Boy, you can learn a lot when you're doing it five nights a week. The two big clubs were Folk City and the Gaslight. They were almost interchangeable. There were two minor differences. The Gaslight had no booze, but it was in a better location. So what each lost in one, it made up in the other.

The bar called the Kettle of Fish was *the* hangout. The biggest reason was that you didn't have to go too far to get there. We used to hang out there day in and day out. We used to eat at Minetta's Tavern all the time, right on MacDougal and Minetta. We really enjoyed that place. The White Horse was a hangout and later the Lion's Head. The Limelight was a big gathering place also. We used to meet the Clancys there and have some beautiful singing. A drink would show up every once in a while, I seem to recall.

But it was really the Kettle of Fish where all the ideas, gossip, songs, and friendships were exchanged. A typical night was sitting at the table right up front by the cigarette machine. There were constant comings and goings, and the cast of characters included Bob Dylan, Phil Ochs, Dave Van Ronk, Eric Andersen, and David Blue, plus various wives and chicks.

JESSE COLIN YOUNG: Roger McGuinn was doing Beatles impressions all the time. McGuinn was the one who picked it out. He kept saying, "This is what's going to happen next." And he was right. He was so excited about it, too. I remember talking to him in the street one day and he was completely wired by the idea. The Beatles' music just turned his head around.

TOM PAXTON: Folk music declined because the quality declined. Folk music originally became popular because of the unutterably ghastly commercial pop that was popular, like Fabian and Frankie Avalon. Then the Kingston Trio happened and blew the whole folk scene open. Folk started dying out because the Beatles and the Rolling Stones were putting out good commercial rock. The rock music got better. They were in control. The young listener finally had some real good commercial music to listen to. They also lost interest in folk when they weren't getting drafted anymore. They weren't being sent to Vietnam to get killed. They didn't need to connect with a message.

We loved the Beatles. They put out great music which was infectious. We weren't closed-minded about just folk music and our own songs. We realized the importance of groups like the Stones and the Beatles.

It was a very competitive time, but healthily competitive. When you hear a good song there are two things you can do: one—Destroy your guitar; two—Say, "I want to do as well." The competition created inspiration. There was a friction there. When you rub against good people it's bound to wear off.

There was a hide-out room above the Gaslight where we could hang out. Once Dylan was banging out this long poem on Wavy Gravy's typewriter. He showed me the poem and I asked, "Is this a song?" He said, "No, it's a poem." I said, "All this work and you're not going to add a melody?" He did. It was "A Hard Rain's Gonna Fall."

ERIC ANDERSEN: David Blue was always on the streets. He had more fucking stories than anyone else.

He was also a real pothead. Phil Ochs would dabble in it but was very paranoid; so David would score for Phil and end up stealing the pot from him. But Phil was so paranoid he would keep giving David more money and David would keep taking more pot.

MARC ELIOT: At the beginning, no one in the "in" crowd liked David, except for Phil Ochs. Phil thought he was a tremendous performer and songwriter. Later on, people started coming around to his music. David's music was all romantic. Phil's was all political. In fact, David, Phil, and Dylan were an interesting threesome when it came to writing about women. David would write about women who most people didn't know—the exotics; Dylan wrote about the universals; and Phil didn't write about them at all.

David was a character. He would be offended if someone told him he looked like Dylan, yet he looked like that on purpose. After he would get off stage, instead of saying, "What did you think?" he would say, "Hey, wasn't I great?" He was so arrogant and complex those ways.

JAKE JACOBS: Someone once said David Blue was a Bob Dylan clone. If Dylan changed his hairstyle, David would change his hairstyle. If Dylan would wear a white shirt buttoned to the top, then David would, too. He was ornery and arrogant and abusive.

David used to spend hours in front of the mirror just getting ready to go out. He was very vain.

I learned a lot from him about songwriting, singing, guitar playing, and the scene. He was the muse. He was the Greek chorus.

ERIC ANDERSEN: Joni Mitchell had taken care of David for years. She told me once that she was going over her books, and there were more checks made out to David than there were to the phone company.

Once he called her because he was desperate for money, he was being thrown out of his apartment. So she got the money to him. The next day, just by chance, she runs into David on the street in the Village and he's standing there with two dozen roses.

He had taken the money and bought the roses for his new girlfriend. Joni understandably flipped out and David typically remarked back to her, "Come on, Joni, why do you have to be such a bitch?"

JAKE JACOBS: Fred Neil was a local celebrity. He had groupies. He had people carrying his guitars. He had people giving him drugs.

MICHAEL MANN: Freddy Neil was an enigma. He went in until the water was up to his neck and then he got out. And that was every time.

PAULA BALLAN: There were a bunch of musicians who got lost. The first musician that I knew of who got lost was Fred Neil. People like Mike Mann learned a lot at the feet of Fred Neil. When a musician copies somebody's style, like Mike did with Fred, you also copy their lifestyle. You idolize the person. The person is on drugs, then you take this for what the style is as well. Look at Mike now.

HOYT AXTON: That bass voice Fred had! He'd hit those low notes very clearly and straight ahead. What a great singer. Freddy influenced me a lot as far as singing goes.

MICHAEL MANN: There were great musicians, musicians of quality. There were people who you will never hear of again who were talented beyond detail. Dino Valenti became a legend and went out to the coast to join Quicksilver Messenger Service. Lisa Kindred was one of the great, great singers of folk music. Steve Stills was here and we had a sort of duo. All these famous names came out of the Village. Some of the strange group names came out of jokes and lines from the Village. It was terribly funny then. Everything was funny. There was so much head action going on. The streets were full of it. You couldn't move without picking up somebody else's ideas.

I didn't come to see anybody at the clubs. I came to see me. I came to find out what I could do in front of an audience, what effect I could have in front of an audience.

BARRY KORNFELD: Michael was a phenomenal guitarist. He was something really special on guitar, and then he got involved in some weird things.

TERRE ROCHE: The first night I met Michael Mann, I was with Mark Johnson and here comes this guy I used to see in the street. He came up to us and said, "Hi Mark."

I was shocked. I said to myself, "Mark knows this guy?" Next thing I know, he's walking along with us to the apartment and I'm thinking to myself, "What's wrong with this picture?" I don't want this guy coming to my house.

Anyway, he came over and there were about five of us sitting around the apartment. Michael was his crazy self and he was playing the guitar and I was really impressed even though every once in a while he would go right off the neck and stop playing the guitar. But when he was playing, he was a really good player. Eventually, everyone left.

The next day, Michael came back. We heard the doorbell ring. We look out and we said, "Oh, God. It's that guy." So we let him in, and he started hanging out at our house. He must have come over there every day for the next two years. He'd come over and we'd make dinners and I tried to help him out.

At one point, I called up a schizophrenic association and asked them about megavitamin therapy. They said to bring the person in. I said, "I'm talking more about slipping it into his food."

Michael was very dodgy, and he knew exactly what I was up to. I think he had a lot of women react to him the same way I did. There's something very attractive about Michael. He's like this little boy gone awry. You think, "I want to help this guy."

Michael is a certified Village character. Everybody knows him and likes him. Local businesspeople and performers often help him out financially. Tourists who pass him on the street most likely think he's just another street bum. In the summer, he usually sells rare books and records. When he's on a good streak he's very pleasant company.

MICHAEL MANN: I learned how to play guitar from Mike Bloomfield. Mike, Roy Ruby, and I were the triumvirate of our private high school in Massachusetts. At that time Bloomfield was a top guitarist in Chicago and he was playing gigs by the time he was sixteen—studio stuff. He was one of the best of the studio boys from that time. He started playing when he was fourteen, and by the time he was sixteen he was already recorded. And Ruby was no slouch. Ruby was like a 219 IQ who loved jazz. They're both gone. It wasn't drugs—the closest I can get is the sky opening and a big voice saying "Hurry up please, it's time."

The last time I saw Mike Bloomfield was six weeks before he died. He came in and told me that Roy was no longer with us. I was very sad, and he mentioned it just in passing because he knew how much it would hurt me. I asked him how he was doing and he said, "I'm only on Valiums and I'm cutting down." And I said, "Just cut it out completely. Another one's gone, and that only leaves the two of us." And six weeks later I walked into the Figaro and someone told me Mike Bloomfield was gone.

It didn't end, it faded. You can still watch words and lines and ideas shine like neon lights in the thin air on any Village street. You can look up and you can pick up whole verses that haven't been written yet. There was a real lasting intelligence. The bars of hip conversation. You start an effect that way and it continues, it progresses.

At the time it was rather well known that the light at the end of the tunnel was the headlamp of an oncoming train.

LOUIE BASS: Phil Ochs was a nice fellow when he was sober, but he was very seldom sober. He used to come into Folk City always drunk. One night he came in and Mike Porco wasn't in. He wanted me to give him ten dollars. He said, "Mike said it was okay for you to give me ten dollars, he'll give you ten dollars." Then Phil would say, "Then give me a drink. Mike said it was okay for me to get a drink anytime I want." I said, "It's probably true, but I'm not authorized to give it to you. You have to come in when Mike is here."

Phil got very upset and argued with me until I asked him to leave. I practically had to throw him out. The next thing I know, Phil is out in the street, panhandling. When people wouldn't give him money, he would curse at them.

One time he came into the club with two baling hooks. I took them away from him. When he left, he forgot that I took them. He thought that Mike took them. He went over to Mike and asked him for his hooks back. Mike didn't know that I took them, and Mike told him that he didn't have them, and Ochs got in an argument with Mike. Finally, Mike got him to leave without them. They were very dangerous weapons. He could have hurt someone with them.

There was a fellow playing on the street one night with his guitar case opened. Phil came by and dropped a hundred-dollar bill in the guitar case.

ED McCURDY: I was very fond of Phil when he would allow me to be. I think his death was an absolute obscenity. People said he was hell-bent for destruction and you couldn't do anything about it. Nobody tried very hard. Mike Porco did. He gave him sanctuary when no one else would.

MICHAEL OCHS: Phil was the best singer-songwriter of the political movement. His non-political songs stood strong also. He really stretched melodies, the way no one did before. Neil Young said that his own melody writing was greatly influenced by Phil's.

He was in total awe of Dylan, he wanted to be as big and famous as he was. They had a give-and-take relationship. When Dylan wrote new songs he would play them for Phil, and Phil would think they were great. Dylan was the king of the mountain and he played it to the hilt. What happened to Phil was, he dug a hole too deep. He started to have no opinions on anything, and for Phil, that was bad. He lost his ego in the manic binges of false energy. He had a desperate need to accomplish something and it wasn't coming with his songs. He felt that there was no more purpose.

He will always be remembered as a social activist and poet through his songs which have proven to be enduring.

SONNY OCHS: Phil started getting attention right away. When he got to the Village he started writing political songs, and, God, he was knocking them off right and left. He had written practically all his famous songs by '64. It was like coming off the press one right after another.

He was like a music machine. He would buy every magazine available, listen to the news and every time he'd hear a story like William Worthy's, he would write a song about it. Everything he wrote about he turned into poetry.

JOHN SEBASTIAN: The first time I heard Timmy Hardin, I said, "This guy is a genius." Timmy came into the Village in about 1963 or '64. My house was one of his first stops, because I knew everybody he knew. Tim had heard my playing at Fred Neil's shows.

My first meeting with him really characterized Tim and his incredible self-confidence. He showed up at my house the day before we were to do a recording session together. He said to me, "John, I think you're great, and tomorrow you're going to be even better because you'll be playing with me."

Now this was in an era when everybody was trying to subvert their ego. It was the beginning of the hippies and peace and love. But Timmy was incredibly aggressive and extroverted, but he was able to back it up with tremendous strength as a songwriter and player. And he was right—I never did play better than I did at that session. A large part of Timmy's presence was his involvement with heroin.

Tim Hardin (Armen Kachaturian, copyright © 1975)

VINCE MARTIN: Timmy Hardin never was in charge of himself. I remember him singing those beautiful songs he wrote.

Oh God, Jesus, what beautiful songs. He hung out with Bobby Darin. He was a feisty guy. He was a mean guy. Not terribly pleasant.

STEVE MANDELL: At the time, you would never admit that you liked rock-and-roll. When I first met Dylan at a party, he was secretly introduced to me as "a really good rock-and-roll piano player." You had to be a closet rock-and-roller.

There was a strong sense of family. There was a feeling you belonged. In the folk days, it was very supportive. Once rock-and-roll came around, the jealousies came out.

ROGER McGUINN: The first time I met the Beatles was in 1965 in London. We had just played a little club. Derek Taylor, who had formerly been their press agent, was working with us in the same capacity, and he got us together. They came down to the club to see us, and after we got done with the show, we all went to this room upstairs and we all sat around. It was kind of an awkward meeting. We weren't too comfortable with each other. We all asked each other questions. Lennon was interested in my little glasses. He wanted to know what they were all about. I showed them to him and he didn't think they were very practical because they were hard to see through. Crosby, of course, was getting to know everybody, being the flamboyant character that he was. Chris, Michael, and Gene sort of kept their mouths shut. I was kind of not believing the whole thing was happening. It was a big move for someone who only a short while before was scuffling around the Village.

A couple of months later, when the Beatles came over to America for their second tour, they invited us up to their house. They sent a limousine down to pick us up. That was very exciting, going up there.

They had rented the Gabor mansion in Beverly Hills. So all these limos went winding up through the hills. You had to fight your way through screaming girls

Roger McGuinn

who were hanging off the gates and the walls and the cliff. It was just insanity. There were hundreds of girls all over the place trying to get a glimpse of the Beatles.

We finally got inside and Joan Baez was in there. Ringo was having a sandwich and we all sort of stared at him. He looked at us and said, "Don't mind me, only eating." George was real friendly and we got to talk. George and John and Crosby and I went into the bedroom and all these security guards were walking around, so we went into the bathroom for a little more privacy. We closed the door and sat on the floor with these guitars and started playing.

Crosby and I had just gotten into Eastern music, like Ravi Shankar. We started playing our impressions of that for George and John. They had never heard anything like that before, so they were real interested. This was around the time of "All I Really Want to Do." We had already had a number one song with "Mr. Tambourine Man," and it was before "Turn Turn Turn."

At the same time we were working with Phil Spector. Dylan was around at that time, too. I remember at one point Spector turned around and said to me rather facetiously, "You're in with the in crowd."

ALIX DOBKIN: One night it was quite late at Gerdes, and we had just finished the third show on a weekend night and Jim McGuinn came in. It was way before the Byrds. He was so excited about this new group called the Beatles. "I Wanna Hold Your Hand" and "She Loves You" had just come out and he just loved them. He loved the music, the sound. So, just before my set ended at the very end of the night, he asked me if he could come up on stage and do "I Wanna Hold Your Hand" with me. He was way ahead of his time.

GEOFFREY STOKES: I first met Roger McGuinn when he was playing banjo with the Chad Mitchell Trio. He gave me my first dope. It was probably 1961. It happened at a party. I came into the room knowing full well, if I ever had this first puff I would be an addict forever.

ROGER McGUINN: I was out in L.A. working at the Troubadour, and Gene Clark was in the audience and he heard me and liked what I was doing. He said, "Let's write some songs together." So we wrote a couple. David Crosby came in one night, and he started singing harmony with us. We asked him if he wanted to join us, and we had the nucleus of the Byrds. We started rehearsing and we were off and running.

Crosby knew Jim Dickson who brought us into a studio to record some demos which later turned out to be the album "Pre-Flyte." We found Michael Clarke, who began to play drums. And Chris Hillman learned to play bass—he was a mandolin player. Jim ended up being our manager.

We hoped that the Byrds would be successful, but we were mostly concerned if we could play a strong enough beat so people could dance to the music. We all came from a folk background where the beat wasn't that important so we weren't real rhythm conscious. We knew the songs and we knew how to pick, but just keeping the beat was a challenge for us.

Dylan's road manager sent our manager a copy of "Mr. Tambourine Man," the dub with Bob and Jack Elliott. Our manager said, "This is going to be a hit," and, of course, we didn't know. It didn't really sound that way to me. But we said we would learn it, and we did.

It seemed like we became overnight sensations. But it simmered down towards the late sixties. Our biggest hits were in '65 and '66. It was a very heavy time. We were suddenly riding in limousines. The whole time seemed like a party. That sudden success and fame was difficult to get used to. Many of us came out of modest folk roots and the small clubs. People like Michael Nesmith, John Sebastian, and John Phillips were soon part of the Monkees, the Lovin' Spoonful, and the Mamas and the Papas. Everyone had a successful band. We were making money; girls would camp out at our houses; and our songs were becoming number one.

LOUIE BASS: I remember Simon and Garfunkel performing "Sounds of Silence" for the first time at Folk City. They sang it at some sort of college reunion. At that time I never thought they would make it. They didn't sound as good as some of the other acts. It was the first time they tested it out publicly. They went over well because it was all their friends.

BARRY KORNFELD: Paul Simon and I met in the Village, and I ended up playing on the album *Wednesday Morning, 3 A.M.* Paul and I eventually went into the song publishing business together.

We recorded the album in the spring of '64. Paul and I were on guitar and Bill Lee was on bass. It was released in the fall of '64, and it was a totally acoustic album. "Sounds of Silence" is acoustic on that album. The album did nothing—maybe three thousand in a year.

One DJ at an album-oriented station really liked "Sounds of Silence." He suggested that it should be electrified, which eventually happened. They over-dubbed a rock rhythm section. The electric "Sounds of Silence" came out about a year later, and I remember Paul was pretty pissed off. The decision to call them Simon and Garfunkel was also made without Paul's input by their producer, Tom Wilson, who was also Dylan's producer. There was already a duo called Art and Paul on the scene. So they couldn't go with that. Paul came back from England and his recording was electric, his act was named, and the cover was a fait accompli. Lucky for him.

One night we ran out of musicians, and Emmylou Harris was walking down the street with a guitar, and I went up to her and said, "Do you play?" She said, "Yes." I said, "Would you come in and play?" She had a sweet voice and an angelic look. She ended up playing a lot for us at the Four Winds.

One night Peter Tork came back to the Village. His group, the Monkees, was the hottest thing going. He was running down the streets crazy and wild because the girls were chasing him and he was trying to get away from them.

BETTY SMYTH: I ran many baskethouses during the sixties and seventies. The Why Not? was the longest-running baskethouse. It opened around 1961 and closed close to 1970. Most of the clubs were very small places. What we did was pull the people in and throw them out again. We charged a lot of money for coffees. We were in it to make money and that's what we were doing. But politically we had a lot of trouble. They gave us licenses and then took them away. The city and politicians were really ruining it.

At this time, Gerdes was a much better club than the clubs we were running. We were running tourist-attraction-type places. Gerdes was like the Copacabana of the folk houses. Gerdes had a liquor license. My god, all the singers wanted to play there.

Around 1966 the Village was starting to die. They were advertising race riots. There was never a race riot in the Village. The people that lived there for sixty years wanted this hubbub to stop. They were harassing us like crazy, and folk music was dying out. I went into Trude Heller's, which was on Thirteenth Street, and I saw that they had a rock group there and the place was jumping. It was the only place in the world where they charged a two-drink minimum charge at the bar. I said she must be doing something right.

I ran a club for my friends on Third Street which held about two hundred and fifty people. So I hired a rock-and-roll trio, which was the worst trio ever. Ever. I just wanted to experiment. If it worked so close to the Village, why couldn't it work *in* the Village? The place was called the Music Hall, and I was the first one to bring rock-and-roll into the Village. I couldn't believe it, it worked. The place was packed.

Now my daughter is involved in the music business. Her first performance was at Gerdes singing a Cat Stevens song.

PATTY SMYTH: It was a unique experience growing up the way I did. I grew up around music and exciting people, and there was always a sense of something special going on and I was right in the middle of it.

My first performance was at Folk City. I was fifteen. I joined my friend Alana on stage and played guitar and sang. I was incredibly frightened, but it was very

Patty Smyth and Betty Smyth

thrilling. I was very lucky to be a part of that whole scene my mother was involved in.

Within the club world of the Village there were many different musical and social territories. The Gaslight and Folk City were similar in the people they booked and in their ambiance. Folk City was the magnet—kids came from all over the country to the hoot nights there. Later, the Gaslight gave a stage to more contemporary acts like Bonnie Raitt and James Taylor, while Folk City tried to hold on to folk music for as long as possible.

The Bitter End was slicker than Folk City and the Gaslight, and it hired more established acts. As Emmylou Harris recalls, "You had to be a big name just to get third billing there." The Cafe Au Go-Go was big enough to accommodate the new rock bands and many blues acts as well. The Gaslight took over the Au Go-Go. The Gaslight Au Go-Go name was meant to attract the whole spectrum—from singer-songwriters to full-tilt rock bands. The Night Owl leaned toward the psychedelic, drug-oriented music. In the early sixties, Tim Hardin, Fred Neil, and their crowd hung out there, and then folk-rock groups like the Lovin' Spoonful came through. The Night Owl is a paraphernalia-and-poster shop today.

LOUIE BASS: Around the middle to late sixties there were hippies in the Village. They lived in a group like ten, twenty, whatever could fit in an apartment. They slept on the floor—that's the way hippies lived. They were decent kids, though. They weren't rowdy.

PAULA BALLAN: It was the time when the Village was going through the vanguard of changes. Here's where it all got tried out first, questioned, talked about, touched, and played with before it went out to the mainstream.

You might not have lost your virginity in the Village, but it was certainly where it was tested a lot more often!

ED McCURDY: I hated rock when it came into the Village scene. I think the term rock singer is a misnomer. You can't play rock and sing at the same time. It desensitizes due to the nature of it. It's that overproduced sound that's based on distortion and electronics, and you can't have music this way.

Malcolm X, the Black Muslim leader, was assassinated in 1965 and there were outbreaks of racial violence throughout the year. Both Selma and Watts made their way into the American headlines. T.S. Eliot died and Ralph Nader's Unsafe at Any Speed *became a bestseller. Folk-rock was in full swing with acts like Barry McGuire, the Byrds, Sonny and Cher, We Five, and Lovin' Spoonful. "What the World Needs Now Is Love" signaled the battle cry of the hippie generation.*

In 1965 and 1966 the U.S. began to counter the British invasion. Groups like the Supremes, Mamas and Papas, Monkees, Righteous Brothers, Young Rascals, and Simon and Garfunkel were taking back the airwaves. The mid-sixties even saw the forerunners of punk achieve chart success with songs like "Tears," "I Fought the Law," and "Psychotic Reaction."

FOLK MUSIC PLUGS IN
AND · TURNS · ON

· ·

· · · · · · · · · · · **F**olk-rock was now just one of the major movements in the emerging rock culture. Soul music was flourishing. The year 1967 saw the release of "Respect" by Aretha Franklin, "Soul Man" by Sam and Dave, "I Heard It Through the Grapevine" by Gladys Knight and the Pips, "Cold Sweat" by James Brown, "I Was Made to Love Her" by Stevie Wonder, Wilson Pickett's "Funky Broadway," and Marvin Gaye's duet with Tammi Terrell, "Ain't No Mountain High Enough."

Folk-rock itself was becoming more country-tinged. Buffalo Springfield debuted their album of the same name in 1967. Band member Stephen Stills' song "For What It's Worth (Stop, Hey, What's That Sound?)" went to number seven that year, and out of this band, Crosby, Stills, Nash and Young, Poco, and eventually the sound of the Eagles would form.

Van Morrison broke off from Them and made four songs for Bang Records, one of them "Brown Eyed Girl."

The Smothers Brothers Comedy Hour first aired in February, 1967 and began a long, stormy relationship with CBS and its censors. Many of the brothers' guests were antiwar and left-wing. Pete Seeger, long blacklisted from television, sang his Vietnam protest song, "Knee Deep in the Big Muddy." After many fights over material and outspoken guests, CBS cancelled the highly-rated show in 1969, replacing it with Hee-Haw.

RANDY MASTRONICOLA: A lot of people, from an outsider's viewpoint, think that the Village was really artsy and Bohemian and had a real liberal sensibility. People fail to recognize that internally there is a strong Italian-American community that can be as constraining as any hick town, USA.

The established corner-boys and social club guys viewed the artists and musicians as outsiders and hippies. They didn't understand them. I did. I was intrigued by them and it opened me up at a really young age. Those guys were threatened and intimidated by anything creative because it wasn't within them to begin with.

I would go to school and hang out and play stickball, and then I would walk down MacDougal Street and it would be like walking through a carnival on acid at nine years old.

We were constantly taught by the nuns in school and by our families to stay away from MacDougal Street and Washington Square Park because that wasn't our element. We were told to stay in the internal neighborhood and not the peripheral scene that was burgeoning. We were told that the Bohemians, Beatniks, and hippies were the seedier aspect of life—the junkies and child molesters. The older Italians couldn't understand the new ideologies being espoused by the newcomers to the Village. They felt that their children shouldn't have contact with the other side.

Well, we did get to the other side because we were curious about it. The ironic part is that the kids who listened, who stayed away and remained on the street corners and the church steps were the ones who became the dope addicts. It happens to communities, anyway. The hippies had little to do with it. Those kids became the people their families tried to protect them from.

From all over the country, longhaired, flower-adorned, glassy-eyed kids would flock to the Village. It was where they could hear the music they liked, live with whomever they liked, buy their costumes, and acquire their drugs. Marijuana, LSD, and various other hallucinogens were not only the rage, they were a public statement. The hippies were tuning in, turning on, and dropping out. Instead of coming to the Village to pass on the words of Woody Guthrie, they were in the Village to extoll the teachings of Timothy Leary. Suddenly, Woody Guthrie's "Pastures of Plenty" took on a different meaning.

Dissent and rebellion were the passwords. Many of the young runaways were coming to a place where they knew their opinions would be reinforced. Strangely, a large number of the runaways were from liberal, middle-class, suburban families, and their expressions of rebellion sprang more from a need to assert their individuality than from any political motivation.

There were many things to protest and everyone had his or her own pet cause. Button and poster shops flourished and were as much a part of the Village scene as were the coffeehouses and clubs. Every hippie had a button and every button had a statement. There were a lot of issues.

There were people who were concerned about the war in Vietnam. There were people devoting themselves to ending the draft. Interest in civil rights was dying down in the white community, but interest in ethnic pride and power was on the rise in the black community. There were those who wanted the drug laws changed and others who were just attracted by "peace and love."

The Village streets were like a carnival during these years. Young girls with flowers in their long, blond hair and stars painted on their faces would wander the streets innocently looking for a place to crash. Young boys with long hair, army jackets, and joints hidden in their Marlboro boxes would wander the streets looking for young girls with flowers in their long, blond hair.

For the first time, young blacks would come to the Village, proudly displaying their Afros, and sporting jackets with raised fists embroidered on the backs. Midwestern parents would be walking the streets posting "wanted" and "reward" signs for their runaway kids. The Doors would be blasting from stereos in apartments on Bleecker Street. Donovan could be heard wafting from someone's tape recorder on MacDougal. A car would speed down Sullivan Street blaring "The Ballad of the Green Berets" from its radio. Groups of kids would stand on the corner of Sixth Avenue and Third Street, next to the Waverly Theatre, making plans to see Yellow Submarine *or scalping tickets for a Jefferson Airplane concert at the Fillmore. This was the time when John Phillips was famous for fronting an exciting new folk-rock band called the Mamas and the Papas, and not, as one young kid recently described him, "MacKenzie Phillips's father." But it's nice to know that some things haven't changed. Jimi Hendrix was then, as now, being played at deafening volumes on radios in Washington Square Park.*

Many legitimate organizations like the War Resisters League, the Black Panther Party, and Women Strike for Peace used the Village as a vehicle to spread their cause and recruit new members. The Village was filled with people who were viewed as directionless: but, in reality, they were being offered and were following many directions. It was a time of searching and discovery, and, whether or not you were taking drugs, the Village was mind-expanding.

In the mid-sixties, folk music gave way to folk-rock, and a whole new renaissance began in the Village. Once again, there was a new surge of popularity for the Greenwich Village music scene. Formerly a mecca for folk fans, the Village now became a center for a new and exciting blend of influences called folk-rock. Instead of the regulars being Ramblin' Jack Elliott and Cisco Houston, they were now the Youngbloods, the Lovin' Spoonful, the Byrds, and the Blues Project.

By going electric, Dylan had once again changed the sound of folk music, and everyone else was catching on fast. The tiny music shops on Bleecker Street started stocking amplifiers and pick-ups, and the usual window displays of acoustic Gibsons and Martins gave way to Les Pauls and Telecasters.

Folk sections in record stores were being trimmed while rock sections were expanding. Radio stations were playing groups with names like the Strawberry Alarm Clock, the Lemon Pipers, Moby Grape, Iron Butterfly, the Holy Modal Rounders, and Ultimate Spinach. Many women forsook the straight blond, trimmed-hair and idealistic look of Mary Travers, and the solemn, Gypsy-madonna image of Joan Baez for the free-spirited, unkempt, less innocent look of Janis Joplin and Grace Slick. Women were beginning to weary of this enforced purity.

Their male counterparts gave up the well-scrubbed collegiate look of the Kingston

Trio for the unrestrained sexuality of Jim Morrison and Jimi Hendrix. "My God, I don't know how I stood it all those years," laughs Dorene Internicola, a former madonna-type who found herself seduced by the sexy antics of Jim Morrison.

DORENE INTERNICOLA: When I was twelve I used to dream about being a musicologist and tracing the roots of songs like "Mary Hamilton" and "Barbara Allen," and going down to the Village to hear people like Doc Watson, Joan Baez, and Bob Dylan. I even once had a barber cut my hair like Mary Travers's.

But all of a sudden, the whole scene changed. A bunch of us had an apartment across from the old Fillmore East, on Sixth Street, and we used to sneak in or listen from our roof to people like Janis Joplin, the Grateful Dead, and Jim Morrison. The whole lifestyle just turned a lot more decadent. There were more drugs, more sex, and the music got heavier, more electric and psychedelic. All of a sudden the Village seemed to be mimicking the Haight-Ashbury district in San Francisco.

It was a lot of fun, but it was also much angrier and more cynical. We didn't believe we could change the world anymore. The war was going on in Vietnam despite all our protests and the heroes were dying, like Bobby Kennedy and Martin Luther King, Jr. So we turned away from marching for peace, and towards just having a good time. It's not that we stopped believing in all those things, we just felt more hopeless and powerless.

So personal freedom became very important to us—getting by on no money, sneaking into concerts, everybody sleeping in the same bed, and surviving on spaghetti dinners and marijuana. It was fun, but you couldn't really do all that stuff and be a madonna anymore.

ERIC ANDERSEN: It was a tumultuous time—raw, sexual energy. Dope was coming around; and political and sexual tumult. I was very much involved in understanding relationships. I was having a hard enough time figuring out what I wanted; I couldn't attempt to try to figure out the world. So my stuff was more introspective. I couldn't write a song about Vietnam. People just cared about good writing. They didn't care if it was political.

BILLY JOEL: During the sixties I wasn't a joiner. I didn't agree with the war in Vietnam, but I wasn't going to join in demonstrations. It sort of had a Nuremberg Party-rally thing to it, which I backed away from. I didn't like the knee-jerk atmosphere.

It was the same way I listened to Dylan. I remember everybody sitting around smoking pot trying to figure out what the hell Dylan was talking about. I always had a deep-seated suspicion that a lot of what Dylan was talking about wasn't anything—it just sounded good. He was using words like a musician would use notes to create a certain sound. A guitar player would use a fuzz-box to get a distortion. It was still a guitar playing; it was just a distorted guitar. I think Dylan found the fuzz-boxes in the English language. I think a lot of it is nonsense. But a lot of creative, well-done nonsense. The protest songs he did were pretty straight-ahead. They were cool. But I wasn't into the Country Joe and the Fish stuff at all. It wasn't musical to me. Dylan was musical in a lyrical way.

ELLEN McILWAINE: I came to the Village in 1965. A lot of people were into purist acoustic music, and I came up here with my amp from Georgia. I had an acoustic guitar with a pickup and it was plugged into an amp. A lot of people didn't think it was cool at all, they thought it was gauche. Over a period of time they accepted me, although there still might be some of those guys who want to beat me up.

I used to play with Jimi Hendrix. I don't think Jimi ever played with women before. There weren't that many women around. I played the piano. I didn't play guitar when he played with me. He played lead guitar. He sat on a barstool and he played and didn't try to steal the show and act macho and everything.

It was real interesting getting to know him, because he was real difficult to get to know. I don't know if anybody ever really did. He was withdrawn. Music was the way he communicated—music was everything. He lived it and breathed it. He was always interested in hearing everybody. I never heard him put anybody down.

When I was playing with him I called my manager at the time, and I said, "I found a guitar player." And he said, "Well, who is he?" I said, "You've got to come down and hear him, his name is Jimi Hendrix and he's really good." He said, "I heard about him." I said, "Well, come hear him." He said, "No. No. You don't want him in your band, he's black." I said, "I don't want you to be my manager."

Rampant commercialism made for strange bedfellows. The Monkees, invented by TV executives and backed by the music of Tommy Boyce, Bobby Hart, and Neil Diamond, began to tour in 1967 and 1968. Peter Tork, onetime Village hopeful on the baskethouse circuit, was suddenly a household name. Mickey Dolenz, their drummer, spotted Jimi Hendrix in England in 1968, and Hendrix opened for the Monkees in the United States. He was usually booed by the teenagers in the audience as they sat there wincing through "Purple Haze," waiting for the Monkees to hit the stage with "Last Train to Clarksville."

VINCE MARTIN: One day, there was a knock at my door and it was Peter Tork. "Peter," I said, "what the hell are you doing here?" "I'm on tour," he said. "I'm one of the Monkees." I said, "Who are the Monkees?" I didn't own a TV. He said, "Come on . . . 'Last Train to Clarksville'?" I said, "That's you?" The last time I saw him, we were singing for baskets out in the streets. He said, "You got any time?" I said, "About three weeks." He said, "Come with me."

I packed my bag, turned out the lights and locked the door, walked downstairs, and there was a big damn limousine. We went to a fancy hotel. Jimi Hendrix and Circus Boy and all the rest of the Monkees were there. It was Jimi's first American tour. He opened for them. He bombed. I said, "Peter, why are you subjecting Jimi to this?" He said, "I love him. He's got to work."

Peter said, "This is incredible. I'm a millionaire. Shit, Vince, anything you want is yours." And for the next three weeks, I was in their own plane with the Monkees logo and a red guitar on the side.

We sat around in the hotel room, bare-assed naked—me, Steve Stills, Jimi Hendrix, and Peter, jamming, with detectives outside the door.

PETER TORK: I arrived on the Village scene the winter of '61, and stayed there for about two and a half years. I played guitar and banjo. I came to the Village for glamour, excitement, hippiedom, the liberal lifestyle, free love. I was on the basket-passing circuit in the smaller clubs, like the Basement, the Cyclops and the Id. I later played Gerdes.

What I was working towards was to be in a group. When the Beatles hit, where were all the folkies going to go? But I also wanted to be a folk music performer.

A lot of what I did was hanging out, feeling for the first time that I was part of the scene, walking down the street and seeing people I knew, doing a little flirting. People were coming to the Village to sit down and have a cup of coffee and hope to find the free love that was supposed to be all around. The character that I was on *The Monkees* was developed on the stages of the Village clubs.

DANNY KALB: The Village wasn't free from controversy. When Dylan went electric, everyone in the Village got mad, huffed and puffed, and went immediately to the store that sold electric equipment. Everyone went straight for it. Folk music was no longer the property of a few politicos.

It was so ridiculous anyway. Electric music has its roots in folk music with zydeco and country-and-western. I always played rockabilly and electric music. I loved Chuck Berry, Muddy Waters, and the Beatles. Blacks always used electric instruments. People complained about folk music going electric, but what about all those city folk, the blacks who were playing electric blues since 1930!

PAUL BUTTERFIELD: I don't know what the big deal was about the Newport Folk Festival when Dylan played electric. It was the only direction to go in. I don't think it really made that much of an impact. We were just up there doing

The Monkees: (top) Peter Tork, Mickey Dolenz; (bottom) Davy Jones, Mike Nesmith

what we do. Dylan said to me, "Ya wanna play?" and I said, "Yes." No big deal.

LINDA SOLOMON: Mike knew he should bring in electric music. He wasn't against growing when necessary. He was against adding an additional microphone. He wasn't about to put any more money into Folk City than he had to. One other reason why he didn't want to get into rock too heavily was drugs. He felt very strongly against drugs, and in those days, all it meant was grass. He just didn't want any grass on the premises. None. He felt it was bad enough to deal with people like Phil Ochs, who had a serious alcohol problem, and others; or when Bob Shelton would get drunk and obnoxious and loud.

ROLAND MOUSAA: When the Village was in its prime there was a lot going on. People like Linda Ronstadt, Joni Mitchell, Jackson Browne, and a lot of the

California singer-songwriters were coming to make it in New York. In the Village they met up with the hometown kids like Loudon Wainwright, John Sebastian, and Maria Muldaur. I remember, the night I met Linda Ronstadt she sat right on my lap. She had really pudgy cheeks. She had just broken up with the Stone Poneys, and "Different Drum" had just been a big hit. She said to me, "I really want to do big hits." I said, "Go back and do the old hits." She used to hang around with Emmylou Harris. She used to hang out a lot.

Kris Kristofferson used to hang out a lot too. Dylan, Allen Ginsberg, David Amram, and Kristofferson were hanging out together. Janis Joplin was helping out Kris at that time.

I saw Janis when she was at Folk City. In fact, one night I saw Jimi Hendrix and Janis Joplin walking out of Folk City together. I'll never forget it. I was walking in and they were just walking out. The whole audience was following them out.

DAVID BROMBERG: I met Emmylou Harris in the baskethouses. She used to sing a lot of Paul Siebel's songs. I always thought she had a great country voice. She always had a great voice and was a beautiful woman and had a beautiful manner, so it wasn't any surprise that she was successful. It took her a while to realize she wanted to be country. She had gotten involved with the whole Village folk scene in which only old country-western was respectable. She became popular in Nashville by resurrecting some of the old country-western songs. She and Gram Parsons had their ear on a part of music which it wasn't yet hip to like.

ROLAND MOUSAA: I was with John Hammond, Sr. the night he showcased Bruce Springsteen. John asked me to sit with him. Bruce did all these poetic songs and John kept saying, "This guy is great. This man is fantastic." I wasn't sure. I kept trying to understand. He was different and he had all kinds of imagery in his songs. He never really stated anything. He was very wordy and he looked kind of like Dylan. He was exceptionally nice to everybody, even though he was very nervous because he was auditioning for John Hammond. Emmylou Harris was a familiar face in the Village, also.

EMMYLOU HARRIS: The Greenwich Village music scene was very important to me because that's where I met people like Paul Siebel, Jerry Jeff Walker, and Townes Van Zandt—musicians who were great influences. I got turned on to Jimmie Rodgers there, and there was a lot of bluegrass around. I was a fan of Townes Van Zandt's for years. I met him at Gerdes. He wrote "Pancho and Lefty" and "If I Needed You," both of which I recorded. When I first came to Gerdes I was doing everything from country to Dylan. Folk City was my bread and butter. I was doing some Paul Siebel tunes. Some Jerry Jeff Walker tunes.

Emmylou Harris (Don)

I did some Paul Simon songs; also Hank Williams, Buck Owens, Judy Collins. I was very eclectic.

ROLAND MOUSAA: Burt Reynolds took an interest in Seminole Indians and my friend was going to give him a Seminole coat, so we had Burt meet us at Folk City. No one knew who he was. He wasn't even famous at that time. We were talking about all sorts of things and he said to me, "If I hang out with famous women, I'm going to become famous." The Village was full of these chance meetings with people who would go on to become famous. Everybody was hanging around trying to be famous.

By 1968, the record business was a billion-dollar giant. Executives lavished money on groups that used to play for forty dollars a night in Village dives. If television could invent the Monkees, then record companies could shop around and develop their own supergroups. For every band that had crafted their sound over years with virtually the same personnel (the Beatles, the Stones, the Grateful

Dead, the Band) there were new "instant" phenomena manufactured every day. After struggling, musicians themselves found it impossible to say no to all that money. So rather than opting for a record company that would enable them to grow and experiment, many groups went for the big money. On paper, the Electric Flag, led by Buddy Miles and Mike Bloomfield, looked great. Before they ever appeared in public, they had a record contract. Columbia sold a lot of records but the band died in six months. Cream was an "instant success." Eric Clapton, Jack Bruce and Ginger Baker could barely stay in the same room together— popularity had inflated their egos to the breaking point—but the band managed to sell millions of dollars worth of albums without the benefit of a hit single.

The market was glutted with hundreds of bands, and the competition for radio airplay was stiffer than ever. Listeners were thus treated to the likes of "Jumpin' Jack Flash," "Dance to the Music," "Everyday People," "Born to be Wild," and "Hey Jude."

Bands that were not created in the studio had to develop somewhere, and the Village was as good a place as any. There was an abundance of musicians and a diminishing number of clubs. The Village was extending further east, and city venues were still important to play because of their close proximity to the heart of the music industry.

PEGGY DUNCAN: I used to encourage Mike to hire certain bands because they were big tippers. Folk music fans tip very little. So do folk musicians. John Denver came in one night, spent fifty dollars and didn't leave a tip. Rick Danko from the Band is the complete opposite. Not only does he tip the waitress and bartender, but he also takes care of the soundman. You can tell he's a nice guy even from his music. He's one of the few musicians who is equally powerful solo as he is with his group. He does old Band songs, some of his own songs, and he has an incredible positive energy. He's friendly, warm, and talented. He's a top-notch musician who satisfies his audience, and that kind of feeling even flows through to the bartender. People tip better when they're having an up time.

IRA MAYER: I had done a number of reviews for the *Village Voice* of Buzzy Linhart's live performances, and when he came out with one of his albums, I reviewed it for the *Times*. I didn't mince words. I said the album sucked but that he was good live.

I went to Folk City to see Buzzy and all of a sudden, in the middle of his set, Buzzy says, "This next song is for Ira Mayer and anyone else who thinks they can bring down an artist who's trying to do his best. *Fuck you, Ira Mayer!*" And he launched into some song. The girl I was with fell over backwards in her chair.

SAM SHERER: I used to come to Folk City and watch Peter Stampfel every time the Holy Modal Rounders played. I used to love watching him play fiddle and I was amazed at how he improvised. I recently asked him how he was so lucid at improvising and he said, "Oh, I'm taking lessons now. When I was doing all that I was on drugs."

PETER STAMPFEL: I was originally from Milwaukee. I came to the Village and moved to the Lower East Side, because the Lower East Side was hip. Being twenty-two years old, I was extremely interested in being hip as possible, especially because I was from Milwaukee. I used to come to the Village with various friends and sneer at this and sneer at that. The Village was more square because it was more expensive, more established.

I got to New York and met all these banjo players who could pick circles around me. There were only two fiddle players. When I came to New York, I heard about all the banjo players in town and I wanted to know who was the best banjo player. You know—"Who's the fairest in the land?"—and everyone told me Luke Faust. I didn't get a chance to hear Luke until about a year later. He completely knocked me out. His voice sounded very traditional. He was with the Insect Trust along with Robert Palmer, the writer for the *New York Times*.

There were two of us in the Holy Modal Rounders until Dec. '64. Then we had a backup band with Ken Weaver on African drums, Tuli Kupferberg, and Ed Sanders on baby organ. There were no gigs until '65. I broke up with Steve Weber after about six months. He was flipping out and he was refusing to work on new songs. He would hitchhike to gigs because it was cooler to hitchhike than take a bus. We were the Holy Modal Rounders but we were also the Fugs backup band. The whole thing was the Fugs.

My wife Antonia and I started taking speed and pissed away a couple of years. I ran into Sam Shepard in October of '66. I was in a pawn shop and this guy came up to me and said, "Hey, are you a bass player?" I said, "Yeah." I learned to play bass that summer. He said, "Me and this guy are looking for a bass player to play with us. I play drums and he plays guitar."

I didn't know he was an Obie-winning playwright until several months later. He was a totally humble person. We formed the Moray Eels. He was our drummer. This was '66–'67.

The Holy Modal Rounders were asked to do a record for Elektra and I said I would if the Moray Eels were involved. Shepard had met the director Antonioni and was working on the dialogue for *Zabriskie Point* at this time, so the timing was good. So we made the record called *The Moray Eels Eat the Holy Modal Rounders*. After we made the record we had an attack of nostalgia and put the whole thing together and made it the Holy Modal Rounders again.

During the summer of '68, Sam was writing *Operation Sidewinder*, which had

The Holy Modal Rounders, 1967: John Wesley Annis, Sam Shepard, Peter Stampfel, Steve Weber, Richard Tyler (Terri Thal)

a lot of our songs in it. He was also going to write a play for the Rolling Stones, so he didn't have time to be a Rounder. He was a Moray Eel–Rounder from early '67 to early '69.

Riots followed the assassination of Martin Luther King, Jr. Bobby Kennedy was shot in a hotel kitchen in June after winning the California Democratic primary, and Yippies told millions to come to Chicago for the convention in August, 1968. If the Yippies were calling for a "constitutional convention," then the city of Chicago was calling for twenty-five thousand troops. Phil Ochs sang at an anti-birthday party for LBJ—"It's always the old who lead us to war; it's always the young who fall." Over the next five days, Chicago was a bloodbath. "The whole world is watching" was the chant on Michigan Avenue as the police and National Guard troops charged the crowds. The whole world watched the "police riot" for a long week. It was one of the darkest, ugliest weeks in American history.
While some kids were fighting it out in the streets in the big cities, others in

small towns were trying to "find" themselves. Self-expression was the byword and if you weren't fighting it out in the political arena, you were certainly searching for your identity in some way. And music was often the means of self-identification.

BILLY JOEL: The Rascals were the biggest group locally. They were the Beatles of New York. Blue-eyed soul was the preferred music. We were still playing the hits, but we were leaning towards Wilson Pickett, Otis Redding, and Sam and Dave. To get ideas we would go to the bus station in Hempstead, which had the greatest record store. To this day I've never seen anything like it. It had every single by every soul, rhythm-and-blues, or Gospel artist that you could find. This is how we picked out what we were going to do in the show. We were going to do white arrangements of black music.

We tried to do a couple of originals. This was the era of psychedelic self-

Billy Joel, 1982 (Kat Wolfe, copyright © 1982)

expression. We weren't really an acid type of group. The white soul movement was lifted from R&B. We didn't relate at all to the California sounds like the Jefferson Airplane and Quicksilver Messenger Service. It was all bullshit to us. Our thing was arrangements more than material.

All those clubs had those weird sixties names—the Bugaboo, the Hullabulaga; and everything else was something *à go-go*. Everybody was wearing paisley, flowered, Tom Jones balloon shirts and love beads. We were more the striped shirts and the vests with bell-bottoms and engineer boots. We looked like the Blues Magoos. I was in the Hassles from '67 to the end of '69. Then I had a power duo with my drummer. It was me playing organ through amplifiers and he was playing drums. There was this huge wall of sound. There were twenty gigantic amplifiers. We predated heavy metal, actually. The name of the group was Attila. We were going to destroy the world with amplification.

It's funny because a lot of people perceive me as a mellow kind of Buddy Greco piano-man kind of guy, but I really came out of hard rock, and I survived it. The drummer was John Small, who was also the drummer in the Hassles. Attila only played about five gigs. People walked out of the place, it was so loud. They used to look at us in shock—"What happened to the Hassles?"

In 1969, the Hassles had gone heavy metal, and the Stones played catch with the Beatles: the Beatles released Abbey Road *and the Stones came back with* Let It Bleed. *The Band released their second album, and Creedence Clearwater Revival continued their streak of top ten singles. The Who released* Tommy, *a ninety-minute rock opera written by Pete Townsend.*

A splinter group from the Students for a Democratic Society took their name from a Dylan song—the Weathermen took part in the Days of Rage in Chicago, smashing windows in the Loop.

The Tenth Annual Newport Folk Festival was to have been James Taylor's chance to smash into the big time, but the emerging star was given a short set during the daytime "Young Performers" concert on Sunday. Taylor told Jan Hodenfield of Rolling Stone, *"I waited all weekend for this . . . and they only let me play fifteen minutes."*

The Scene, Steve Paul's rock club just west of the theater district in Manhattan, closed after five years. Paul had an enormous influence on the New York music scene and was responsible for bringing Johnny Winter, the albino blues guitarist, up from Texas. The Scene gave many top bands a rung up in their early days. Jimi Hendrix, the Doors, the Rascals, Blood, Sweat, and Tears, and the Chambers Brothers all appeared there. Jimmy Page and Jeff Beck had jammed there; so had Richie Havens and Joan Baez, B.B. King and Jimi Hendrix; even Tiny Tim had mixed it up with the Doors!

Steve Paul wasn't the only club owner in trouble. By the end of the sixties, torn by changing traditions, styles, and finances, Mike Porco found he must face a new crisis. He had to move his club.

For years local Village residents had tried to wipe out the coffeehouses and the "bad element" they brought with them. For the most part, that "bad element" consisted of refugees from middle- and upper-class families who were socially, politically, and musically motivated. Their main offenses were drinking too much, surreptitiously smoking marijuana, or playing folk music too loud. Some were involved in interracial relationships and many were involved in "promiscuous" lifestyles. When the Beatniks and hippies finally moved out of the Village, the street element that stayed—the junkies and derelicts—was harsh and shocking. Drugs, runaways, rebellion, and sex was what the local community thought the Village was all about during the period between 1965 and 1969. The streets were choked with tourists who wanted to see the Beatniks, hippies, and folk singers. When the tourist attraction left, the tourists left. The Village became desolate.

So in 1969, in the midst of this desolation, Gerdes Folk City moved to 130 West Third Street, between Sixth Avenue and MacDougal Street, a building which was once occupied by the notorious jazz and strip club, Tony Pastor's.

By the time the club moved to Third Street, it was already suffering from the musical and cultural changes of which it had originally been the catalyst. Suddenly the club was having difficulty keeping up with the times. Gerdes was moving into a new home in an abandoned building on a deteriorating street that was dotted with strip clubs.

ROGER BECKET: People were very upset when the club moved. It was like an anchor for the whole folk scene. Suddenly it was changing. It was out of the way on Fourth Street, yet at the same time it was such an established, known entity, that moving it somewhere else sort of scared people. They saw that things were transient, nothing stays forever. When the new location opened it was very much like opening a new club. There was a whole new crowd.

The new location made a difference because people are creatures of habit. A lot of the oldtimers stopped hanging out. Also, by this time many of the musicians moved out of New York, and others had moved on to play bigger venues. This is why all of the clubs were suffering.

PEGGY DUNCAN: When Folk City moved to its new location, business went down for about two years. Folk music was losing its popularity. Mike started putting in bands. It didn't really help though, the Village was quite dead.

The Village was not unique anymore. There were pockets of creativity in every small town in the country. Places would be referred to as the "Greenwich Village of Washington, D.C." or "Milwaukee's Village." The music business itself was suffering from the lack of creative spark and everyone was just waiting for the bad years to pass. Their wait was in vain. The trends that were to follow were created in corporate offices and not on the small stages of Greenwich Village clubs. The sixties had been such a creative and heady time that it made sense for the seventies to become a time to sit back and take a breath.

Fortunately the Village still retained its aura, and drew young creative artists to its stages, albeit in smaller numbers. Although the performers who came through the Village during the seventies were no longer a part of a cohesive musical movement as they were in the sixties, the high-quality acts still stood out.

Emmylou Harris came from Alabama and spent her first trip to New York in the baskethouses. Her second trip brought her to legitimate clubs. Phoebe Snow came from New Jersey and followed her idols around. It wasn't long before they became fans of hers. Loudon Wainwright, Steve Forbert, Willie Nile, Steve Goodman, Melissa Manchester, the Roches, Elephant's Memory, and Linda Ronstadt all came to the Village and made headway during the lean years of the seventies.

A highlight in this otherwise bleak decade in the Village appeared during 1971–73. Allan Pepper and Stanley Snadowsky, two young friends from childhood who were booking clubs around town, decided to ask Mike Porco if he needed their services at Folk City.

PAULA BALLAN: In the Stanley and Allan days, Folk City was a place where I would do business, whether I was buying for the [Philadelphia Folk] Festival or selling my own projects. When they were at Folk City, it wasn't just folk music. They played everything. They really opened up the scene.

I liked them. I knew they were trying very hard to take music they really cared about and make it accessible. I often thought there were some shows that they put their own money into, because Mike wasn't guaranteeing them too much money.

LOUIE BASS: Allan and Stanley were strictly business people. They didn't want the waiters and waitresses to be disruptive. They didn't want the shows to be interrupted by selling drinks. Mike didn't quite agree with it but he went along with it. Mike made his living by selling drinks.

Allan and Stanley raised the quality of the music and the level of professionalism at Folk City. It was a difficult job and the times were not making it any easier. Finally, however, Allan and Stanley realized that they could be successful on their own, and they opened their own cabaret-theater showcase, the Bottom Line.

DOUG YEAGER: After Allan and Stanley left Folk City, I would sometimes have acts at both Folk City and the Bottom Line in the same night. Mike would ask me, "So, how's so-and-so doing at the Bottom Line? Lots of people there? Gee, I guess Allan and Stan are doing pretty good. How's business over there? How many people were there? Was it full?" It was never out of bitterness. He doesn't have a vengeful bone in his body. He was just curious and maybe a little envious.

IRA MAYER: I remember when I came to the realization that any time Allan asked me how an act was, I had to remember to ask whether he meant, did I like them musically or were they drawing.

STANLEY SNADOWSKY: Allan and I got into the music business when we were sixteen. We presented some local acts during that time. Ultimately, we founded an organization called Jazz Interactions. We worked at the Village Gate for about a year.

After we finished at the Gate, we presented it to a place called the Red Garter, which is where the Bottom Line is now. Across the street from the Red Garter was Gerdes Folk City. In the sixties, we were at the Red Garter every Sunday presenting jazz sessions, and it was natural that we went across the street and got friendly with Mike Porco.

Mike was in dire straits when we went there in 1971. He was still presenting what he thought would draw people, but wasn't. It wasn't relevant. He forbid almost all electronics until we said, "Hey, you have to do it this way. It's what's happening."

We brought in some packed houses with Dave Bromberg, with Jonathan Edwards when he had his hit "Sunshine," and Martin Mull at the beginning of his career.

ALLAN PEPPER: During that time, a lot of competition started springing up. The Bitter End was very strong, and Max's Kansas City was also competition. Sam Hood, the guy who used to book the Gaslight, was booking our type of talent at Max's.

I believe Mike would have locked the doors in two weeks if we hadn't arrived. It was that desperate. Business was terrible for him. He had cut down the entire staff. The only people working there were a barmaid and himself, and that was it.

It could have been literally the first place electric music would have been played. It would have been a natural move if he understood it, but he quashed it. He took the attitude that what worked before would work again. So he kept doing folk singers. He didn't like electric music. He thought it detracted from the "artiste." When we brought in the electric stuff, he gave us a hard time.

He used to make his money with a Joan Baez or a Judy Collins, and the people

there that didn't get what it needed. And there was a feeling that with all the recognition you would be filled. Well, you're not. It's the "Is that all there is?" syndrome. That's why so many performers turn to drugs. Hopefully, it's a stage.

GEOFFREY STOKES: There was a lot of rampant ingestion of anything that would stand still. There wasn't that much serious smack use. This was, in general, a group of people who stayed up later at night than the general run of society. There was a lot of smoking . . . a lot of drinking. Occasional use of more colorful substances by some, and more regular use by others.

RAMBLIN' JACK ELLIOTT: I have been a big failure at times and I will be again if I don't keep my act together. I went to some alcoholics' meetings. I saw Phil [Ochs] drinking. I saw him on stage one night so drunk that everyone felt embarrassed and sorry for him and shocked with his behavior. I know that I too probably shocked with my own behavior when I was drunk, and probably did not know what happened afterwards. I never even thought I was an alcoholic. I drank to get loosened up. It was a very dangerous threat to my career. I had to deal with it as the enemy. That goes for drugs too. At one point I couldn't stand to perform without being high.

JUDY COLLINS: There's always pressure. This is a very tough business. I think every profession that exists, everybody who's in it always says, "This is the hardest profession. This is the profession where people succumb to drug addiction, alcoholism, suicide." Perhaps the music business profession is in a class by itself because of the coverage we get.

MARSHALL BRICKMAN: I may have smoked a little grass, but I was a nice Jewish boy, I wasn't into drugs. Maybe there is something to be learned from trying to understand or examine the use of drugs as part of the trend towards people doing original work. I think it's completely wrong to say that if you want to be an artist or a creative person you can be undisciplined and that it's a lifestyle which people embrace because it allows you to be undisciplined.

But on the contrary, it's easier to report to an office every day, because at least you have a structure that's superimposed on your life. You get people who are attracted to the music lifestyle and people who are attracted to what seems to be the lifestyle. The lifestyle almost imposes a kind of disorientation and depression on you which I could see leads very easily to drugs, to try and take away some of the pain and disorientation of playing in bars and living at night and getting home at three or four o'clock in the morning—after sleeping for eight or nine hours it's the afternoon. It's kind of a strange gypsy-like experience. It does have a kind of sinister, seductive appeal, but you have to have enormous character in order to live a productive life.

THE ECLECTIC
SEVENTIES

....

In 1971, U.S. bombing raids over North Vietnam escalated and America gave its eighteen year olds the right to vote. Charles Manson was found guilty of murder, and Governor Rockefeller had to deal with forty-two deaths resulting from the Attica prison uprising in New York. Bill Graham closed the Fillmores on both coasts. Female singer-songwriters were proving themselves with such classics as Carole King's Tapestry, Carly Simon's "That's the Way I Always Heard It Should Be," and Joni Mitchell's Blue. "Joy to the World," written by Hoyt Axton, was the number-one song of the year, followed on the year-end list by an array of bubblegum classics like "Knock Three Times" and "One Bad Apple."

Black artists were producing records that represented the black experience. It was the year of Marvin Gaye's classic "What's Goin' On?" Freda Payne's "Bring the Boys Home," "Family Affair" by Sly and the Family Stone, and "Theme from Shaft." Linda Ronstadt's backup band split and formed the Eagles. John Lennon released Imagine.

By 1972, hard drugs were firmly entrenched in youth culture, as was glitter-rock. David Bowie, a cult favorite in England, metamorphosed this time as Ziggy Stardust. Androgyny and heavy electric guitars were becoming the rage. The Band chose brass to back themselves up and released Rock of Ages, a live triple-record set.

The Democratic National Headquarters in the Watergate Hotel was broken into and Richard Nixon's problems began, although he slaughtered George McGovern in the presidential election. George Wallace was shot and partially paralyzed. Angela Davis was acquitted of murder, and Arab terrorists killed eleven Israeli athletes at the Munich Olympics.

Folk artist Ewan MacColl's "The First Time Ever I Saw Your Face," recorded by Roberta Flack, was the number-one song of the year. Don McLean, a Village regular, had a monster hit with "American Pie," and "I Am Woman" was the commercial rallying cry for feminism.

ANNE BOWEN: The Deadly Nightshade was three women playing our own version of power bluegrass, drumless rock, and feminist politics. Pamela Brandt played bass, Helen Hooke played lead guitar and violin, and I played rhythm guitar. We started the Deadly Nightshade to have a little fun and make a lot of noise. "Where did you get a name like that?" was the most frequent question, followed by "Why are you all women?" The answer to the second was simple. The answer to the first we tried to make exotic: "We wanted to honor eggplants and Lucrezia Borgia." But, it was really simple, too. Helen had always wanted to name a band the Deadly Nightshade, and Pamela and I didn't particularly mind.

We put the band together in 1972, and by 1974 we were ready to hit the big time. We were going to make it the old-fashioned way—playing live and building a following. We did a Monday night audition and got a booking at Folk City. We were on the way and we loved it. In other places, we had been regarded, both musically and personally, as somewhat hostile and definitely oddball. But, at Folk City we fit right in. We even liked the interior decoration. The wallpaper reminded me of a club that had fired us after two nights, and the murals were much odder than we were.

DAVID JOHANSEN: I used to live on Staten Island, and I would come into the Village all the time. We used to come in and see groups like the Magicians and the Spoonful, but we'd also come in to see people like Muddy Waters. Boy— Bleecker, MacDougal, and Third were really swinging around 1966. The Cafe Au Go-Go, Folk City, and the Cafe Wha? were the places everyone was going to. People were coming from all over the world to hear the music in those places. And those places were affecting the music all over the world.

I was in rock bands in high school. One band was the Vagabond Missionaries. It was a rock-and-roll cum blues band. We used to pack up our equipment in shopping carts and get on the ferry boat and come down to the Village and play.

Suddenly, the scene sort of shifted and the Village was all boarded up. Everybody who was interested in the music that was coming out of the Village grew up and moved to the suburbs.

JOEY RAMONE: I grew up in Queens, but I never felt a part of it. I kept coming into the East Village in 1967 and hung out. I felt like an outcast. I hung out pretty much by myself. I had some friends, but I came into the city. I just didn't fit in Queens.

In the city there were things like the Electric Circus, the Dom, Lou Reed, and the Fillmore. I hung out, but not in a particular scene. I dressed in an individual way—jumpsuits and pink knee-high boots. I had a sense of defiance and I just felt more comfortable in the Village. I was doing this in Queens and

The Ramones: Joey, Richie, Johnny, and Dee Dee (George DuBose)

it sort of shocked the neighborhood. In the East Village no one cared. There was more creativity in the Village.

BILLY JOEL: I moved to California in '73 and I became Piano Man. In L.A. I was listening to the Eagles and Jackson Browne. L.A. radio is very chauvinistic. They support their local artists. New York doesn't do that. Radio should support their own artists. When I came back to New York, I found that the cutting edge was gone. Places were more commercial. The kids that were hanging around the Village were teenagers from Long Island and New Jersey who had a couple of drinks and decided to go down to the Village and hunt up some drugs or chicks. The signs weren't even Bohemian looking. The facades of the places had been compromised. It looked like Forty-Second Street. It was a rougher atmosphere. Record companies had bought a bit of the atmosphere.

JOEY RAMONE: My favorite bands of the day were the Who, the Beatles, the Kinks, the Beach Boys, and the whole Phil Spector thing. As I got older I got into some of the fifties music like Buddy Holly, Jerry Lee Lewis, Little Richard, and Elvis Presley. One of the most exciting things in life is to discover things that are fresh. I would collect records and go to Woolworth's when records were fifty-nine cents. I had a good singles collection.

Since I was thirteen I was a drummer with bands. In '73 I formed a band with another guy called Sniper. It was a glitter-glamour kind of thing. I was one of the first people to get into Alice Cooper in '72. In '73 I was getting into the Stooges and the MC5, T-Rex, Slade, Gary Glitter. I was a big fan of Lou Reed's. He was a major inspiration. I liked Alice Cooper, but I liked him more when he was genuine. I thought he was a really sick guy—I thought he was great. Actually, I was all bummed-out when I found out he was golfing.

BILLY JOEL: In 1974, the record companies and the corporate powers that be got a hold of the singer-songwriter genre and turned it into cabaret-chanteur-Los Angeles cowboy singers. Slickness had set in. And money had taken over. The places had become less clubs and more showcases. Some of the clubs had gone already. The Gaslight was already out and the Bitter End changed its name and that took away a lot of its magic.

Elton John and Yes were both big at that time. I listened to a lot of jazz. Nobody was really a big influence on me. I was my own biggest influence on me, for better or worse. Some people will say for worse.

RALPH NEMEC: The Village lost most of its carnival atmosphere. There wasn't that much happening. The Bitter End had closed. The famous cafes were closed. The Cafe Wha? tried to revive when Richie Havens took it over but it only did well when Richie played. The Village was dead.

I tried to get Mike to book jazz, to try something new, but no. The locals pretty much had control and were booked constantly. By this time fifty percent was folk, thirty percent glitter rock, and twenty percent more traditional rock. If a group could pull people in, Mike would re-book them. It didn't matter if they were good, as long as they were popular. But Folk City was such a historical landmark, it was more a tourist attraction than a bastion of folk music.

While Watergate hearings filled the television screens during the day, at night Americans watched Kojak *and* Mannix. Kojak *beamed an image of New York as the proverbial tough, crime-ridden but compassionate city. In 1974, the city itself was in bad financial shape, and critics across the country pointed to the welfare-state excesses of New York City in the Lindsay Adminstration.*

The summer of 1975 seemed like it would be a desolate one for Greenwich Village. Most of the clubs were long gone and the few survivors were struggling. Uptown cabarets were the hot venues and few tourists made a night of it in the Village anymore. The downtown performers were despairing and the scene seemed dead once and for all. But something happened that summer that shot life back into the Village. Greenwich Village's favorite son came back.

Bob Dylan returned to a scene much different from when he left in the sixties. Once word spread that Dylan was hanging out, the streets filled again with the

Joan Baez, Bob Dylan, Eric Andersen at Folk City, October 1975 (Mary Alfieri)

curious, the sycophants and the hopeful. During the course of the day, one might run into Dylan on MacDougal, Bleecker, or Third. His presence brought better performers to the Village hangouts like Gerdes, the Kettle of Fish, the Dug Out, and the Other End. They all wanted to be a part of Dylan's new venture—the historic Rolling Thunder Tour.

On October 23, 1975, Mike Porco's birthday, the Rolling Thunder Tour was launched. Amidst camera crews shooting what eventually became Dylan's film, Renaldo and Clara, and a gathering of celebrities, Bob Dylan gave Mike an all-star birthday party which would become the talk of the music world for years to come. Big names remembered what fun it was to play small, intimate clubs.

There had been rumors circulating around the country that Dylan would be playing a small club somewhere. Everyone knew that if Dylan would play a small club it would be Gerdes Folk City.

ALLEN GINSBERG: The first time I performed at Folk City was with the Rolling Thunder Revue in 1975. I hadn't played before because Folk City was Dylan's club. The poets had to find somewhere else to read. The top musicians had Folk City.

It was a big night. There was a poetry reading at St. Marks with Robert Creeley and Ed Sanders of the Fugs. There was a party at my house afterwards, and Dylan came with his camera crew. Later we went down to Folk City. Bette Midler and Phil Ochs were there and they sang. I sang "The Nurse's Song," accompanied by Denise Mercedes, whom Dylan liked a lot. She wore a red rose in her bosom that night. Bette Midler ended up on my lap . . . or was it Dylan's lap? She ended up in everybody's lap over by the wall. She was great. She was a lot of fun. The full band was there, all the musicians from the tour. Phil Ochs was very affecting. It was a big party. It was a night everyone could try out and find out what they could do.

ROSIE: I came by Folk City because I thought it was just going to be a birthday for Mike. I ended up being the MC.

Everybody came in about eleven o'clock and the show got started. All these people got pushed in front of me and I had to introduce them. I was trying to get some of the new people on. There was one person everybody wanted me to put on, and I kept saying, "Just a minute," and they pushed him right up. It was Bob Dylan. I said, "Who are you, Bob Dylan?" He said, "Yeah." The people around said, "Rosie, this is really Bob Dylan." And I said, "Yeah, so are a million other people telling me they're Bob Dylan when they come to Folk City." He was a little tense, but he was very sweet and I'll never forget his blue eyes.

I said, "Are you really Bob Dylan? If you *are* Dylan, do I get a kiss?" and he kisses me on the cheek. And I said, "On the cheek? For all this struggle? Don't I get a sexy kiss?" And he kissed me on the lips.

I came back on stage and everybody kept saying, "Put Bette Midler on." And I kept saying, "Who? I have other people to put on, I can't push them aside." I introduced her as Betty Miller.

I liked her. I thought she was a very good entertainer. She was a little wild.

I don't think she did the whole song because I said, "Look, we have other people." I announced, "All right. Betty Miller, it was nice having you. Come back again." She said, "Okay, okay, okay." Everybody was having fun, even Dylan, and Dylan never laughs.

Allen Ginsberg and Patti Smith got up. They looked like a pair. It was like the sixties. Patti was very, very quiet, and she came dressed all in black. She sat there and didn't make a sound. Compared to her, Bette Midler was the complete opposite. Patti Smith was the sparkler and Bette Midler was the firecracker, the dynamite. Bette was having a good time, drinking up her beer, sitting with nice-looking guys. Patti Smith got on stage. Did her thing. Very nice. That was it. She went back to her seat.

Finally, they brought out the cake for Mike and as I was presenting it to Mike, the cake fell accidentally. They said that I let it drop, but that's not true. I started eating it off the floor. I bent down, put my fingers on it and said to Mike, "The top is still clean, honey." Everybody was laughing, even Dylan.

David Blue, Bette Midler, and Allen Ginsberg, Folk City, 1975 (Mary Alfieri)

At the end of the night, Phil Ochs said, "Rosie, please put me on." I don't know what was between him and Dylan, but it was very important for him to play. He said, "I want to do my best, I want to do it for everybody and I want to do it for Bob." He sang five songs. The audience loved him. He never sang that well, even on his regular shows there. He yelled from the stage, "Bobby, Bobby, Bobby." I think Dylan was getting ready to escape and Phil yelled, "Bobby, Bobby—you, this is for you." And Bob Dylan never turned his head. I felt so sorry for the both of them. I'd never seen Phil Ochs act that humble or wanting something that much. He was a loner that night. He sang "Changes," and you would have tears in your eyes. Some people who were just getting up to leave sat back down.

In the summer of 1975, after the fall of Saigon, over two thousand discos started up across the country. Estimates had two to three hundred discos in New York alone. Previous top grossing concert attractions were suffering because of high ticket prices and their not-so-danceable music. Suddenly the superstars of the sixties and early seventies were being considered dinosaurs. With disco, the clientele became the show.

The music itself became more saccharine although the lyrics began to get more suggestive. Songs like "Love to Love You Baby" and "Love Machine" became big hits. A new pastime was seeing how outrageously racy album covers could get, with the Ohio Players occupying the winner's circle. But still, a quality act like Phoebe Snow could still be recognized.

Records became longer and DJs became essential. Clubs with non-live music became the rage. But not downtown. On the fringes of Greenwich Village a whole new scene was forming; and Patti Smith was becoming the great hope for live music in New York City.

The seventies music market wasn't as accepting as it was in the sixties, but the artists who came through this era endured. Emmylou Harris, Melissa Manchester, Phoebe Snow, Linda Ronstadt, Steve Forbert, Loudon Wainwright, Willie Nile, the Manhattan Transfer, the Roches, Sammy Walker, and David Bromberg were all Village-based artists who first gained popularity in that time.

SAMMY WALKER: When I was singing in the coffeehouses in Atlanta and north Georgia, I used to fantasize about playing Gerdes Folk City in New York. I heard about it through the years from reading about it, and all the people who had played there were all the people I admired when I was a teenager growing up in Georgia. Folk City was *the* place in my mind. So the first time I got to sing there was a big thrill for me.

The first time I met Phil Ochs was in 1973. Phil had just given a week's worth of concerts in Atlanta. In between sets, he would come out to the lobby and talk

Sammy Walker at Folk City, July 1975 (Jody Miller)

to his fans and I was right there with him. He was one of my idols. I remember asking him about Gerdes Folk City. I asked him if it was still around and he said, "Yeah, it moved to Third Street." Of course, being from the Atlanta area, it didn't mean anything to me. I didn't know what street it was on to begin with, but it was good news to me to know the club was still going after all those years.

A month later, Phil was going to have his farewell performance and one of the things he was going to do was to introduce me to New York. That was my first live appearance. I had been on the radio a couple of times and we had just gotten through making the first record for Folkways. Shortly after that I got a record deal with Warner Brothers.

JANIS SIEGEL: I had a group called the Young Generation when I was twelve years old. Richard Perry was our producer. We made a couple of singles. We lasted all through high school and through the first year of college. We used to play the West Fourth Street subway station. I was in Laurel Canyon up until I met Tim Hauser.

TIM HAUSER: There was a quality about Janis that was so special. It's very rare when you see a white girl sing like that, and she could deliver a line. Sometimes she sounded like Aretha. She has a quality that sets her apart. It's something so special, so unique, I get goosebumps from her.

JANIS SIEGEL: Laurel Canyon's music was acoustic harmony music with a big emphasis on folk. I was writing quite a bit. We were starting to get very influenced by people like Tracy Nelson and songwriters like Eric Kaz. We did some Joni Mitchell and Cat Stevens songs. We were also becoming a little influenced by jazz. The emphasis was on three-part harmony and our guitar playing was adequate. That was the time of the singer-songwriter types. We would do the songs of people that we would meet down in the Village.

I found it a very exciting time. It was very supportive among the musicians. There were no rivalries. Everyone would help each other. The Village was still the place to be even though it was the tail end of the big scene there. In one night you could play three or four different places.

We played the streets. We did it to make money and it was fun. We would go into a restaurant and start singing and get enough money to pay for a meal.

We were three girls from Brooklyn and we thought the ultimate place to live would be Laurel Canyon. We were also heavily influenced by Joni Mitchell. That's how we got our group's name.

Folk City was part of our route. We would drop in to see what was going on. You would always see someone good. Our rounds were mostly hoot nights, and all that depended on the MC. The MC was the god. He would decide who would go on. Sometimes you'd wait for hours. But you'd just wait. You had to work your way into that scene. The MCs had to get to know you, and if they thought you were good you'd gain their respect.

I joined a group called Trust Me and I found it extremely exhilarating to sing without playing a guitar. The more I was with Trust Me, the more I was getting tired of Laurel Canyon. I had met Tim Hauser when he was driving a cab and we became friends. He was in the Manhattan Transfer and he told me he wanted to re-form the group. The idea of four-part harmony was thrilling to me so I quit Laurel Canyon just as we were about to get a record deal. This was in 1972.

One night I'm singing in the Village and years later I'm performing with Ella Fitzgerald at the Grammys.

TIM HAUSER: I hung out in the Village when I was very young. Since the late twenties my parents had a house on MacDougal Street. In 1959 I went to the College of Complexes, a bastion of the Beat scene in the Village. As a teenager I was always very curious about the flyers for poetry readings all over the Village.

The Manhattan Transfer (Armen Kachaturian, copyright © 1974)

It was my first exposure to a side of life other than suburban middle-class life. My curiosity was always whetted by the Village.

In college I was in a group called the Criterions. It was a rhythm-and-blues group. We couldn't get much work so we got into folk music. At first it was just to get work. Then I got completely absorbed in it.

My folk group was the Troubadours Three. We weren't good instrumentalists, but we were great singers. I started performing in the Village in 1962. We used to get booked with Bill Cosby. Sometimes we were his only audience.

We couldn't really break into the "in" crowd in the Village, because we didn't live there. In the early seventies I spent all my time in the Village totally in awe and so much wanting to be a part of it. We suddenly had a tight clique—Barry Kornfeld, Dave Van Ronk and Denny Doherty, who later was in the Mamas and the Papas. We were all a bunch of snobs. We thought we were hot shit and we mistreated a lot of people. I guess we figured that's how we were treated when we first came in.

The Troubadours Three were more commercial than the usual fare and that was frowned upon. If you were a fan of the Kingston Trio, you were very un-hip.

In 1972, I met Janis Siegel who was singing with Laurel Canyon, and we eventually re-formed the Manhattan Transfer.

My experience in the Village was invaluable for my later career. It was one of the most enjoyable times of my life and the quality of music was so great. It was very intimate. You could get into the singer. It was more subtle. That's how I developed as a singer.

It was a very human kind of thing. Even though it got big-time, it was never "big-time." The intensity was in the lyric, not in volume.

There was a buzz that was sweeping the country and it was happening in the Village. I relish those times. I was privileged to be there, and history tells us how really magical it was.

LOUDON WAINWRIGHT: I came to the Village in earnest to make it when I was writing my own songs around 1968. I had a job in a macrobiotic restaurant. I was sleeping on people's floors. I was writing all the time and playing the hoots. I was doing everything you were supposed to do.

I was very lucky because not that much time elapsed between the time I got to the Village and the time I got my record deal. The record business was really booming in the late sixties and early seventies. It was a combination of luck and that they were signing a lot of people. I got a record deal fast, I think, because they felt that folk music was going to come back into vogue with the ascension of James Taylor.

When I came in '68 the scene was not happening. Everybody had moved to Woodstock. I stuck it out and I recorded my first album for Atlantic in 1969 and it came out in 1970.

Loudon Wainwright

The early seventies crop included me, David Bromberg, Steve Goodman, John Prine, Bonnie Raitt, and Tom Waits.

SUZZY ROCHE: The music became your whole world and there was nothing else but that. Someone would write a song and everyone would listen to it. It wasn't exactly the most loving, caring, friendly scene, but everyone was paying attention to what everyone else was doing.

The sixties was the first time that the fame and the glory happened. So now in the leaner times everybody was going after that fame and glory. I remember Steve Forbert hitting town saying he was going to be a star.

STEVE FORBERT: When I got to New York in 1976 from Meridian, Mississippi, I was interested in everything. I wanted to do the hoots and I enjoyed playing CBGB's, opening for people like John Cale and the Talking Heads when they were a trio. I also have a lot of country in my style so it fit right in with CBGB's concept of country-bluegrass-blues.

I got into New York by train, and I checked into the Twenty-Third Street Y. I thought I should come right down to see these places in the Village right away. This way I didn't build things up and get nervous. I came into Folk City and asked when the hoot was and I saw all these flyers around for the new Village songwriter-poets and I wondered how good they were.

It was very exciting to me to be around all these people who were very serious about writing songs. It was a gas. I knew right away I was in the right place. It was a live club scene. A song exists in the air. Sing the song and see what the people like.

That was probably the most fun time of my life. singing around and living off chicken piss.

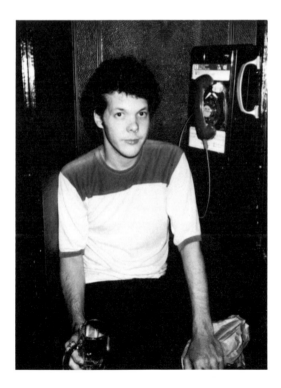

Steve Forbert at Folk City, 1985 (Karen Garthe)

I was bugging Mike for a gig for a while. He'd say, "You gotta getta da following." It was Catch Twenty-two. How did you get a following if you were playing the streets?

The streets were pretty good money, better than the clubs. You could sing for about twenty minutes and get about twenty bucks.

In 1977, Mike finally gave me an opening-act spot. I opened for a loud blues group. Mike used to ask me to do other people's songs so he could tell whether I was good or not. He used to say, "How can I tell if you are good, if I'm not familiar with what you are singing?"

I just wanted to sing and write songs for a living. I wanted to stir up as much dust as I could. I'm still working on it. I hardly feel like I've accomplished what I want to do.

I always hated being called "the next Bob Dylan." It showed a lack of creativity on the part of journalists. It's an easy tag, an easy way to sell magazines. It's difficult to be looked at as yourself.

My southern influences were important to me. I reacted a lot to Elvis and Jimmie Rodgers, who's from my home town. I liked pop music more than the Dylan label implies.

Phil Ochs had a much more difficult time fighting the Bob Dylan label.

DAVID AMRAM: The last time I saw Phil Ochs, he was having a concert at Folk City and he asked me to come down and play. He called and said, "Dave, you have to come down here. We need some different kinds of music." He was very upset, and he was having a very hard time at that point in his life.

When I came down I could see he was having so many troubles. He forgot he had called me. I said, "You just called me up and here I am." He said, "Dave, my God, excuse me. You have to pardon me. I'm kind of under the weather." He asked me to get up and play something. I played Pakistani flute and a jazz piece, and then I made up a blues for Phil. He was sitting at the bar and enjoyed it so much that he came up and started playing, making up the lyrics and improvising. He was having a good time. That was the last time I ever saw him.

OSCAR BRAND: Phil's songs themselves were banners, slogans. But he didn't sing with fire. He was a driven writer and a good performer.

Phil would have been ten times bigger if he needed it more. He always seemed to get in his own way. I think, in a way, he hated himself as he got successful. He didn't want to become that kind of person. Phil was an anomaly. He was shy at the same time he was bold.

One night, I met him on the street as he was going to Folk City. I asked him

Phil Ochs

how he was doing. He said, "Great. I'm writing again. I'm going out West. It's going to be terrific." Soon after, he committed suicide.

Phil Ochs died on April 9, 1976, at his sister Sonny's house in Queens, N.Y.

But for all those bad-luck stories, there are also performers who found good fortune in New York City.

JERRY HARRISON: My first involvement with the New York music scene was when I was with the Modern Lovers. We seemed to be more well-known in New York than we were in Boston, which was our home base. We only played New York a couple of times, but we were very popular amongst the music critics centered around Danny Fields and Lillian Roxon and Steven Gaines; and later, Lisa Robinson.

The first time we played was at a private party. Then we played at the Mercer Arts Center. We played a very notable gig opening for the New York Dolls on New Year's Eve, 1973. So I feel there was this scene around the Dolls and the Mercer Arts Center.

Jerry Harrison and David Byrne (© Stephanie Chernikowski)

Right around when the Modern Lovers broke up, the CBGB scene began. Around that time some of the Modern Lovers were talking about working together and Richard Hell and Tom Verlaine started talking about forming Television.

JOEY RAMONE: I always wanted to make it from when I first started coming into myself. I knew this was what I wanted. What we did was genuine. We are four unique individuals, and all the guys are talented. Johnny created his own sound. His sound changed the world in a sense as far as guitar playing. A lot of people used to hate us because they studied at Juilliard for twenty years. We just made it off the bat and they were working their asses off forever. We created a unique and definite new sound that I feel revolutionized rock-and-roll in '74. Even today, the evolution stems from what we did back then.

LOUDON WAINWRIGHT: When a person gets a record deal, people get excited because they think they might be next. In a way that's true. It usually happens in spurts. Record companies don't know what the fuck is going on so if the critics say something is happening down here, then Clive—or whoever—will come down and check it out. And if somebody gets signed, record executives get paranoid and think that they're missing out on something, so they sign some people. Then it all dies down and they all get dropped.

SUZZY ROCHE: One night in Folk City, Linda Ronstadt and Phoebe Snow came in to see us. They were extremely noticeable. They would clap and laugh at our jokes. We'd sing a line and they'd yell, "Brilliant." We felt like little bugs. They came backstage and shook our hands. Linda said things like, "Marvelous writing." I've never been comfortable around famous people, and I was always sure that I was the one energy that the critics didn't like.

PHOEBE SNOW: Linda and I came to see the Roches one night. John Rockwell originally turned her on to the Roches. When she was in town I saw her and said that I was a big fan of the Roches and she said, "Me too. I just got turned on to them. Let's go down to Gerdes and see them."

They sang "Married Men," which was a song I had my heart set on for a long time, and Linda heard it and started elbowing me. I said, "Do you like that song?" She said, "I love that song." "How much do you love that song?" I asked her. The two of us were having a cackle party back there. I said that I wanted to do it. She said that she wanted to do it. We both ended up doing it.

The Roches are really droll, and when they met Linda it was like, "Oh, hi." I was almost peeing in my pants.

SUZZY ROCHE: I met Loudon at Folk City. Maggie and him were having some sort of . . . nothing. He was sort of chasing after Maggie. I was sitting at the bar and Mark Johnson suggested, "Why don't you go over and talk to Loudon." Mark was trying to get him away from Maggie. He was interested in her. I had no idea who Loudon was. I thought he was kind of square and too straight looking.

Loudon finally came over and started talking to me. I was flattered that he was talking to me. Then he offered to walk me home and when we got to my place he said, "Well, you know, do you wanna . . . do you want me to stay here tonight?" And I said, "No, I think you better leave."

Months later he came to my door with a McGarrigles record and handed it to me and asked me to go out on a date with him. I always ask him, "What were you doing?" because all of the songs on the record were these poor, heartbroken songs. We met in Folk City and spent many nights together at Folk City. We had lots of fun there, for sure.

LOUDON WAINWRIGHT: "Making it" is a very hard, difficult, weird thing, and talent has very little to do with it. In the beginning it's necessary to have a lot of talent and to maintain a lot of talent, but after a while, talent isn't the issue anymore. There are things like luck and discipline and politics and the weather. You could become this year's big thing and be finished in a short while.

The Roches (Irene Young)

SUZZY ROCHE: I didn't have sense that anything was going to take off. When John Rockwell came down to review us, I was thinking about an act he had reviewed the week before, an act of three sisters from West Virginia. He gave them a terrible review. I remember thinking, "He's going to hate us." I'd gone to see those other people, and I really identified with them. I thought we were just like them. Then I thought, "He's going to tear us apart."

He wrote a front page feature in the *Times Arts and Leisure* section about us, and he took a few other people like Steve Forbert and George Gerdes and singled them out and basically said the Village scene is happening, and these are a few people that are happening in the Village.

Rockwell picked our album as Album of the Year, and that was a great help to us. He wrote that, and a hundred people around the country wrote the same exact article.

Everybody else who was playing was saying, "Why wasn't I mentioned in this article?" I think right there was when things started to break down into factions.

DAVID BROMBERG: I met Phoebe really early on. After seeing Bonnie Raitt play, this girl followed me saying, "Mr. Bromberg, Mr. Bromberg." I'd never been called Mr. Bromberg in the Village before. She said, "Hey, I write songs and I can sing." She sang really well and played good guitar and we became friends. The girl was Phoebe Snow.

PHOEBE SNOW: I had a friend who was a couple of years younger than me, and he had a jugband. In 1969, I had a big crush on this guy. He wanted to manage me. He heard me play and sing one of my obscure little blues tunes. He said to me, "You know, you really have talent and you should be heard." He took me to WBAI, the listener-supported station. It was four o'clock in the morning, and I played a couple of songs, shaking so hard and just drooling from nervousness. People called in at four o'clock in the morning and said, "Who was that?"

After that he said, "You know, there's an amateur night circuit and you ought to play there." I said, "Oh God, you mean in front of people?" I was mortified. I wasn't born yesterday, but the idea of getting up in front of people was horrifying. In school, when we had an oral book report, I would be sick that day. So singing in front of people is like taking your clothes off, by comparison. Since I had a crush on him I let him manipulate me into it, which is probably the hippest thing I ever did. So I did it and people clapped. It wasn't like they stood up and trashed the place, but they clapped.

One very funny experience was when Bruce Springsteen was showcasing on an amateur night. I was supposed to follow him. The MC moved me. My idol, John Hammond [Sr.], was sitting in that audience. I went into the ladies' room and cried. I followed John Hammond out of the club strumming my guitar, yelling, "I can sing! I can play the guitar! La, la, la, la." And John Hammond just went, "Bye."

Tracy Nelson, Robbie Woliver, and Phoebe Snow at Folk City

The MC decided to put his girlfriend on before Springsteen. When I came out of the bathroom I saw Springsteen going out to the sidewalk. Trying to keep a stiff upper lip, I said, "Excuse me, Mr. Springsteen. How did you . . ." and I lost my composure and started crying—"How did you get John Hammond to discover you?" Bruce said, "Oh, that's okay, you'll get discovered too." And he's patting me on the back. I recently saw him and he said he will always remember that night, that it was hilarious.

I never expected what happened to me to happen. It was one of the greatest shocks in my life that the album was successful. It was a low-budget, unassuming, quiet little album. Most of the disc jockeys around the country liked it.

I started off in folk clubs playing an acoustic guitar, sitting in a bridge chair. Not exactly a polished performer. And my first record out of the box went gold and platinum. I didn't know what to do. I never fronted a band. I never played a hall larger than 100 people. I never toured. I was a total novice. I knew nothing. I had no mistakes behind me. I had nothing to learn from. Don't make it right away. You have all of the time in the world.

Some of the people around were very angry. I think there was some resentment. How come you made it and I didn't? Which is a perfectly organic, natural way to respond.

LIBBY TITUS: I grew up in Woodstock, New York, which I considered a deadly bore. At least in 1959 and 1960. I would come to the Village every weekend. My aunt lived in the city. I was only thirteen. I would hang out and look in on the clubs. There was so much energy you could feel it. I was drawn to it. I was a singer at thirteen, too.

Everyone flocked to Woodstock starting in 1963. My territory was being invaded and it was thrilling. I was to Woodstock what Maria Muldaur was to the

Maria Muldaur, Libby Titus, and Carly Simon at Folk City (Marion Kahan)

Village. We were both neighborhood girls in neighborhoods which were becoming the in place to be. The Village was the urban version of Woodstock.

As a writer I was terrified by Dylan. At every line of his songs I would say, "What did that mean?" What if he hears my song? Does this measure up to a Bob Dylan line? That's stupid because poetry shouldn't be a competitive, commercial thing. But I personally was inhibited by him.

During the Woodstock years he had this definite hierarchy around him. First there was Bob Dylan. Then there was Sara [Dylan]. Then there was Albert Grossman. Then Albert's wife. Then Robbie Robertson. Then Robbie's wife, Dominique. Then there were the other Band members. Then there were the Band members' wives. Then there were the Band members' girlfriends. And so on.

I loved Albert Grossman. He was brilliant and eccentric, to say the least. He's hospitable and very clever. In the whirlwind of all the insanity he kept his head on his shoulders. If only I had listened to everything he had told me to do. He was like a computer brain.

When my success happened with "Love Has No Pride," the Band treated it as if it happened to their baby sister. They were so proud of me and supportive. But those were very heavy times.

With the formation of the New York Dolls in late 1971, a new New York style began that would culminate in punk rock five years later. They sounded a lot like the Stones (especially the guitar of Johnny Thunders, a veritable xerox of Keith Richards's playing), the Stooges, and the Velvet Underground. The Dolls dressed in women's clothing and wore outrageous makeup.

Lou Reed left the Velvet Underground and went into seclusion. He later moved to England to begin his solo career in 1971. Elephant's Memory, formed in the East Village by drummer Rick Frank and Stan Bronstein, got their musical exposure in small clubs and roadhouses, and forged a street-band reputation. When John Lennon was looking for a band, they were recommended and Lennon immediately signed them up. All kinds of New York alliances were being formed at this time, most of them were grounded in hard rock and accompanied by increasing drug use.

DAVID JOHANSEN: The Dolls got together in '72 for about three years and tried to breathe some life in the scene with rock-and-roll in the classic sense. Our big drive was to have fun playing our music, get an audience and fill joints up. We played all over—Kenny's, Au Go-Go, Max's, Mercer Arts Center. The Mercer Arts Center was a great place. It was ten rooms in a hotel on Broadway and Mercer. There was an experimental video room, a cabaret room, a theatrical room. The experimental place, the Kitchen, started there. We started on Tuesdays in the Oscar Wilde Room. Then we moved to the bigger theatre where *One*

David Johansen (Marion Kahan)

Flew Over the Cuckoo's Nest was playing. It was actually a great place. A lot of things going on at one time.

We were kind of like the house band at Max's. It was booked by Sam Hood who used to run the Gaslight. It was really eclectic booking policy. They would book the Wailers, Bruce Springsteen, the Dolls; *and* they would have Waylon Jennings. It was fun to be there. We predated the CBGB scene. Later on you had the Talking Heads, Patti Smith, and the Ramones. We used to just hang out at Max's and at Nobody's, Charlie Chin's bar on Bleecker Street. A lot of rock people hung out there.

IRA MAYER: When I started hanging around, the people who were playing were Kris Kristofferson and Rita Coolidge, who I think made love on the Gaslight-Au Go-Go stage the second night that they met, and I was there. It sure looked like it from where I was sitting. She was playing the Au Go-Go. I forgot where he was playing. They had met on a plane coming to New York, if I remember right, and they timed their set so they could each appear with the other. And I remember the two of them doing strange things around the microphone stand. It was a lot of fun.

BARBARA DANE: I was scheduled to play around April 30, 1975, and that's when the war in Vietnam ended. I turned the night into a celebration. There were people all over town who wanted to celebrate and didn't know what to do, so they all ended up at Gerdes. We were running through all the antiwar hits. It was a glorious night and Mike didn't know what to make of us celebrating "the enemies'" victory. He didn't seem to mind. It was jammed and he did all right at the bar.

RICK FRANK: I came to New York in 1967 and formed a group called Elephant's Memory. It was a group of jazz players who played rock-and-roll. We were like vagabonds. We traveled around New England; a lot of lounge jobs; bowling alley gigs. One of the first times the Elephants worked with horns was at Folk City. Stan Bronstein, who was playing with Tito Puente at the time, and I got an offer from Allan Pepper to play Folk City. The horn section was very progressive and innovative. We were ahead of every trend in New York. We had a jazz following and an R&B following.

Through the seven or eight years we played there I kept trying to get Mike to upgrade the place. I was one of the few people he listened to. I kept my shoes in the toaster oven in the kitchen. That upset him. I tried to explain to him that you needed a dressing room in order to keep your shoes out of the toaster. Either get a toaster for each band member or get a dressing room. And he did. He really respected us. He treated Elephant's Memory far better than other groups. He became loyal to us because we stayed loyal to him. We didn't play neighboring clubs.

John Lennon was looking for a working band. At that time we sounded like the Stones with horns. We did a live concert on WLIR with Billy Joel, and Lennon heard it and I got a call instantly about meeting him. It was a funny thing, because most of the people in my group were not Beatles fans.

The first message I got was to show up at an apartment at 150 Bank Street where John and Yoko lived, and deliver a picture of the group. He said he wanted to make sure we were all psychos. So we delivered the picture but I didn't get to see him. The next day he called, and I was told to come to the Record Plant, and within minutes he was asking me to overdub a drum part on a concert he had done at the Apollo.

Following that, he wanted to come down to a little studio in the Village called Magna Graphics. I brought John down there to meet the rest of the Elephants. They were waiting for me to show up with John Lennon, which was amazing enough; so not only do I show up with him, I show up with Yoko, Phil Spector, a couple of Spector's girlfriends, and the whole tribe. The studio could comfortably hold four people. We ended up jamming for four or five hours.

John would call whatever group that was working with him at the time the

Plastic Ono Band. We were the Plastic Ono Elephant's Memory Band. As accessible as he would like to think he could be, he definitely had a sense of who he was all the time. Except he'd like to run around and get loaded with a bunch of crazy guys. It, in a way, insulated him from danger.

John taught us the whole ethic about talking to the press. You know, make things up because they're going to make things up anyway. He compared the

Plastic Ono Elephant's Memory Band: (top) Gary Van Scyoc, Jim Keltner;
(middle) Stan Bronstein, Wayne "Tex" Gabriel, Adam Ippolito;
(bottom) Rick Frank, Yoko Ono, John Lennon (John Gruen)

period of time working with the Elephants to when the Beatles were in Hamburg. That mixed feeling of greatness. People had a difficult time dealing with the tough image he had when he worked with us. We didn't know him as the family man who had cleaned up his act, as he was in later years. We were with him when he was a drug-influenced maniac.

Our connection with Lennon was taken so badly by some people that it left many bitter feelings. Many people took us as rejecting them. A lot of people wanted favors from us. But we were just trying to survive and we weren't rejecting anyone.

LENNY KAYE: All those bands in that crowd—the Patti Smith Group, Television, the Ramones, the Talking Heads, and Blondie—we were all in the right place at the right time. There was a need then for music to become more raw, emotional, and primitive. It was time to head back to its grass roots. Music got very stratified. There was a gap. There's a change happening now. Music is getting away from technical rock to more human, acoustic, and poetic style.

Music moves in cycles. There's an underground and an overground. Then the underground becomes the overground and a new underground comes up. We were the new underground. By "we" I mean the bands, the fans, and the journalists who covered it all.

There was a great sense of cooperation between the bands. We were all friends. From just saying, "Hey, great set," to hanging around together. It was a small world. We used to play a lot with Television. The Talking Heads opened for the Ramones. We were all in the same social circles.

I thought Television was the greatest. At the time, I was editing a magazine called *Rock Scene* with Richard and Lisa Robinson. It was the chronicle of CBGB's life. We tried to promote the scene.

BUZZY LINHART: I came to the Village in 1963 as a folk singer from Cleveland. Folk City was the first place I went to and was the first place I sang. It was strange to me because it was more like a bar than a folk club on the regular folk circuit. Steely Dan opened for me there in 1972.

Carly Simon and I were dating for a while and I set her up with Eddie Kramer to produce her first album. She was very shy and I was cutting an album and Eddie was co-producing for me. He and Carly decided to cut my song "The Love's Still Growing" and I played on a few other songs.

And I've had songs recorded by Bette Midler. Bette was dating my drummer Luther Rix. She was working at the Continental Baths and she used to come in and see us every time we played. She came up to me one night at Folk City after our show and told me that she decided to take a record deal with Atlantic

Buzzy Linhart (Armen Kachaturian, copyright © 1974)

and that she was going to use my song "Friends" on the album. The last time Bette and I sang together was at the Folk City party for Bob Dylan's Rolling Thunder Tour in 1976. Bette and I closed the show singing "Friends" together.

LENNY KAYE: The Patti Smith group began playing at CBGB's in early '75 for nine weeks straight, four nights a week. It gave us a chance to continuously work out an act. We worked pretty much on improvisation. We became a real band after that gig. It was also around that time that we were signed to Arista.

were the Long Island groups like the Vagrants and the Rascals. After that was the Village folk-rock scene with bands like the Magicians and the Lovin' Spoonful. So by their very existence, the Dolls gave a certain focus to the glitter–New York rock scene that gave us groups like the Forty-Second Street Harlots, the Miamis, and Teenage Lust.

It was a rock-oriented, hanging-out scene in the seventies. Every Sunday, I would go down to CBGB's and watch Television. They were very raw at that time but I was fascinated by what they were trying to achieve. Television would be followed by the Ramones and the Stilettos, which was Debbie Harry's group. All the bands were playing for each other. There wasn't much of an audience at that time. Also there was Club 82 which would tie together the glitter and rock scenes. All those bands were proud of their uniqueness and individual ideas.

"Because the Night" made it to the top fifteen in 1978, and *Easter*, the album it was on, did well on the charts also. In fact, our debut album, *Horses*, went top forty.

Patti was extremely inspirational. She had a great enthusiasm for the creative energy of art. There was the personal side of her, which was very warm and funny. We used to giggle a lot and tell jokes and sit around and have good times. There was something very little-girlish about her. She also had very set ideas about pushing herself and making sure that neither she nor anyone else she was working with was content with what was. She was working for what could be. That's why the band split up. When there was nowhere else to go we decided to go on to new things.

I first got into Patti as a fan when she was an actress in a Jackie Curtis play at La Mama. I still remained a fan throughout my association with her. She's one of the great creative minds of our generation. Music is not the foremost thing on her mind right now, I suppose, but I'm sure we haven't heard the last of Patti Smith.

JERRY HARRISON: When Mickey Ruskin ran Max's, it was his personality. He really wanted it to be a bar for his painter friends, but it became a hangout for rock stars. He thought they were okay but he wasn't that excited by them. He was much more excited about Bill deKooning coming around. Mickey's clubs always had an integrity to them. At the beginning, Max's didn't have bands playing, but later on when the Modern Lovers started coming to New York they had started their policies of having bands playing. Then Mickey moved to the Local and Max's was bought out, and that's when Max's started competing with CBGB's for acts. Then he went to the Lower Manhattan Ocean Club, which was a very odd combination of a place to perform and a big restaurant.

CBGB's best quality was that it was long and narrow and it had great sound.

And if you particularly didn't like the band that was playing you could go to the back of the club and wander outside and have a conversation with someone and wait for the next band to come on. It really facilitated people just hanging out there. Because it was long and narrow, the front rows filled up very quickly, so that any band with fifty fans felt like they were playing to an audience. The things that made CBGB's an optimum site for underground music were that you could fill up the front, the sound was good, a number of bands could play, and you could choose your distance.

JOEY RAMONE: In 1976 when we went to England, there was no punk. The press started calling us that because of "Judy Is a Punk." The big music over there was pub-rock-Dr. Feelgood, Brinzley-Schwartz. We went over there and we were selling out places for three thousand. Over here we were playing for three or four hundred people. We were sort of being treated like royalty. That's the summer "punk" exploded. We were the incentive and inspiration. These kids kept coming up to us telling us we were the inspiration for their bands. Those people later became the Sex Pistols and the Clash. All these kids were hanging around with red and green hair. They kind of dubbed it "the summer of hate."

The year 1976 saw Jimmy Carter trying to create a down-home feeling in the White House while young kids were glitzing it up in the discos and the few rock clubs that were sprouting up all around the Lower East Side. The Sex Pistols were shocking Britain and Elvis Costello was wowing the Americans. It was also the year of the Talking Heads' record debut.

The record-buying public decided that they would prefer to listen to their records in a club where they could dance, show off their clothes, and meet members of the opposite sex. Suddenly records that the mainstream audience never heard of were working their way up the charts. The passionless disco craze was continuing its impersonal, yet glamorous rise.

The intimate Village clubs gave way to large, loud, bass-heavy discos. Record companies were able to create their hits in a studio. They didn't need the Gaslight, Folk City, or Au Go-Go. They didn't even need an act that was intact, they would create one to sound like the record. Instead of "memorizing every breath that Joan Baez took," as aspiring singers like Libby Titus did in the sixties, in 1977 they were home lip-synching to the number one song of the year, "You Light Up My Life."

But something interesting started to happen during the late seventies. Sneaking onto the charts were old Village names like Carly Simon ("Nobody Does It Better"), Peter Yarrow (writer of "Torn Between Two Lovers"), Rita Coolidge ("Higher and

The B-52s (Fred Schneider, second from right) March 1983 (The B-52s)

Higher"), and Linda Ronstadt ("Blue Bayou"). The disco trend was almost im-
possible to break through, however. In 1978, the Bee Gees had five of the top six
songs and their album Saturday Night Fever *sold over thirty million copies.*

The backdrop to all of these musical happenings was the death of America's
rock hero. Elvis Presley was found dead in his bathroom at Graceland on August
16, 1977. He was forty-two years old.

FRED SCHNEIDER: I thought disco was shlock. We'd go to discos to be disruptive.
We'd go in and start dancing wildly. When everybody was performing the ex-
aggerated graceful disco moves we would be throwing each other on the floor,
laughing and yelling. But it did make people say, "Ooo God, I hope there's
something else out there to listen to." Luckily the new-wave thing came along.

JERRY HARRISON: Everybody's talking about a sixties revival, but I don't think the sixties really ended until the early seventies. There was a distinct decision to try to get away from what had become of sixties music, which was excessive versions of songs. It started with fascination with the blues, and it became more electric. When it first started off, with people playing jams, it sounded really great, but then it became this excessively boring thing. Then you had groups like Yes and these kinds of monster-groups of people who seemed like they had no commitment at all. The one thing that bound the people at CBGB's together was the idea of having shorter songs that were about something and having commitment to the music. Simultaneous to this was the coming of disco, and how powerful that became.

Disco was important because it made people more aware of dance, and offered the sense of things being continuous. One song would lead to the next song. With the Ramones the songs would be only separated with this mass count—one, two, three, four. Very early disco was really great. Then it became formula-acts and dull. It was all technique. It also gave the choice of whether you were going to see live music or not. It made live music something that you wouldn't take for granted. So acts became more dramatic. Before disco, the bands were just back-up. After disco the bands had to become dramatic and exciting and had to be something you definitely went to watch as well as to listen to. You didn't really necessarily go to see a band to pick up girls, you went to really see what they did and maybe you'd meet girls.

JOEY RAMONE: Every ten years people get disgusted with what's not happening. It's a reaction. What we were doing was a reaction. We put the fun and excitement back into rock-and-roll, like what Little Richard and Gene Vincent were doing. It was spontaneous. We were writing great songs that were three minutes again instead of forty-five minutes. We took out all the boring things like guitar solos and, in concert, the tuning up. We got rid of the stupid clichés. We played great songs and we put the spirit back into rock-and-roll. There was a time when you had to be serious, but rock-and-roll was meant to be fun. People used to say that we were stupid or minimalists or dumb. At that time there were about five or six songs on an album, because there would be about a half an hour of guitar solos. We cut out all the bullshit.

It wasn't just disco that was bad, there was all this heavy metal shlock. Now the high-energy metal bands are combining our style with something else. A lot of the new bands consider the Ramones, along with early Black Sabbath, as influences. Groups like Motley Crue—their inspiration is a little obvious and sometimes with groups like that you can hear some of *your* songs in *their* songs.

TOM PACHECO: Years ago an artist could grow. He was allowed to develop. He would put a record out and if it showed promise he would be allowed another record and another record. Maybe the third record would be the one. Nowadays you put one record out and that's it.

A lot of the people coming up in the seventies were great but got lost because the music business was so bad. People like George Gerdes. George is one of the greats. Besides being a great songwriter, he's a great comic and actor. Steve Forbert is enormously talented. One day Jack Solomon said to me, "You've got to come see this kid. I know a superstar when I see one." It was Forbert.

I travel a lot and I go into diners and I see families and working men and working women, and I know there's no way these people are going to love the Talking Heads or X. Those groups can't reach those people. Folk music can. The Clash is doing the same thing Phil Ochs used to do.

Ellen Foley

ELLEN FOLEY: I liked acting, but I also very much wanted to be a part of the New York music scene. There was a real talented group of people in the late seventies, like Ian Hunter, Mick Ronson, Debbie Harry, and David Johansen. It was a real exciting time. You knew you were involved with talented, creative people. There was a real camaraderie existing. A lot of the people took off and became famous, but a lot of those people who were in that crowd were musicians who aren't well known.

Some of the artists were very creative and individualistic like David Johansen. His music was heartfelt. He was musical and he was a good performer. We all had to find new ways of expression because of the economics of the record industry.

David put together Buster Poindexter and I put together a cabaret act. This new act that I performed at Folk City was what I perceive as true cabaret. I don't think cabaret has to be that spry musical-comedy thing that you see in theatre bars. To me, cabaret is that pre-war German feeling of people like Brecht and Weill. That's what rock and roll was born from. It's dark, dramatic, sexual, and passionate. The Doors recorded it and it's what David Bowie is doing. It's the pure form. I'd love to do *Threepenny Opera*. Jim Steinmann called me the modern-day Marlene Dietrich.

FRED SCHNEIDER: We played New York before we even played in a club in Athens [Georgia]. Finally the local folk club decided to book us. They were kind of iffy about it until they saw we could draw in a crowd.

Our fans were very important to our success. When we put out our independent single, "Rock Lobster," in 1978, it generated enough interest that the B-52s were able to go to Australia. It was a time when independent singles were being listened to. Radio was receptive too.

The most important thing was that the audience would have a good time. If we made a mistake in concert, we'd start over and we'd all laugh. In '79 we signed with Warner Brothers. There were people at W.B. who liked us and there were others who couldn't figure out what on earth we were doing. But that was normal. The whole new wave thing was such an anti-commercial commercial thing.

Most of the major critics thought of new wave as a breath of fresh air, which it was. It was the whole garage scene again, maybe a little wilder. It was people getting together with or without skills. Just have a good time and do it.

The Rolling Stones, after the lackluster albums of the mid-seventies, released an album that made the faithful happy. The punks seemed to have lighted a fire under Jagger and Richards. Some Girls *came out in 1978 and the Stones played* Saturday Night Live *in its peak years. Bruce Springsteen, wary of going the hype route again after a three-year legal battle with Mike Appel, his former manager, cut* Darkness at the Edge of Town. *Elvis Costello topped his debut with* This Year's Model, *and Blondie went platinum with* Parallel Lines.

The crowds stayed away from Renaldo and Clara, *Dylan's film that featured footage from the Rolling Thunder Tour. He toured New Zealand, Australia, Europe, the U.S., and Japan. A year later, Dylan would become a born-again Christian.*

Two Bronx musicians, Nile Rodgers and Bernard Edwards, formed Chic in 1976. By 1978, their single, "Le Freak," and album, C'est Chic, *changed dance music in a fresh way. Rodgers went on to become one of the hottest producers and songwriters in the business.*

The New York scene continued to foster small pockets of musicians: folkies in the Dylan tradition, rockers following Patti Smith and Television; all sorts of new clubs opening, like Danceteria, Interferon, the Mudd Club, and the return of the sixties hangout, the Peppermint Lounge.

In 1979, Marvin Gaye was instructed by a judge to record an album and pay his ex-wife, Anna Gordy, over $600,000 in royalties. Though it failed commercially, many fans considered the court-appointed double album, Here, My Dear, *to be a masterpiece. Michael Jackson, a Motown lifer who had learned a thing or two in the studio, made* Off the Wall, *a great funk-and-pop album.*

Pink Floyd toured with The Wall, *which was duly constructed during their mammoth stage shows. Sister Sledge (with Nile Rodgers producing) sang "We Are Family," and the Pittsburgh Pirates adopted it as their rallying cry, winning the Series that year. Three peroxided rockers called the Police scored a hit with "Roxanne." The Talking Heads grew stronger with* Fear of Music *and Donna Summer rocked with* Bad Girls.

Every record company was trying to capitalize on the new-wave-punk thing. Many retread formula bands razored their hair, wore skinny ties, and played cheap-sounding Farfisa organs in the hopes of securing a deal like the Jam and the Clash got.

The winter of '79 was a sentimental time for Mike Porco. He was in the process of selling Folk City and no one other than the principals knew. It was getting close to the twentieth anniversary of the club, and Mike wanted to leave with a flourish.

Beginning the second week in December, Mike hosted a reunion celebration that brought back many Folk City alumni and friends. The celebration also was a big shot in the arm for Greenwich Village clubs.

PEGGY DUNCAN: It was nice to see a lot of people I hadn't seen in a while. It was like a family reunion. Everybody was coming in and hugging each other saying, "Oh, I haven't seen you in so long." It was very moving. One funny incident was Alix Dobkin, who is a lesbian singer, commenting on not having kissed so many men in years.

DOUG YEAGER: Mike called me up and asked me if I would help him put together a twentieth-anniversary show. I said, "I think you need someone who is highly respected by all the people in the business, and who is an entertainer and a personality to be the MC." We decided that Bob Gibson would be the perfect person. We put together a letter which we sent to all the important people in the business signed by Bob Gibson and Mike Porco, inviting them to the Twentieth Anniversary Week. National Public Radio recorded the entire week. Some of the people who came were Don McLean, Tom Paxton, Odetta, Cynthia Gooding, Ed McCurdy, Oscar Brand, Jean Ritchie, Hedy West, Brother John Sellars, and a lot of new people like Loudon Wainwright and the Roches.

It got a lot of publicity. There were a lot of beautiful moments, and at the end of each evening, you would have twelve to fourteen people on stage singing together.

One of the most moving things was Ed McCurdy getting up and singing his song, "Last Night I Had the Strangest Dream." The whole house was singing at the top of their lungs. Ed had been paralyzed, on his back, for nine years prior to the twentieth anniversary. It was a very moving moment. The week was very, very special and a landmark in folk-music history.

BOB GIBSON: One night there was the most fabulous moment. Jean Ritchie got on stage and sat down with the dulcimer across her lap and started to sing some mountain ballads. Some of the young kids' eyes started to glaze over. They weren't going to give this music a chance. Then she did a song of hers that she said Emmylou Harris recorded, and she played a song that they all recognized from Emmylou's records and they realized that this old gal from the hills could write a song that could be a pop success. All of a sudden they all sat up straight and listened to Jean.

I was watching some of the kids watching Odetta, and they were awed. It was a wonderful week to watch the newer kids and the people who had been around a long time mix. We were all celebrating something different—the event and what the place meant to all of us.

THE EIGHTIES:
JUST · LIKE · THE
GOOD · OLD · DAYS

....

With The River, *released in 1980, Bruce Springsteen collected more fans and toured for eighteen months worldwide, landing in New Jersey, as usual. The controversial Clash put out a triple album, and in a strange move included a song by an outsider who just happened to be Folk City regular Tymon Dogg. The Clash's* Sandinista! *was not the only auspicious release of the year. Warner Brothers had their hopes set on Minneapolis's favorite son, Prince, a funky new-wave version of Sly Stone and Jimi Hendrix. The album was* Dirty Mind.

One of the darkest days in contemporary musical history was on December 8, 1980 when a twenty-five-year-old with a handgun shot John Lennon down at the Dakota apartment entrance on Seventy-second Street in New York City. Lennon was pronounced dead on arrival at Roosevelt Hospital. There was a series of tragic deaths of talented musicians in a short period. Tim Hardin, Harry Chapin, and Bob Marley left us a rich legacy of unique styles. Harry Chapin also left us the charity World Hunger Year.

The start of the decade had us in doubt. The country was at a pivotal point in its history and everything seemed to be on hold. The Village scene, too, was stagnating. It needed to be regenerated.

LESLIE BERMAN: Sonny Ochs was my oldest friend in the world, and when I heard that Phil had died I immediately called Sonny. There was chaos in the Ochs household and chaos in my household because my fiancé had died nine days earlier. I couldn't come down from Syracuse, where I was living, for Phil's funeral or to console my dear friend. I couldn't handle it. I also was not able to come down for the memorial concert, but I returned soon after. Sonny and I decided to do something to pay tribute to Phil.

We thought it would be appropriate to spend some money from Phil's estate to do something for songwriters in Phil's memory. In the course of some months we formed a non-profit organization that was to do something in that regard.

In the spring of '78, we decided we had procrastinated long enough and I planned a songwriters workshop which was held at Folk City. Phil felt that it was important to make space for somebody new, so we decided to put songwriters together with industry people and other songwriters, and in turn help these songwriters work out their own direction.

The Songwriters Showcase started on the heels of the Phil Ochs Songwriters Workshop. The whole thing happened so rapidly. One day we're doing the Workshop, the next day the Showcase; and the next day Mike sells the place. That's what it seemed like, at least. Time collapsed then—it was actually two years. It made perfectly logical sense that it would turn out the way it did. This was the right time for the Songwriters' Series. It really perked up the Village music scene. This was the right time for the right people to take over from Mike. The club and the scene got a real shot in the arm. There was excitement in the Village again. The Village songwriters came into national focus again.

In 1980 the Village was buoyed by the success of albums by such alumni as Willie Nile, the Roches, Carolyn Mas, and Steve Forbert. The Village was attracting more press and industry people. The economy was improving and the streets were getting crowded again. On a weekend night, Kenny's, Folk City, the Other End, CBGB's, and the various jazz clubs which were just beginning to open were packed with patrons. Frustration turned into hope.

The renewed connection with the press was an important one and many writers began to surface, happy to find new blood to write about. That important connection between the Village and the press was alive again for the first time, really, since Robert Shelton left for England in 1965.

Ironically, the one publication that was not supportive of the Village music scene was the Village Voice. *The* Voice *was more interested in the punk scene, which had not yet found its way to the Village.*

The Voice's *disinterest was frustrating, but it really didn't have much effect. The Village was now making it back into the national spotlight. Acts began to get written up, and, if nothing else, the Village performers regained new purpose, credibility, and exposure.*

FERRON: Stephen Holden's review and eventual follow-up feature on me in the *New York Times* was a tremendous boost. He's so honest. He's not into hype. Many other reviewers picked up on me after his pieces came out.

SUZANNE VEGA: Stephen Holden's review of me was what finally got my record company to sign me.

STEPHEN HOLDEN: I don't think I have that power. It was Suzanne's talent that got her signed. My article may have given her the extra push, but it would have happened anyway.

I felt Folk City was an oasis of an ongoing sensibility that seemed to disappear almost everywhere else in New York. When I saw young performers creating great songs in unique styles I knew that this tradition was going to go on and would continue. There was still a strong audience for it. The new folk music was not anachronistic or dead. It was very much alive and progressive. There was an ambiance at Folk City that was lost in New York.

Some artists have to be explained. The ones with intellectual depth are the ones who attract the writers. People who got record deals through writers were artists like Patti Smith, Laurie Anderson, Lou Reed, and Suzanne Vega. It was that their intellectual tradition created the need and desire for writers to delve more deeply into their work and bring it to the attention of the public.

ANDY BRECKMAN: Fred Kirby, the "new acts" reviewer for *Variety*, changed my life. His review literally turned me around and changed my life. I was working for minimum wage in a mailroom, sorting subscription flyers by zip code. Within a week of that review, I was in an office at Rockefeller Center with a secretary saying, "More coffee, Mr. Breckman?"

FRED KIRBY: Originally I wrote for *Billboard*; then in 1971 I went to *Variety* and worked under the "new acts" policy. I wound up doing most of the Village clubs.

There was a tendency to only write about the headliners, but I could think of opening acts that were headliners in a couple of months.

I felt that if I wrote about an opening act accurately, then possibly I could help the act get to the right place.

I remember one night the electricity went out at Folk City when the Manhattan Transfer was playing there. They went on and did a great acoustic set, proving to me how really talented and adaptable they were.

The list of names Fred Kirby reviewed during his tenure with Variety's *"new acts" column is a remarkable who's who. It is also a good indication of the rise and fall of different scenes and venues.*

Some of the acts Kirby reviewed as "new" include: Melissa Manchester, Bonnie Raitt, Billy Joel, Stevie Wonder and Wonderlove, Jackson Browne, Bruce Spring-steen, Chick Corea, Tom Waits, Chuck Mangione, Yoko Ono, Joan Armatrading, Patti Smith, Charlie Daniels, Phoebe Snow, Freddie Prinze, Tower of Power, Rick Springfield, Ashford and Simpson, Leonard Cohen, Blondie, Talking Heads, Richie Havens, Lou Reed, Andy Gibb, Elvis Costello, B-52s, Carly Simon, the

Police, Kris Kristofferson, and Prince. All of these acts were reviewed in Village clubs.

LENNY KAYE: It's the creative momentum that you really remember. You never really thought about who was going to make it and who wasn't. Everybody was one of a hundred guys. There were so many ifs, ands, and possibilities. It's the same in any scene. In the early folk scene Dylan was just one of the crowd. He could have been Fred Neil. He could have been Phil Ochs. He could have been Tim Hardin. Who knew? The same with the seventies rock crowd. We were just a bunch of working bands.

Blondie was based on the girl-group sound. The Talking Heads were based on rhythm-and-blues. It was the beat that got them across. David Byrne was into Bohannon records. I'd go over to their loft and listen to all these R&B records. They tapped into the burgeoning disco craze without hurting their integrity. They were open to all sorts of good music. David Byrne going down to Folk City to see someone remarkable like Richard Thompson is the same as him playing Bohannon records. He's open to different influences.

We were all so connected it was hard to differentiate us. For example, Patti Smith's player Ivan Kral used to play with Blondie. We tried out keyboard players in Blondie's loft. The scene doesn't happen on stage. The real inner dynamics of a scene happens between sets, after the show, during practice, and during the rest of the day.

During the past five years, many new forms of music have found a home in the Village with the jazz market being the healthiest. Many new jazz clubs have opened and are doing quite well. The Blue Note has distinguished itself as New York's premier jazz venue, joining the venerable Village Vanguard, Seventh Avenue South, Greene Street, and the historic Village Gate. Rock is well represented by Kenny's, the Bitter End, CBGB's, SNAFU, Irving Plaza, the Peppermint Lounge, Rock Hotel, and Danceteria. For a more eclectic program, there's the Bottom Line, Folk City, the Pyramid, the Cat Club, the Lone Star, and Tramps, each club offering everything from folk to rock. There is the Reggae Lounge and Sounds of Brazil (SOB's) for those looking for ethnic music, and the Duplex, Jan Wall- man's, Don't Tell Mama, and Paper Moon for cabaret and easy listening. The most popular experimental performance spaces are the Kitchen, P.S. 122, and Inroads. There are the many little new-rock clubs that are dotting the streets of the East Village's Alphabet City—Avenues A, B, and C. Opening and closing daily, just like the baskethouses twenty years before, these clubs have such enticing names as Downtown Beirut and the SIN Club (Safety in Numbers). Some have more practical names like 8 BC (located on Eighth Street between Avenues B and

C, of course). These clubs provide the burgeoning East Village sound with venues ranging from the dark and dingy to the slick and trendy. Then, of course, there are such trendy discos as Area, the Limelight, and Heartbreak. The Village is once again a vital musical community.

But one of the most popular trends of the eighties seems not to be music. The comedy craze is sweeping the country and you can see it on almost every block in the Village. There's the Comedy Cellar, Sweeps, Comedy U., Comedy Grand; and comedy has become a part of the regular program at the Bitter End, Folk City, Bottom Line, Paper Moon and the Duplex.

Comedy might be on an upswing, but the rock scene in the Village is as healthy as it could be. Bands from all over the country are coming to New York where they seem to be getting signed by major companies almost the minute they play

Robin Williams with comedy-night MC Jane Brucker at Folk City, summer 1983 (Marion Kahan)

the city. Many of these bands were introduced to New York at Folk City's innovative Music for Dozens series but they all paid their dues in their hometowns—L.A., Minneapolis, and Boston. However, it was New York where they were able to garner the important press, and to showcase in front of the record industry.

Music for Dozens was the most farsighted music series to take place in recent years. Originating as Two Nights of This, by Marilyn Lash and Frank Maya, it was conceived as a showcase for mostly unorthodox up-and-coming rock bands, with a very low admission price. When musician-performer Frank Maya booked the series, the acts were mostly "art bands" and performance-oriented acts. Frank stopped booking the series to pursue his own career, and Michael Hill and Ira Kaplan took over and renamed the series Music for Dozens.

IRA KAPLAN: I was working at the *New York Rocker* as a record review editor. I used to come to Folk City to see George Gerdes, Peter Stampfel, Two Nights of This, and a few other things. When Michael Hill, the editor at the *New York Rocker*, was asked to book the Music for Dozens series, I volunteered to do it with him, because he didn't want to do it alone. We wanted to put on good, low-cost shows.

We were a good combination, because I liked more of the sixties-based stuff, and he liked the performance-oriented stuff more than I did. We would book groups that we wanted to see and were curious about. A lot of the bands we knew by word of mouth. We put on bands that deserved the attention and the series was incredibly successful.

MICHAEL HILL: On one night, we booked V-Effect, an avant-garde Lower East Side band, playing with the Neats, a traditional, four-piece rock band. We liked cross-pollinating the audiences. On good nights it worked, and sometimes we alienated people. But, for the most part, people would meet each other socially, who would never be in the same room together. I was as much interested in what was going on at the bar as I was in what was going on on stage. Musicians, writers and people on the scene, all together. And the price was right. People who were living hand-to-mouth could afford the three-dollar cover charge. Another night that had a good mix was with Mofungo, a popular East Village band, the Dangerous Birds, a Boston rock band, and Mr. Baxter, a band that played hypnotic, drone, meditative music. It was a very large crowd that night and a nice unusual mix of people and music.

All the bands of tomorrow played there yesterday.

Audiences and performers alike treated each other as equals in a way you couldn't in another club. We brought a ragtag community together for a time. It was a real rock-and-roll community. It's true—you don't know what you've got till it's gone.

We started on November 17, 1982, with three nights of music. That gave us the big push. One of the biggest shows that we had was on January 27, 1983, with the Morrells and the Violent Femmes. The Morrells got a great write-up in the *New York Times*. There was a line down the block and that show *made* the series. The Violent Femmes got their offer with Slash records the day after the show and they are now one of the biggest selling groups on that label. Wim Wenders came to see them one night. One night, the Blasters came in and jammed with the Femmes.

There was one night when the Willies, the Trypes, and Yung Wu performed in one show. They got great coverage in the *New York Times*, and it was the first New York appearance of the Feelies in their new group.

A lot of the groups that played now have record deals. The Trypes are on Coyote. The Dream Syndicate made their first New York appearance at Music for Dozens, and they are now on A&M Records. All the A&R people from all the record companies showed up that night. Beat Rodeo is on IRS. The Minutemen, a big independent band which was on the *New York Time*'s Best of List, is on SST Records. One of the best shows, which was really significant, was on April 13, 1983. It included the Replacements (now on Sire Records), the Del-Lords (now on EMI Records), and the Del Fuegos (now on Warner Brothers Records). All have become substantial bands. You'll never find anything like that again. You can never get them assembled in the same room again. It was a major event. The first time Husker Du played "Eight Miles High" was at Folk City. The club inspired them to learn it. It was later released and is a real cult favorite. The Plugz are on Enigma Records. They were Bob Dylan's backup band recently on *The David Letterman Show*. They are now called the Cruzados, and they're signed to Arista. The first New York appearance of the 10,000 Maniacs was at Music for Dozens. They are now signed to Elektra Records. The Fleshtones played the series as the Hex Breakers, and Exene and John Doe, from the group X, along with Dave Alvin of the Blasters, played an acoustic set as the Knitters.

Our anniversary show consisted of some of the best new groups in rock-and-roll—Beat Rodeo, Ben Vaughn, the 10,000 Maniacs, the Last Roundup, John Zorn playing be-bop, Peter Stampfel and the Bottlecaps, and a number of ad hoc groups like the Hanna Barbarians, made up of members of some of the best bands around.

It's amazing to think that this happened only in the course of a year. It was music history happening at Folk City.

At the end of 1984, Folk City's landlords insisted on rigid sound requirements as a prerequisite to signing a new lease. The requirements were prohibitive, but some soundproofing was completed so that the landlord and tenants would not

hear the music coming from the club. During the course of the soundproofing,
booking restrictions had to be taken under consideration.

MARILYN LASH: Music for Dozens became a casualty of the sound-requirement
problems Folk City was having with its landlords. These Wednesday-night programs were unmercifully loud, which was a major factor in Folk City losing its
lease. We wanted to keep the series going, but we had to hold back on electric
music until some soundproofing was done. Ira continued to try to book bands
doing acoustic sets, sandwiching a cult B-movie between the music. We even
sold popcorn. This Mumblin' Music for Dozens series didn't work out, and Ira
was frustrated in his futile search for acoustic bands.

  After a brief hiatus, we worked out an arrangement with Tom and Jim Wyn-

Folk City co-owners Joe Hillesum, Marilyn Lash, and Robbie Woliver (Irene Young)

brandt, who had recently produced and promoted a successful acoustic all-star benefit night for the homeless at CBGB's. They were interested in running a series that would take Music for Dozens one step further. They wanted to book Wednesdays with big-name rock acts in a performance that was different from their regular fare.

JIM WYNBRANDT: The point of the series was to feature known artists and musicians doing performances that were different and out of the ordinary. It

Kristian Hoffman, Ann Magnuson, and Robert Macke (Teddy Lee)

would provide an experimental space for them to try new things. Also, the audience is exposed to different facets of a performer.

I invited artists who were capable of that sort of reaching and growth to do something unique and exciting. It added a spark, a freshness to what they were doing. The sound restrictions played into our hands.

Our opening show was Lenny Kaye, and Hoy Boy and the Doys. Later on we presented Annie Golden, who was in the band the Shirts, and starred in the film *Hair*, and in the Broadway show *Leader of the Pack*. She did original songs with a single guitar and piano accompaniment.

Richard Hell from the band Television presented his first public poetry performance. Suzanne Vega was on that show. It was a daring mixture and it worked. It was Suzanne's introduction to the new-wave circuit.

Ellen Foley, who starred in the TV show *Night Court*, performed an evening of cabaret. She had a successful rock career and her show with just piano accompaniment was a large departure from her rock-and-roll act. She never did anything like that before.

David Johansen did his first public performance of his work-in-progress, "The Poet's Cafe."

Helen Wheels, the heavy-metal muscle-builder, did an acoustic set, which is something she doesn't do every day. She's written songs for Blue Oyster Cult and is an all-around tough girl. It was great seeing her in that acoustic context, although she was pretty loud.

Eric Bogosian and Ann Magnuson, two of the top performance artists, did a show together that was spectacular. Joseph Papp came down to see that show.

Sylvain Sylvain of the New York Dolls did a night of his favorite rock songs, all done acoustically.

John Lurie did a solo-sax appearance. He was formerly of the Lounge Lizards and the star of the film *Stranger Than Paradise*. The last time he did that solo-sax appearance was at Carnegie Hall.

There were lots of others—Hoy Boy taking requests from the audience of their favorite TV themes, Kristi Rose performing solo, and Pianosaurus's first of many performances to follow. Pianosaurus plays toy instruments. There was also the Last Roundup, Ned Sublette, the Squad, and some Village favorites like Mark Johnson, Michael Fracasso, Ilene Weiss, and David Massengill.

We had a great time doing the series. It was interesting, it was fun, and it got an amazing amount of press. But we just ran out of acts.

So it was time to search once again for someone to run the successful Wednesday new-rock series. The next pair to come along was Pat DiNizio, leader of the band the Smithereens, and Todd Abramson. They called their series the Big Combo, and they combined the avant-garde direction of Two Nights of This, the trendy and unlikely bookings of Music for Dozens, and the aspect of big-name acts performings in unfamiliar styles that the Wednesday Night Music Series offered.

PAT DINIZIO: We had to be creative with the bookings because of the sound requirements. Since its inception there have been wall-to-wall crowds enjoying such unlikely bills as Steve Forbert playing acoustically with an accordion back-

would try to get the crowd to participate with the music. That's what they would do inside the clubs, but on the street the MCs would just rhyme and make their own songs while the DJ would play old rock records like Billy Squire's "Big Beat," Aerosmith's "Toys in the Attic," and Queen, and just keep the first four or five bars which were all beat. They would keep the beat going constantly. Instead of the DJs cutting the beat over and over, the beat boxes came in.

Bands used to be out in the streets at block parties and they just got played out, because a band can't play all day every day. A band is a show and a DJ makes it a party. Soon the MCs got to be as good as the singers. Nobody wanted to bring a drum and set up and mike the whole drum up. You just bring the beat box, it was much better.

Rock and rap wasn't the only hybrid. There was also rock and performance art.

STEPHEN HOLDEN: Frank Maya is a wonderful, zany showman. The most interesting thing about Frank is his wild, hysterical, nervous energy that can catch up an entire audience.

His songs may sound frivolous at first, but they are very intelligent statements dealing with breaking out of a cultural claustrophobia. A lot of it is a funny, ironic commentary on growing up in suburban Long Island.

He breaks out of a sense of confinement. He presents the serious thoughts he has in a funny way. There's a wild, liberating sense of fun and being naughty. He's playing with popular culture and he's breaking free from the conformity.

FRANK MAYA: In 1979 and 1980, new wave was already being considered slick. Debbie Harry was considered new-wave. "Art rock" consisted of odd poems which didn't rhyme. The "noise" bands were purposely playing dissonant stuff. You didn't care if the chords were right for the melody. We were trying to combine these three elements. We thought that if they began to play more mainstream clubs like Folk City it would get attention from record companies. It turns out that the record people and the press did pay attention but the straighter crowd never came in. If anything, they left.

The hot clubs of the early eighties were CBGB's, Inroads, the Mudd Club, Club 57, and Folk City for Two Nights of This, and later Music for Dozens. The downtown sound was starting to get into respectable venues. The important up-and-coming bands from the downtown scene were Three Teens Kill Four, V-Effect, Mofungo, and Barbara Ess. People like Laurie Anderson came from a more sophisticated scene. They didn't do anything without grants. I never saw Laurie Anderson bumming around clubs.

DAVE ALVIN: The Blasters all grew up in Downey, California, and we got together in 1979, because we were all leading sort of desolate lives being fry cooks and working day jobs. Then I found out that Johnny Rotten and I were the same age, so I decided that maybe I could still play rock-and-roll. So we got a band together in order to sort of keep our sanity.

I call our music electric folk music, because we take all the folk traditions— whether it's hillbilly, blues, or ragtime—and play it through amplifiers. We don't play these types of music straight. It's like the way Muddy Waters had to take Son House and make it into Muddy Waters. On his first recordings he sounds like he's trying to be a Son House–Robert Johnson imitator. Then ten years later when he was in Chicago he sounds like Muddy Waters. He may be doing some of the same songs, but it's a different style. On one hand we're like music historians, in that we're so engrossed in those styles, but at the same time we consider ourselves as contemporary as David Bowie or Duran Duran. The same is true of Los Lobos, because they also keep a lot of those traditions alive.

The Knitters at Folk City: Dave Alvin, John Doe, Exene Cervenka (Jon Zeiderman)

The Blasters play electric folk music, where the Knitters, on the other hand, got together because Johnny Doe and I would sit around when I was working on songs for our album, *Nonfiction*, and he was working on *More Fun in the New World*. We'd get together and Johnny would say, "Hey, I wrote this song," and I would say, "Well, hey, I wrote that." We'd play guitar together. Johnny was just kind of learning how to play guitar, and Exene would come by and we'd start singing songs together, and we'd say, "Hey, this is fun."

Then it started getting serious. The Blasters were on hiatus and X was on hiatus. So we decided, "God, this is fun, let's keep doing it." That's when we came to New York and we performed at Folk City. Johnny was very nervous about playing the same stage that Phil Ochs once stood on.

It's very different from the Blasters and X. With those groups it's all very loud, where in the Knitters it's kind of laid-back, and you can become a different personality. It's as valid a thing as either of our bands. Even though people think it's fun, the Knitters are real serious for us.

It's fun for me to hear the songs that Johnny and Exene are writing, because I'm used to writing songs with three chords and pretty direct lyrics, while they're not. They're used to eight chords and hazy, confessional lyrics. My idea of a perfect song is "Waiting for a Train" by Jimmie Rodgers, which is folk music.

I was turned on to Big Joe Turner and Carl Perkins records when I was a little kid. At the same time I was getting turned on to Phil Ochs, Bob Dylan, Dave Van Ronk, and Eric Andersen. From one group I learned to love the beat and from the other I learned to love the lyrics. The Village music scene of the eighties was something I was interested in. I was sorry I missed that time. But I hung out in the Ash Grove, which was California's authentic folk club.

JAM MASTER JAY: This was always my music. There were all these rhymes you hear now, there were tapes of them—Grandmaster Flash, Cold Crush, Kurtis Blow. The MCs were always out doing their thing. I also listened to contemporary music like the Jackson Five or Chaka Kahn, really everything they played on WBLS, like the normal kids did. That wasn't the best though. I always said that if I had the chance to make my own radio station I would only play what I like, which is straight-up hard rock like Black Sabbath, *Toys in the Attic*, and Billy Squire.

Run and D.M.C. were real good, and they were always beefing about other records. I would say, "This is a def jam [great record], listen to this." I felt that you couldn't be as good as them because they were on the radio. But Run was always saying, "We're gonna make a record. We're gonna be better than them." Run might have idols, but he always felt that he was better than this person or that person. He never admits it. He used to say, "Hey, if my thing was on wax, everybody would like this, too."

CHARLIE CHIN: There's a large number of young white people who write songs that have no particular meaning except "How clever am I?" You would go to a folk festival and notice that of all the black performers, practically none of them were under fifty. Why is that?

John Hammond, Jr., has made his career on playing Afro-American music. He's the first guy to say so too. But it does seem strange how he has been able to get over so many times with this, and yet at the same time, the people he learned that music from couldn't get over with it.

In 1983, there was a special event held at Folk City. Libba Cotten was celebrating her ninetieth birthday with a concert at Gerdes and she was garnering as much press as any current rock star would. Featured on the cover of the New York Daily News Weekend Section, *she filled the club with admirers and fans who wanted to pay homage to the legend. They thought they were going to see an old lady go through a nostalgic set. What they ended up seeing was Libba's agile fingers picking away at the guitar like no one they'd ever seen.*

MARILYN LASH: So many people came down to see her just to be part of history. She's influenced so many people. Even the Grateful Dead does one of her songs!

She's an important symbol to women and women musicians. And who hasn't sung "Freight Train" a hundred times in their lives? Everyone came to see this little old lady and were blown away by the most spry spirit in the house. She was nimble, intelligent, beautiful, and full of humor. Seeing her was a moving and important experience for many people.

When they brought out the ten-piece cake with each piece designed as different cars in a freight train, Libba was standing on stage smiling and waving at everybody. There wasn't a dry eye in the place. That woman has a lot of class.

CYNTHIA GOODING: It isn't as much fun now as it was in the early days of folk music. There's so much infighting and jealousy now. In my day, you worked for weeks at a time, now it's one show and there are so many people after that one show. It's a hard life. Shows used to be twenty minutes. Now they're at least forty-five minutes long.

FRANK MAYA: Danceteria started to become an important rock club. In one quick set you would have tremendous exposure. It started booking these bands after they were introduced in legitimate clubs or at Two Nights of This. Danceteria didn't give you a start. It gave you the big booking for nine hundred dollars. Folk City's Music for Dozens was always the hip series to play, although it didn't pay much.

Now it's the Lower East Side scene. Places like 8 BC and the Pyramid. The

Pyramid books all sorts of talent—drag queens, theatre, music, and film. The "in" crowd moves from club to club. It's the fashion-and-music-scene crowd. The scene has been happening on the fringes of the Village for a while. Kenny's Castaways and Folk City were really the only two clubs left in the Village in the late seventies and early eighties. A new scene had to open.

I liked folk music although I never wanted to do it. I was disappointed with the folk music of the late seventies and early eighties that was being presented at Kenny's and Folk City. I kept thinking that nobody had the kind of power anymore that Joni Mitchell and Peter, Paul, and Mary had. Then one day I saw the Roches and I said, "Well, here it is." Odetta is someone else who had that kind of power. I met Odetta and took a few voice lessons with her. I also wanted to give her songs, but it wasn't quite her style.

The New York music scene is becoming very healthy again and it's very encouraging. A lot of East Side bands are getting signed, a lot of the old "noise" bands are becoming commercial, and the club scene is picking up.

LENNY KAYE: In 1980, I formed the Lenny Kaye Connection. We played the Ritz, Irving Plaza, the Peppermint Lounge. My music is more traditional than Patti's. I didn't try to write more avant-garde, because I was in no rush to do anything that wasn't really what I do. I'm content with it being a vehicle to express myself. I still have time to write for Elektra, produce Suzanne Vega, and play with other people like Jim Carroll and Ned Sublette. I've been in rock-and-roll for twenty years now, and I'm in no hurry to do anything that isn't true to me.

DAVE ALVIN: The seventies were a time when everybody who wasn't into disco or hard rock was told they were uncool. One good thing about punk rock was that it kind of said that you could do whatever you want and be cool. That's why now you see Phranc or Chris D., the ultimate punker, going acoustic. The seventies were not the greatest musical times. It went back to Frankie Avalon, Tommy Sand, and Bobby Rydell. It was formula rock-and-roll. It's like new wave now—they have the formula down as to how you're supposed to look. You look like Wham! or you look like Duran Duran. You have synthesizers. The folk revival that's happening now is a reaction to that. They're saying that if rock-and-roll is such a calculated, commercial thing, then they'll just pick up their acoustic guitars! When that turns into a gimmick, we'll have the Monterey Folk Festival and all plug in again.

One of the reasons people lost interest in folk music was that it got clichéd with a lot of the sensitive singer-songwriters. But Bob Dylan is at his best when he's sensitive, and he's not a wimp. He has a hard edge to him. Phil Ochs was never a wimp. You don't really have too much to hide behind when you're up there with your acoustic guitar.

JOAN BAEZ: Society changes and it's difficult enough to deal with those changes. When I was young, my mother would look at someone and say, "They're *on* something." And I would innocently say, "Oh no, mother. Whatever do you mean?" Now I go into my son's room and look at his record album jackets and say, "God! These people look like they're on drugs." And he'd casually say, "Yeah, they are."

GORDON GANO: When the Violent Femmes came to New York for the first time, it was exciting because we were getting great reviews, and critics tend to read each other's work. We were really on a roll. Before we even had an album, we were in the *New York Times*.

The Violent Femmes: Brian Ritchie, Gordon Gano, and Victor DeLorenzo (Irene Innes)

BRIAN RITCHIE: It was thrilling. We stayed in a hovel in Alphabet City.

VICTOR DELORENZO: We were very bemused. Here we were, playing in New York, and they like us! We heard that they weren't going to be responsive. When we got back home we read this wonderful review in the *Times*. Another big break for us was when Chrissie Hynde saw us playing the street underneath the marquee of a theatre where the Pretenders were playing, and she asked us if we'd like to open the show for them, which we did.

BRIAN RITCHIE: When we came back to New York, we played Folk City in the Music for Dozens series. The place was overpacked and it was a real gas. It was a fantastic experience. Nowhere else in the world were there so many fantastic groups playing together. And there were always lines all around the block. As a performer, that's a real gas to see.

VICTOR DELORENZO: It was a great billing with the Morrells. A lot of the bands who are really hot now and making waves now came out of that series. Groups like the Del Fuegos, the Replacements, and the Femmes got a lot of attention playing there. The place was always packed with critics and record company people. I thought it was befitting that Folk City would host such a series. The intimate atmosphere encouraged people to actually take notice of what was going on. It was a real hip thing to be a part of.

MARILYN LASH: T-Bone Burnett was playing as part of the New York Folk Festival. That night we got a call from Elvis Costello's road manager. He informed us that Elvis would be arriving for T-Bone's second set after Elvis finished his concert at Radio City Music Hall. We doubted he'd make it because we knew his record company was holding a post-concert party. He showed up at Folk City instead, and with an entourage that included Paul Carrack from Squeeze, Nick Lowe, and Dave Edmunds.

No one in the audience knew he was there and they certainly weren't prepared for what was to come. Burnett finished a song and then announced that he had a friend in the audience who he would like to invite up. As Elvis walked towards the stage and people began to recognize him, the polite applause began to get louder and more enthusiastic. By the time he was on stage and everyone registered who he was, the place went wild.

Elvis and T-Bone performed for about forty-five minutes. The highlight had to be their rendition of "If You're Going to San Francisco (Wear Flowers in Your Hair)," "So You Want to Be a Rock and Roll Star," and a few other folk, rock, country, and original songs.

After their performance Elvis sat back down in his seat and a line of two hundred people stood patiently waiting to talk to him and get his autograph. He patiently greeted everyone. I've seen this reaction before. It's when a performer of his magnitude finds the joy in playing a small, more intimate room than the venues they are used to.

Elvis Costello and T-Bone Burnett at Folk City, summer 1984 (Thom Wolke, copyright © 1984)

Although it was the most popular, rock was not the only type of music finding a productive base in Greenwich Village. Traditional and contemporary Irish music and women's music were all finding the Village to be a springboard for national recognition.

Since 1980, women's music finally had a legitimate home where women of a specific political consciousness could gather, feel comfortable, and not be exploited.

influences like Bob Dylan. I didn't hear Bob Dylan until I was twenty-four. It's strange to me when people compare me to him. Some people ask me what my influences were, who influenced my phrasing. My mother influenced my phrasing. She is French-Canadian and she spoke French most of the time and that affected my phrasing.

One day Gayle said to me, "Someday you'll be able to play in New York." By this time I knew what it was and what it meant and I started to tremble. My first appearance in New York at Folk City I spent downstairs for the most part, passing out. I was so scared, I had an awful migraine.

I thought it would be scary and oppressive. I thought people would be cold and not like what I was doing. But I was warmly accepted and it opened up a whole new understanding that people are suffering the same kind of things all over and that what we're all involved in is very communal.

WENDY NEWTON: Irish music found a home at the Eagle Tavern and Folk City, where fans knew they could see the top acts of the genre. I first became involved with the New York clubs in January 1981, when Mick Moloney told me he got a gig at Folk City and I decided to promote it. The night that I was there to see his show, it occurred to me that it would be fun to put Irish music in the club.

Since then I've promoted an annual Irish Festival around St. Patrick's Day. A lot of people come and have a good time and remember it and come back again with friends the next time. And that carries through to all the Irish shows that are presented in New York. It's a great event, the Irish Festival. Even *New York Magazine* gave it top billing over the St. Patrick's Day Parade one year.

One of the most popular acts is Touchstone. A group that combines American mountain music, bluegrass, and traditional Irish music in a very progressive rock sensibility. The traditional people recognize the sound, and the bass rhythm and the beat appeal to rock audiences. Also there's the Irish Tradition, a most talented group that brings in an audience that would otherwise *never* come to the Village.

MATT MOLLOY: Irish music is gaining popularity because it is so good. Irish music has the same general appeal in Montana as it does in Brittany. People are willing to give it a try and after they hear it, they're hooked. You only have to prove it once and people come back.

Green Linnet is a great record company to be identified with. Wendy Newton is straight up. The record business, unfortunately, is riddled with sharks, but Wendy is trustworthy and is doing so much good for Irish music. She goes for the dramatic—like us signing our record contract at Folk City on St. Patrick's night. Who knows what they're doing by the time that night is over?

In the 1980s, another wave of Village artists were easing into their success.

Loudon Wainwright became a popular concert and recording artist. The Roches, too, were breaking house records across the country. Steve Forbert had a top-ten hit with "Romeo's Tune." Willie Nile was opening for the Who during their tour. Carolyn Mas had a charted hit with "Stillsane." Steve Goodman was one of the most highly respected songwriters. Emmylou Harris was winning Grammy Awards.

A new group is ready to take off. Now, the names being talked about are Ilene Weiss, Lucy Kaplanski, Frank Christian, Suzanne Vega, Sammy Walker, Deidre McCalla, George Gerdes, Casselberry and Dupree, the Song Project, David Massengill, Christine Cavin, Mark Johnson, Ferron, and Frank Maya.

HERB GART: Towards the end of 1979, I felt the energy of the Village starting to feel like the creative energy of the early to mid-sixties. The big difference was, in the sixties kids used to come into my office and say, "Listen to me. Listen to my songs. Listen to my music." Today they come in and say, "Listen to my product." Now people are coming to the Village specifically to showcase. They used to come down to live and to grow. There was comradeship, a sharing of talents. Now it's more isolated. Nobody is teaching nobody nothing.

ILENE WEISS: I had been performing in Chicago and I decided to check out what was happening in New York. I came to Folk City to see a show and I was very impressed by the music. On the way out I asked the doorman when the open stage audition night was.

I came back five months later specifically to do a hoot. I had gotten to a level in Chicago where I would have to start hustling there to achieve a certain status or I could go to New York and hustle there. I had seen Talking Heads and I identified with their synthesis—intelligent funky music. I was so excited by them that I figured only in New York could all that come together.

I was kind of chummy and superficially involved in the social scene and making what might have been political progress. But I couldn't deal with that sort of political maneuvering. I was becoming part of the scene and I became easily discouraged.

One of the things I have to deal with that I can't deal with is self-promotion. I just can't do that. The non-creative business-type things are what would hold me back. I want to play with a band, but actually putting the band together is the problem. The idea of playing rock-and-roll and playing with other people is very appealing. When I play solo I have a good time by interacting with the audience. The idea of continuing writing songs and combining that with performance, music and theatre is what appeals to me—earning a living at artistic expression.

LOUDON WAINWRIGHT: Ilene is an excellent songwriter. She's intelligent and humorous and she combines that with a sometimes wild, sometimes tender stage presence. You can't help but love her. She's a natural.

TOM INTONDI: In 1978 a group of songwriters starting formalizing our song-swapping nights. We were doing things that were more workshop than performance, but this eventually led to the formation of the Song Project.

For one week in February, 1978, we put together a group that would perform songs by other people. We were doing one song each by twenty-four different people. It was a one-shot deal.

I fell in love with vocal harmonies. I liked it better than a band and better than the singer-songwriter thing.

In 1980, I was approached by Folk City to start up a Song Project that would be a group in the true sense and that would tour and play as a constant entity. In June of that year, Martha P. Hogan, Lucy Kaplanski, Gerry Devine, and I began to perform as the Song Project with weekly performances every Sunday at Folk City. This new line-up represented a large spectrum of new songwriters who were suddenly flocking to the Village again. We got through sixty songs and fifty different songwriters.

GERRY DEVINE: The Song Project was a band with a mission. We were going to turn the world on to these great Village songwriters. It had its moments but it started to fade for me. The ironic thing was the closer we were getting to commercial success, the more I was shying away. We played the Bottom Line a couple of times, and Allan was trying to help us get a record deal. We started getting more press—good press—and more interest, but it wasn't what I wanted. I didn't want to devote my energy to it. The more the Song Project became a group, the more I wanted my own group.

I was in the Floor Models and the Song Project concurrently for a while. I quit the Project in Christmas of '81. I met Andy Pasternack at Cornelia Street and we were immediately simpatico. One of the things I liked about the New York scene was its new-wave sensibility, and Andy had that. I liked his writing and that he played twelve-string all the time. A lot of his tunes had the mid-sixties kind of pop feel. So we formed the Floor Models.

One of our first gigs was opening for Marshall Crenshaw at Folk City. We were being heckled by someone in the audience. The heckler is now our drummer.

The Village music scene is the most creative environment in the world. It's produced some artists who have changed the sound of our culture and is still doing it. A community that produces such a wide variety of talent like the Song Project, the Smithereens, Michael Fracasso, Lucy Kaplanski, Mark Johnson, George Gerdes, Ilene Weiss, Suzanne Vega, and the Floor Models can't be all bad.

TOM INTONDI: The minute I first saw Frank Christian perform I knew he was more musically inclined than most. Everything was so clean. Hearing a solo guitar sound like that is amazing. His song "Where Were You Last Night?" has the quality of a standard to it. You listen to it and say, "Did Ella Fitzgerald and Count Basie ever record this?"

He brought a very advanced level of musicianship to the Village scene.

STEPHEN HOLDEN: Frank Christian is the latest and most talented in the long line of blues-oriented singer-songwriters. His songs evoke a very sensual, Bohemian existence in New York. His smoky, sultry voice is halfway between classic blues singer and crooner. If properly recorded, he has a real future. He's a very strong, very talented, acoustic blues traditionalist. His song "Where Were You Last Night?" is one of the most anguished songs of sexual jealousy I ever heard.

FRANK CHRISTIAN: The Village myth really intensified for me in 1977. It seemed to be a place to be accepted as an artist and achieve notoriety. Even though folk music was not in vogue, singer-songwriters were, and that's what I was seeking.

I spent months before I got a number at hoot night. There were about seventy-five comedians waiting to go on. Rosie, the MC, didn't know me, so I couldn't get a good number. I couldn't stay there all night and that was really frustrating.

The scene wasn't especially viable, financially. Mike was running the club like he did twenty years ago. But there was good music happening. I thought things would get better when the Roches, Carolyn Mas, and Forbert took off, but they didn't.

Folk City was the best of times and it was the worst of times. I always hung out there. I think of how many different girls I have broken up with on the pay phone in Folk City. The height of thrill and the depth of disappointment happened at Folk City. It was all very romantic. Sitting at the bar feeling miserable. The dim lights, strong feelings, going to the kitchen to kiss.

One night, this woman came up to me at the bar, grabbed me and gave me a prolonged kiss. What seems like a half-hour later, when she was through, she said to me, "Oh, I'm sorry. I thought you were someone else."

DAVE ALVIN: I'm encouraged by the current music scene. I like groups like X, the Minutemen, the Replacements, Rank and File, Los Lobos, and the Blasters. The American bands are strong again. New York doesn't really have a scene anymore, although there are great groups that come out of New York. The Ramones are still the spiritual figurehead of the whole rebirth of American rock-

and-roll. They were there ten years ago and they're still around doing the same thing. The Del-Lords are another good New York group.

You just have to go through a lot to be a musician in New York. You have to get a place to rehearse on Thirty-Fifth Street and you have to get your equipment there and all that crap. The club scene is so based on playing at four o'clock in the morning before a select clique of people as opposed to in the prime of the L.A. scene, where you are playing at eight o'clock at night in front of a lot of kids. That makes a healthier scene. But there are no new Go-Go's, Blasters or X's. The clubs are all closed down in L.A. The big thing in L.A. now is the folk and poetry scene. That seems to be happening all over the country. It certainly seems to be happening again in New York and that was the home of it all.

MARILYN LASH: We asked Stephen Holden to write a feature on Suzanne Vega. He couldn't until she was a weekend headliner, so we immediately gave Suzanne a Saturday night. Unprecedented for a local act, she sold out all of her shows and has done so ever since. Stephen's article sent a current of excitement through the record industry and Suzanne was soon signed to a major record deal with A&M Records.

As with other Village artists who found success, Suzanne is now confronted with the hopes and jealousies of her fellow musicians. For many years Lucy Kaplanski has been a good friend of Suzanne's, and as a singer, one of the main interpreters of Suzanne's songs.

LUCY KAPLANSKI: When I first heard about the record deal, I was so excited for Suzanne. She absolutely deserves it and I love her, but there was another part of me that felt like a knife just went through it.

The sentiment was not very different from Jack Elliott's when Dylan was first reviewed by the Times. *And just to complete the circle, one of Suzanne's most important reviews mentioned that she was "the best singer-poet since Bob Dylan."*

Suzanne projects a distinctly cool, aloof persona on and off stage. One night, fellow songwriter Vincent T. Vok brought a bucket of ice to Suzanne's dressing room and asked her to "please keep this cold."

STEPHEN HOLDEN: The first time I saw Suzanne at Folk City, she reminded me of Joni Mitchell, but she wasn't as polished. She wasn't quite ready. But she's grown a lot. She still reminds me of Joni with her cool hauteur. She has an innate elegance in everything she does, and at the same time she has a New York urban sensibility that reflects a street experience that Joni never had.

New wave has been a very important influence on her, especially Lou Reed. She has a very pared-down, Zen-like vision of the city. Her emotional relationship to the city is described in diamond-hard images that are extremely precise.

SUZANNE VEGA: I want my audience to find me as I am. I don't want it twisted. I don't want an image created for me. Once, I wore a little flowered dress and

Suzanne Vega (Victor Podesser)

I was so concerned about people looking at my knees. Here I was, singing these serious songs and no one paid any attention to how strangely I was presenting it. People say I have a strong image and it's partly created by the fact that I like to wear black and clothes that are too big. I used to be compared to Joni Mitchell and I want to present myself in a different way. I wear an oversized black jacket when I perform. I feel I could hide in it and add an element of formality. It doesn't reveal too much.

Suzanne was one of a number of new artists who used Folk City as a springboard.

STEPHEN HOLDEN: If Woody Allen had taken up folk singing, he would be Andy Breckman.

ANDY BRECKMAN: Ever since I was a child I knew about Folk City. In the summer of '76, I came to the city with that as my destination. It was the Mecca of folk music. I saw two movies before I moved to the city. One was *Next Stop Greenwich Village*, and I had my bags packed. The other was *Taxi Driver*. It was a tough decision.

Anything good that's happened for me has happened through Folk City. The club has been a focal point of my life. Meeting my wife, finding my manager, breaking into TV, and getting my initial review in *Variety*—all the crucial points of my life are tied in with Folk City. I'm still creatively living off the fumes of those years.

I came because I was after a record deal. Anyone even peripherally involved in the music business I looked at with some awe. Carolyn Mas had just been signed to a record deal around '79, and it was like news from the Mount—it can be done. Someone from the Village has done it. When I hit the Village, she was big news. The scene had been pretty much dead up until Carolyn Mas.

The hope was so palpable there, you could feel it. Everyone thought they were the next Bob Dylan. The hope and optimism in the Village was so amazing. Everyone worked so hard, except me. I never rehearsed. I never practiced. In fact, on one of my biggest gigs, when the record companies finally came down, I came out and began to play. I hit the second verse and my mind went blank. The only time I ever practiced was on stage and I'm not innately musical.

I remember one show, I found a note in my guitar from my manager that said, "Don't forget to practice." I found this note a month after he put it in, when I was getting ready to go on stage. I practiced so infrequently that I was constantly bleeding, because I kept losing my callouses. I'd bleed all over the guitar and the stage. Some of my blood is still on the Folk City stage.

JIM WANN: One of our most fun shows, and the show when the Dinettes joined us for the first time, was with the Bermuda Triangle. Before this we only played Folk City as the Pump Boys. The thing I remember most about that night was that the Bermuda Triangle's audience is like a cult and they memorize everything the Bermuda Triangle did and they kind of adopted that involvement with us too. When the chorus came around, you could see the wheels turning around and by the next time they had part of it and by the third time you knew they could sing all of it. It was a lot of fun playing to them.

BERNADETTE CONTRERAS: It was always interesting working at Folk City, because there was such a parade of personalities. José Feliciano, Shel Silverstein, and Al Kooper would come in and perform guest sets. One night Irene Cara was there dancing in the aisle—it looked like a scene straight out of *Fame.* Within a week, David Byrne, Donna Summer, Carly Simon, J. Geils, George Thorogood, and Madonna came in. Just recently Warren Beatty, Dustin Hoffman, Julie Christie and Elaine May came in the same night. Leonard Bernstein came in one night to see his daughter perform. One weekend Linda Ronstadt and Bob Dylan came back to the club. Folk City is never a boring place and you never know who might be sitting next to you at the bar—or who might be in that audience watching your performance.

ROGER BECKET: Once, after a show, a very loaded girl with a very loaded .45 tried to pick me up at the bar and she was very boisterous. The Porcos, who are very sharp, picked up on what was going on and came up to me and said, "Roger, we want to talk business with you in the back," and took me away and hid me until the girl left. They told her that the bar was closing and got rid of her. On a real serious threat they were always on top of it.

One really funny experience at Folk City was one night, the millionaire Huntington Hartford came in with a couple of chickies. It was especially funny to me, because when I was a kid, my first job was at the A&P, which he owns. That's one thing about Folk City. You never knew who you were going to see.

WENDY BECKET: The streets were great in the Village. There were all sorts of people hanging out. We like to talk to people and we met a lot of interesting people just on the streets.

One day, we started talking to a young girl who was telling us about her interest in music. She was fourteen and she and her friend were just learning to write and they would play us songs they had just written. She was Cyndi Lauper.

They would come over to our house and we'd play songs together. We'd go to Folk City a lot and check out the music.

Cyndi would sing in a voice exactly like Joni Mitchell, really high and clear and sweet, and the songs she wrote sounded just like that too. This went on for about a couple of years, and we didn't see her for a little while.

We later ran into her when she was in the Blue Angel. She started coming over again and sang us new songs. She told us about this technique she found in her voice which would sound like a harmonic, at the same time singing her main note, almost like singing a chord.

She completely changed her vocal style from the sweet vibrato, high soprano to no vibrato, or a very, very, fast vibrato to a chest voice. Also, the songs she had written were really good.

STANLEY SNADOWSKY: They were lovely people, Roger, Wendy, and Sam. We used to book them before they were Bermuda Triangle. We booked them when they were just Roger and Wendy. They had a big local following and they were very nice people. Sam came along and I watched her develop from just playing tambourine to all of a sudden becoming an integral part of the group.

PENNY SIMON: I love the Bermuda Triangle. They were a staple of mine. The audience loved them. They even love them more now. They lived at the Four Winds, practically. They were the Village. They were real family. They encouraged me to act stupid.

RICK FRANK: The Bermuda Triangle is one group I used to like to see. They were incredible. They were very mystical. If I had to answer, "What's the one act you'd go to Folk City to see?" I'd have to say the Bermuda Triangle.

WENDY BECKET: Folk City is like my favorite uncle. I feel a great deal of loyalty and affection.

ROGER BECKET: Folk City has been such a big part of my life. One reason, is the longevity of it. It has outlasted a tremendous number of places. Our karma is all tied up there. It's like family.

LIBBY TITUS: Bobby Neuwirth recently called me up about doing a gig at Folk City. I hadn't done anything in a while. I had terrible stage fright. I really practiced for it and it was amazing how many people came that night, and that I got such good reviews. Mac [Dr. John] played piano. Hughie MacCracken on guitar. It was a great band. The review in the *Times* called me "Blossom Dearie of the punk-rock generation." I love Blossom Dearie. Coming back to Greenwich Village and doing that gig was very important for me.

The early days in the Village were remarkable. There was a heart to the country and a common cause which was peace and liberation and civil rights and growth. The heart was Greenwich Village. And the heart was hopeful and romantic and alive. It was like a meteor falling to earth. It has to shine and shine and shine and dim. Nothing that magnificent can keep on that long.

Folk City is the symbol of the beginning of things. You've arrived. This is it. It is something that has always been there and will always be there. It's classy to sing at Folk City. It's a good name to drop. Before I had ever been to Gerdes I imagined it to be this huge pavilion. It was a political place almost. The priests of the culture were at Folk City preaching.

John Cale, Richard Thompson, David Byrne, and Bob Neuwirth at Folk City, 1983 (Marion Kahan)

The eighties are in full swing and the music business has busted wide open. The Village streets are filled with record company A&R men and women. The Village clubs are frequented by music journalists and the young musicians are coming to the Village in droves. Just like the old days.

The acoustic sound is coming back into vogue as is the Beatnik sensibility. People are beginning to realize that the new-wave attitude and the Beat attitude are very similar. As in the sixties, performers are looking at the artists who came before them. The Blasters' recent recording of Gary Davis's "If I Had My Way" is as powerful a rendition as Peter, Paul, and Mary's in the sixties. When a young girl goes home and learns a Cyndi Lauper song on her guitar—that's the folk process at work and it's no less valid than when Bob Dylan was learning Woody Guthrie songs.

A lot of different styles, approaches, attitudes, and personalities formed the history of the past twenty-five years of the American music scene. During these years, Gerdes Folk City reflected society's changes and helped create a large part of what we were listening to, how we were dressing, and what we were thinking about. Through the people who passed through Folk City's doors, the history of a culture can be traced. From these personalities' reminiscences and impressions— on their performances, their friends, their social lives, their politics, and their aspirations—a colorful tapestry of an important segment of time is woven.

Gerdes was one of many influential clubs that were based in the Village. Only Gerdes Folk City, the Village Gate, the Village Vanguard, and the Bitter End remain. Obviously, neither all the history nor all the influence was spawned in Folk City alone, but there's no question that a substantial amount was. The Rolling Stones never played the club, but the Rolling Stones were influenced by the acts that did play the club. And certainly Bob Dylan's influence twenty-five years after his debut cannot be diminished or underestimated.

Greenwich Village, also, was not the only cultural center in the country during the past twenty-five years, but it was certainly the place which many of today's well-known performers came to try to "make it." Folk City and Greenwich Village are longtime havens for America's musical (and sometimes non-musical) heritage, from the traditional Ed McCurdy to rocker Elvis Costello.

Greenwich Village offers the freedom and ambiance for a healthy cultural community. It is constantly undergoing change and always surviving it, but now it seems as if the Village has met its match. In 1985, in what seems to be its most creative and popular time in the past fifteen years, Greenwich Village is faced with a squad of bulldozers, high rise apartments and a rash of fly-by-night boutiques. It has already withstood drastic face-lifts and gentrification.

It's difficult to believe that its rich history will survive when you pass by the NYU dormitories that have taken the place of the Cafe Wha?; when you can buy falafel where the Folklore Center was; when expensive jewelry is what you find in the dark nooks and corners where baskethouses used to exist; when Korean vegetable stands and Indian clothing shops occupy the storefronts where people once gathered to talk about important issues over espresso; when fast food joints have taken over the rooms where Bruce Springsteen, Joan Rivers, Billy Joel, Linda Ronstadt, and

Woody Allen honed their acts; when street musicians are afraid to play in Washington Square Park because of the heavy drug element firmly entrenched there; when people seeking Folk City are advised to look for the well-known landmark next door, the MacDonalds.

NYU owns a large part of the Village discussed in this book, and it's sad to realize that such a rich piece of American history is at the whim of the everthreatening NYU bulldozers. Twenty-five years constitutes but a small part of the culture that will be buried under the new NYU library where students will only be able to read about the colorful world that their new buildings have replaced.

Folk City will thrive wherever it is. Its history is too strong not to endure, and its present generation is too strong not to break through. The music is the center of it all. It goes on and will continue to bring it all back home, no matter where that home is.

WHO'S WHO IN

HOOT!

....

DAVID ALVIN: Guitarist and lead singer-songwriter of the rock band the Blasters. He also performs with John Doe and Exene Cervenka of the band X in a country-folk trio called the Knitters.

DAVID AMRAM: Musician, ethnomusicologist, and composer. Amram is also a long-time Village resident.

ERIC ANDERSEN: Composer of such classics as "Thirsty Boots," "Violets of Dawn," and "Blue River," a duet with Joni Mitchell. His songwriting style tends towards the romantic and he is considered one of the more progressive leaders of the sixties singer-songwriter clique. He recently started his own record company, Wind and Sand.

HOYT AXTON: Co-writer of the Kingston Trio hit "Greenback Dollar." Another song of his, "Joy to the World," has become a best-selling classic. He has also enjoyed successful careers as a recording artist and actor. He was featured in the popular film *Gremlins*.

JOAN BAEZ: Long considered the Queen of Folk Music, Baez was originally an interpreter of traditional music during her early years in Cambridge, Massachusetts. However, her greatest commercial success was achieved in the seventies with "The Night They Drove Old Dixie Down" and "Diamonds and Rust," a biographical song about her relationship with Bob Dylan. She is still considered a top international concert attraction and she continues to donate much of her time and money to social and political causes.

LILLIAN BAILEY: A member of the early circle of folk-music enthusiasts, which included Susan Rotolo and Bob Dylan.

PAULA BALLAN: A musician and folk-event organizer. She was the former program director of the Philadelphia Folk Festival, and she currently books the Nassau Folk Festival.

LOUIE BASS: Mike Porco's brother-in-law. He was a waiter and doorman at Folk City from the early sixties to 1980.

CAROL BELSKY: A songwriter orginally from New York and currently living in Phoenix, Arizona.

LESLIE BERMAN: A singer-songwriter, organizer, and music critic. She has written for the *Village Voice* and *Rolling Stone*. She currently lives in England and has been covering the mine workers' strike. She is a co-author of the Folk Music Resource Book. Leslie co-founded the Folk City Songwriters' Concert Series in 1978.

BERMUDA TRIANGLE: Originally a duo in the sixties, Roger and Wendy Becket became a top college attraction when fiddler-drummer Sam joined the group in the early seventies. They have recently split up with Roger and Wendy returning to performing as a duo, and Sam returning to finish college.

KURTIS BLOW: One of the original rappers who has greatly influenced a generation of rap artists. He is currently a popular recording personality.

DAVID BLUE: Actor, songwriter, and musician, the multi-talented Blue was part of the Dylan-Paxton-Ochs-Andersen songwriting clique of the sixties. His song "Outlaw Man" was recorded by the Eagles. He was in Neil Young's film *Human Highway*, Wim Wenders' *An American Friend* and Bob Dylan's *Renaldo and Clara*. His last theatrical performance was in the Canadian production of the *Leonard Cohen Story*. He died in 1982 while jogging around Washington Square Park.

NESYA BLUE: Canadian filmmaker; widow of David Blue.

ANNE BOWEN: A founding member of the all-woman RCA recording group, the Deadly Nightshade. She is currently a producer in New York City.

OSCAR BRAND: Canadian-born singer, songwriter, author, and host of a forty-year-old folk-song radio program on New York's WNYC. His early career was steeped in controversy, he being blacklisted by both the Left and the Right.

ANDY BRECKMAN: Songwriter with a bent towards black humor. Livingston Taylor performs two of his songs. Breckman has appeared on the *David Letterman Show* and *Saturday Night Live*. He was a writer for both shows and is currently writing movies for Warner Brothers. He won an Emmy Award for TV writing in 1981.

MARSHALL BRICKMAN: A member of the folk group the Tarriers, Brickman gave up folk music for comedy writing. As former partner with Woody Allen, he won an Oscar for *Annie Hall*. He now writes and directs his own films.

DAVID BROMBERG: An accomplished musician who has played and recorded with such musicians as George Harrison, Emmylou Harris, and Bob Dylan.

JANE BRUCKER: Actress and comedienne, who established Folk City's Comedy Night. She has appeared in a number of off-Broadway productions and is currently featured on ABC's *One Life to Live*.

PAUL BUTTERFIELD: Blues artist whose band backed Bob Dylan during the controversial electric Newport Folk Festival in 1965.

CHARLIE CHIN: Initially a folk artist, Chin eventually became a part of the popular rock band Cat Mother and the All-Night Newsboys. He was also an owner of the popular Village hangout and bar, Nobody's.

FRANK CHRISTIAN: Guitar virtuoso and songwriter, who combines his mastery of folk, jazz, and blues in a distinctive style which has made him one of the leaders of the current crop of New York singer-songwriters. Nominated for two New York Music Awards in 1985, Christian is currently touring in the U.S. and Europe.

JUDY COLLINS: One of contemporary music's most enduring talents, Collins has incorporated many styles ranging from folk to art song. Her greatest commercial success came with "Both Sides Now" and "Send in the Clowns." She received an Oscar nomination for her documentary *Antonia: A Portrait of the Woman*, a film about the conductor, Antonia Brico, Collins's former teacher. She still records and performs concerts internationally.

BERNADETTE CONTRERAS: Playwright and composer. Her musical, *Sons and Daughters*, is scheduled for a late 1986 Broadway opening.

ELIZABETH (LIBBA) COTTEN: Respected as much for her unique guitar and banjo style as she is for her songwriting, she wrote the classic song "Freight Train" when she was twelve years old. Now over ninety, Libba won a 1985 Grammy Award for best folk album.

BARBARA DANE: Political activist and blues and folk singer who tours extensively, collecting and disseminating "people's songs from liberation struggles throughout the world."

GERRY DEVINE: Former member of the Song Project and the Floor Models, he is currently the leader of the rock band Broken Code.

PAT DINIZIO: Songwriter and frontman of the Capitol-Enigma recording group, the Smithereens. Originally a protégé of Chait, the music-industry mogul, he now produces concerts on his own. He is currently writing a book on Robert DeNiro, as well as a number of screenplays.

ALIX DOBKIN: Performer of traditional folk material during her early career and presently concentrating on writing and performing feminist-lesbian music. She was once married to Sam Hood, who ran the Gaslight cafe.

PEGGY DUNCAN: Belonging to the second of three generations to work at Folk City, she is going into her fifteenth year as bartender at the club.

LIZ ELKIND: Staff member of the Folklore Center and the first doorperson at the Fifth Peg. She now lives in Great Britain.

MARC ELIOT: The author of the Phil Ochs biography, *Death of a Rebel*.

RAMBLIN' JACK ELLIOTT: Once called "the Singing Cowboy from Brooklyn," Elliott was a protégé and friend of Woody Guthrie. He went on to establish his own narrative style, which was a great influence on his own protégé, Bob Dylan. Elliott still tours throughout the country.

LARRY ELLIS: Elizabeth Cotten's grandson.

JOSÉ FELICIANO: Guitar virtuoso and charismatic performer, he began his career at Folk City and the coffeehouses of Greenwich Village. The blind Feliciano won friends and fans alike with his witty patter and first-rate singing and guitar playing. His big commercial success was his recording of the Doors' "Light My Fire." He is currently an international success in the Latin music world.

ELLEN FOLEY: Achieving her initial celebrity as rock-star Meat Loaf's co-vocalist on the bestselling *Bat out of Hell* album, Foley has recorded three albums on her own for Epic Records. She recently appeared as one of the stars of the TV series *Night Court* and is presently performing on the New York cabaret circuit.

STEVE FORBERT: Having released a number of critically acclaimed albums, Forbert's song "Romeo's Tune" was a top-ten hit in 1980. He is now living in Nashville.

RICK FRANK: The leader and drummer of the band Elephant's Memory, which eventually became John Lennon's band. He is currently producing commercials and working with a new band, the Stigalators.

HERB GART: Manager and agent of many top folk acts in the sixties, such as Buffy Ste. Marie, and of folk-rock acts in the seventies, like the Youngbloods. He has also represented the Blues Project, José Feliciano, and Don McLean. He is currently a producer, booking agent, and personal manager.

BOB GIBSON: One of the most influential and well-liked folksingers of the sixties. He is credited with popularizing such performers as Joan Baez and Joni Mitchell. He is considered one of the most prominent twelve-string guitarists. His work with partner Hamilton Camp made him part of one of the top folk duos of the era. He currently runs a folk club in Chicago, where he also produces theatrical shows and performs folk concerts.

ALLEN GINSBERG: Poet and spokesman for the Beat generation. His most popular book of poetry, *Howl*, is considered a classic.

VIRGINIA GIORDANO: Record distributor, theatrical producer and concert producer.

CYNTHIA GOODING: Singer of international folk songs, Gooding was one of the leading female folk singers during the fifties and early sixties. She produced a radio program on New York's WBAI which introduced many singers, such as Bob Dylan, to the listening audience.

WAVY GRAVY: Poet and Beat personality who made the successful transition to poet and hippie personality.

ARLO GUTHRIE: Son of Woody Guthrie, Arlo is best known for his humorous epic "Alice's Restaurant" and his recording of Steve Goodman's classic "City of New Orleans." He performs with his band Shenandoah, and makes frequent appearances with Pete Seeger. He has a highly successful touring career and is as popular an act today as he was when he first began.

JOHN HAMMOND, JR.: Long considered one of the most accomplished white blues artists performing the music of the Mississippi Delta, Hammond enjoys a healthy career touring and recording.

JOHN HAMMOND, SR.: As a record producer and director of talent acquisition for many record companies (most notably, Columbia), Hammond has been responsible for the "discovery" of such diverse acts as Bob Dylan, Pete Seeger, Bessie Smith, Count Basie, Billie Holiday, Leonard Cohen, Duke Ellington, Donovan, and Bruce Springsteen. He is now a consultant for CBS Records and producer of Stevie Ray Vaughan. He is the father of blues artist John Hammond, Jr.

EMMYLOU HARRIS: Grammy Award–winning country-folk singer, Harris's initial success came as a backup singer for Gram Parsons and Bob Dylan. She has since maintained a successful solo career as a progressive country-music artist.

JERRY HARRISON: The guitarist and keyboard player for the Talking Heads.

TIM HAUSER: The original member of the Grammy Award–winning group the Manhattan Transfer. During his early Village days he was a member of the Troubadours Three.

RICHIE HAVENS: One of the most popular and individualistic folk performers,

Havens has maintained a strong career in music for over two decades. His unique tunings, rhythms, and frettings have helped to make him one of the most enduring artists to ever come out of the Village. He is an activist for many causes and is constantly appearing in benefits as well as maintaining a heavy touring and recording schedule. He is currently involved with his own record company and his distinctive voice can be recognized in many commercials.

CAROLYN HESTER: Born in Texas, Hester's beauty and delicate voice made her one of the most highly regarded folk singers of the sixties. Once married to Richard Farina, she and Richard are credited with introducing Bob Dylan to John Hammond, Sr. After giving up touring for a while, she has recently returned to performing to sell-out crowds across the country. She has been very active in the success of the popular Kerrville Folk Festival.

MICHAEL HILL: Formerly an editor at the *New York Rocker*, Hill is now working in the A&R department at Warner Brothers Records. He has written music criticism for many publications such as the *Village Voice* and *Rolling Stone*. He was the co-originator of Folk City's highly successful Music for Dozens series.

STEPHEN HOLDEN: Writer for the *New York Times*, former RCA A&R man, and author of the novel *Triple Platinum*.

JOHN LEE HOOKER: One of America's living blues legends, Hooker currently tours with his band.

DORENE INTERNICOLA: Journalist with the Reuters News Agency and freelance writer specializing in the arts.

TOM INTONDI: Leader of the Song Project, a harmony-oriented singing group which serves as a live song sampler performing material by Greenwich Village songwriters.

JAKE JACOBS: Member of the popular duo Bunky and Jake, and member of the rock group the Magicians. he currently performs with his band Jake and the Family Jewels, and as a solo.

JAM MASTER JAY: The DJ member of the popular rap-rock band Run-D.M.C.

BILLY JOEL: New York–bred pop superstar.

DAVID JOHANSEN: Frontman of the seminal New York glitter-rock band the New York Dolls. Johansen presently performs three different acts: The Poet's Cafe, a musical-in-progress about the early Village Beat scene; Buster Poindexter, a rock lounge act; and David Johansen, a hard driving rock band. He was nominated in an unprecedented twelve categories in the 1985 New York Music Awards.

DANNY KALB: Original member of the Blues Project and highly regarded blues guitarist, Kalb is presently touring with a new version of the Blues Project and with his own band.

IRA KAPLAN: Formerly a writer with the *New York Rocker*, Kaplan now writes freelance on music subjects for such publications as the *Village Voice*. He was the co-founder of Folk City's Music for Dozens series and now performs with his Hoboken-based band Yolotengo.

LENNY KAYE: Producer, songwriter, journalist, guitarist, and performer, Kaye was a member of the Patti Smith Group. He currently fronts his own band, the Lenny Kaye Connection. He was the co-producer of Suzanne Vega's highly acclaimed debut album, and he has produced five anthologies for Elektra Records.

FRED KIRBY: The former "new acts" reviewer for *Variety*, he now covers legal stories for that publication.

BARRY KORNFELD: Folksinger and musician during the sixties, who, for a while, had a publishing partnership with Paul Simon. He is now the treasurer of Musicians' Union Local 802.

MARILYN LASH: Co-owner and booking manager of Folk City. She is also on the Board of Directors of the New York Music Awards.

HAROLD LEVENTHAL: Manager of the Weavers, Woody Guthrie, Cisco Houston, and Judy Collins. He now produces concerts and manages such acts as Pete Seeger and Arlo Guthrie.

BUZZY LINHART: Composer of Bette Midler's signature song "Friends," as well as songs recorded by Carly Simon and others. He is currently touring as a solo act.

PHYLLIS LYND: International folk singer with a background in classical music.

ED McCURDY: Best known for his composition "Last Night I Had the Strangest Dream," McCurdy was a popular figure in the fifties and sixties on the folk music scene. He is currently living in Nova Scotia, where he performs.

BROWNIE McGHEE: The guitarist half of the legendary blues duo Sonny Terry and Brownie McGhee. Since the breakup of the duo, McGhee performs with his own band.

ROGER McGUINN: Beginning his professional career with the Limeliters, McGuinn later joined the Chad Mitchell Trio and toured and recorded with Bobby Darin.

His greatest contribution was as writer, lead singer, and guitarist for the Byrds. He now enjoys a very successful solo career.

ELLEN McILWAINE: Regarded as one of the top female guitarists, McIlwaine's latest album, *Everybody Needs It*, was selected as Best Rock Album of the Year by the prestigious National Association of Independent Record Distributors.

TOMMY MAKEM: Best known for his work with the Clancy Brothers, Makem also pursued an acting career as well as a solo music career. He currently owns the Irish Pavilion, an Irish music club and restaurant in New York City, where he often plays. He recently joined the Clancy Brothers for a reunion tour.

STEVE MANDELL: Guitarist-banjoist who performed on his own and with bands, as a recording artist (on "Dueling Banjos"), and as a backup guitarist for Judy Collins.

MICHAEL MANN: Singer-songwriter and accomplished guitarist who was part of the early Village scene. During his more lucid moments he still retains his musical mastery. He has become a symbol to many of how capricious life can be.

VINCE MARTIN: Singer-songwriter who recorded the 1959 number-one song, "Cindy, Oh Cindy." He performed in the Village for many years where his peers and playing partners included Fred Neil, John Sebastian, Joni Mitchell, and Mary Travers. He now sells real estate in Brooklyn.

RANDY MASTRONICOLA: Village-born and -bred fiction writer.

FRANK MAYA: Originator of Folk City's Wednesday Night rock series, actor, songwriter, and performer. He is one of the leading personalities of the East Village art and music scene.

IRA MAYER: Music journalist who has written for the *Village Voice*, *Record World*, and currently for the *New York Post*.

MATT MOLLOY: Member of the popular Irish band Da Danann.

ROLAND MOUSAA: American Indian singer-songwriter whose song "Indian Prayer" was recorded by Richie Havens. Mousaa ran a coffeehouse in the Village in the seventies which showcased such acts as the Roches and Phoebe Snow in their early careers.

MARIA MULDAUR: Growing up in Greenwich Village, Muldaur went through many musical incarnations, including stints with the Even Dozen Jug Band and the Jim Kweskin Jug Band, and briefly as a teenage rock singer. With husband

Geoff Muldaur, she performed as a duo, and after their marriage broke up, she achieved her greatest success as a solo act. Her commercial high came with the top-ten hit "Midnight at the Oasis." She is currently recording and touring with her band.

TRACY NELSON: Lead vocalist of the country-blues rock band Mother Earth. Her composition "Down So Low" is regarded as one of the all-time greats, and her vocal style is considered to be one of the most impressive in contemporary music.

RALF NEMEC: Former Folk City employee.

BOBBY NEWMAN: Arriving in Greenwich village as a young teenage runaway, Newman became heavily involved in the music and drug scene. She waitressed in many village clubs and became friends with such diverse acts as the Clancy Brothers, Fred Neil, and Tim Hardin.

WENDY NEWTON: The owner of the Irish music label, Green Linnet Records.

WILLIE NILE: Formerly an Arista recording artist, Nile is currently regrouping after years of legal battles and management disputes.

MICHAEL OCHS: Brother of folksinger Phil Ochs, he is a photo archivist and author of the book *Rock Archives*.

SONNY OCHS: Phil Ochs's sister and a radio personality on New Jersey's WFMU. She teaches public school in Queens, New York, and gives private guitar lessons. She is a hootenanny MC at Folk City.

ODETTA: Singer, actress, guitarist, songwriter, recording artist, voice teacher, and performer, Odetta is an accomplished artist in many fields. Her unique style of folk, classical, blues, and jazz has influenced many generations of performers. She is still a popular concert attraction, decades after her start as a performer.

TOM PACHECO: Member of a number of groups including the Ragamuffins, Euphoria (with Roger and Wendy Becket of the Bermuda Triangle), and a duo with Sharon Alexander. The Jefferson Starship recorded one of his songs, and he is still recording and performing with his band.

TOM PASLE: Folk singer and author of books for children.

TOM PAXTON: One of the leading acts on the folk-music circuit. A gifted song-writer whose best-known compositions include "The Last Thing on my Mind," "I Can't Help But Wonder Where I'm Bound," and "Ramblin' Boy." His topical material has given him credibility in political circles and he is often performing benefits for worthwhile causes.

ALLAN PEPPER: Once the booking manager for Folk City, Pepper is now the co-owner of the New York showcase cabaret, the Bottom Line.

JOHN PHILLIPS: Best known as the leader of the Mamas and the Papas, Phillips is the writer of such folk-rock classics as "Monday Monday" and "California Dreamin'." His song "Creeque Alley" is an autobiographical history of the folk-rock era. Phillips is now touring with a reorganized Mamas and Papas which includes his daughter, actress MacKenzie Phillips, and original Papa Denny Doherty.

POEZ: Poet, street performer, performance artist and former Folk City hoot MC.

MIKE PORCO: The former owner of Gerdes Folk City, now retired and living in Florida.

EARL PRICE: A past vice-president of CBS Records.

JOEY RAMONE: Member of the seminal New York punk-rock band, the Ramones.

JEAN RITCHIE: Leading performer, writer, and collector of Appalachian music. Her virtuosity on the dulcimer helped popularize that indigenous American folk instrument. She still performs concerts throughout the country.

THE ROCHES: Terre, Maggie, and Suzzy are three sisters whose precise harmonies and offbeat personalities have attracted a cult following throughout the country. They have recorded four albums for Warner Brothers, the first of which landed on the top-ten list of many critics and was selected as Album of the Year by the *New York Times.* Former waitresses and bartenders at Folk City, they have included their own memories of the club in their latest song "Face Down at Folk City."

ROSIE: A hoot MC during the late seventies, Rosie currently appears in New York cabarets performing her eccentric act comprised of songs and poetry. She is best remembered for her hoot antics which included off-color remarks, malapropisms, and a true desire to help up-and-coming performers. She was the MC of the kick-off party for Bob Dylan's Rolling Thunder Tour which was held at Folk City in 1975.

ROBERT ROSS: Blues singer, guitarist, and songwriter who performs solo and with a band. His song "White Boy Lost in the Blues" was recorded by Johnny Winter. Ross was originally recorded by Victoria Spivey on her Spivey label.

CHARLES ROTHSCHILD: One of the original booking managers of Folk City. He later worked for Albert Grossman and became a concert producer. He is now a manager and agent for Judy Collins, the Clancy Brothers, and Allen Ginsberg.

SUSAN ROTOLO: Best known in the sixties as Bob Dylan's girlfriend and inspiration, she became a symbol of a generation after appearing on Dylan's *Freewheelin'* album cover. She is presently a successful illustrator and is raising a family with her husband in New York City.

BUFFY STE. MARIE: One of the most popular folk stars of the sixties, she was distinguished by a varied writing style and distinctive vibrato. Her song "Until It's Time for You to Go" has become an international classic recorded by countless artists. She recently won an Oscar for "Up Where We Belong," a song she wrote with her husband Jack Nitzsche. She was featured for years on "Sesame Street" and has long been an activist for Indian rights.

LYNN SAMUELS: Popular New York City radio personality whose programs on WBAI introduced many new artists, such as Suzanne Vega, to the public. She is also a former Folk City hoot MC.

FRED SCHNEIDER: Leader and songwriter of the popular rock band, the B-52s.

JOHN SEBASTIAN: In his early Village days, Sebastian played backup harp for many of the more established performers. He eventually formed the Lovin' Spoonful for which he wrote many hits including "Do You Believe in Magic?" "Daydream," "Summer in the City," "Darlin' Be Home Soon," and "Nashville Cats." Sebastian began a solo career after the Spoonful broke up, and scored on his own with the TV theme for *Welcome Back Kotter*. He now performs as a solo act.

PETE SEEGER: A former member of the Almanac Singers and the Weavers, Seeger is considered the greatest driving force in American folk music. He is still politically active and supports social, environmental, and political issues, in addition to encouraging young artists. He was blacklisted for many years, but still remained a popular figure. He now runs the Clearwater, the sloop that has become a symbol for environmental issues, specifically the cleaning up of the Hudson River.

ROBERT SHELTON: Music writer for the *New York Times* who was credited with the popularization of the sixties folk-music scene and the "discovery" of artists like Bob Dylan and Eric Andersen. He left the *Times* to move to England where he is now finishing his long-awaited book on Bob Dylan.

BARBARA SHUTNER: Wife of Logan English, one of the most popular folk singers of the late fifties and early sixties. English performed traditional folk songs and was considered "the fifth Clancy Brother." According to Shutner, they introduced Bob Dylan to Folk City while Logan was one of the club's original MCs and Barbara was working for NBC.

JANIS SIEGEL: A member of the Grammy-winning vocal group, the Manhattan Transfer. During her early Village days, she performed in the folk group Laurel Canyon.

IRWIN SILBER: Political activist, writer, and editor of *Sing Out!* magazine from 1951 to 1967. He co-founded Oak Publications, a publishing company devoted to folk-music themes. He was also the editor of the radical *Guardian.*

CARLY SIMON: Her music career started in a duo with her sister Lucy, as the Simon Sisters. After their break-up, Carly went on to become one of pop music's top female singer-songwriters.

LUCY SIMON: The other half of the Simon Sisters, she is now writing the music for a Broadway show.

PENNY SIMON: Along with her husband, Ed, she ran a number of coffeehouses and clubs during the heyday of the folk-music boom in the Village. Among her clubs were the Four Winds and the extremely popular Gaslight.

PAT SKY: Popular folk instrumentalist and singer-songwriter. His album *Songs That Made America Famous* is considered by many to be a folk classic. He retired for a while to concentrate on building Irish Uillean pipes, but he recently returned to touring. Sky and his former girlfriend, Buffy Ste. Marie, were at the center of the folk music boom.

LARRY SLOMAN: Author of *On the Road with Bob Dylan* and editor of the *National Lampoon.*

BETTY SMYTH: Manager of many coffeehouses during the sixties and seventies. Her daughter, Patty, fronts the rock band, Scandal. Betty currently operates a fur shop on Long Island.

PATTY SMYTH: "The Warrior" was a recent top-ten hit for her band Scandal. She and her husband, rock performer Richard Hell, recently had their first child.

STANLEY SNADOWSKY: Co-owner of New York's the Bottom Line. Former co-booking manager of Folk City in the early seventies.

PHOEBE SNOW: After encountering sudden fame with her modestly produced first album and single, "Poetry Man," Snow had a strong career as one of popular music's most captivating vocalists and songwriters until she stepped aside to care for her handicapped daughter. She has recently returned to recording and touring.

JACOB SOLOMON: A controversial figure on the Village scene in the sixties and seventies, he worked as an agent and manager. Although he had a good ear for new talent, some people felt he couldn't get his artists past the initial discovery stage. "Magic Jack" at one time managed Richie Havens, Tom Pacheco, Lisa Kindred, Hoyt Axton, and Van Morrison. He is credited with orchestrating Janis Ian's success with "Society's Child." He is currently working on "a few secret projects."

LINDA SOLOMON: As a writer for the *Village Voice* and the *Soho News*, and as Robert Shelton's companion, Solomon was a regular on the Greenwich Village scene. She still writes about music for a number of publications.

PETER STAMPFEL: Fiddle-playing leader of the group Peter Stampfel and the Bottlecaps. He is best known as a founding member of the offbeat Holy Modal Rounders. His greatest commercial success came with his scoring part of the soundtrack for *Easy Rider*. He also writes for a number of publications on music topics.

JOHN STEWART: A member of the Cumberland Three and the Kingston Trio. He wrote the hit "Daydream Believer" for the Monkees, and most recently had a hit with his own recording of "Gold." He runs his own record company and is currently touring and recording.

GEOFFREY STOKES: Author and writer for the *Village Voice*.

TERRI THAL: Manager and booking agent for a number of artists from the early sixties through the seventies. With her former husband, Dave Van Ronk, she was considered one of the folk elite. She was involved with the early careers of Van Ronk, Bob Dylan, Tom Paxton, the Holy Modal Rounders, and the Roches. Still a very outspoken and politically oriented woman, Thal now lives and works in upstate New York.

LIBBY TITUS: Singer-songwriter who is best known for her classic composition "Love Has No Pride," which she wrote with Eric Kaz. Her songs have been recorded by Linda Ronstadt, Bonnie Raitt, and Carly Simon. She was married to Band member Levon Helm, and was part of the group's clique during the height of its success. She has since collaborated with Burt Bacharach and Dr. John. She is currently appearing in the Mike Nichol's film *Heartburn*.

PETER TORK: Member of the television and recording sensation, the Monkees. He now performs as a solo folk act in New York City.

HAPPY TRAUM: A member of the New World Singers, a group popular in the sixties, he now performs on his own and with his brother, Artie.

MARY TRAVERS: As a member of Peter, Paul, and Mary, she still travels extensively with one of the most popular folk groups of our time. Travers also continues her career as a solo artist. She was raised in Greenwich Village and spent many years waitressing in Village clubs, before she was asked to join the trio that Albert Grossman was putting together with Peter Yarrow.

DAVE VAN RONK: Once considered for the Peter, Paul, and Mary trio, before it was actually cast, Van Ronk has been a major force on the contemporary folk scene. His blend of blues, jazz, and folk, combined with his mastery of guitar has made him a distinctive stylist. With his gravelly voice, he has been the first interpreter of many contemporary artists like Joni Mitchell and Bob Dylan.

SUZANNE VEGA: The critically acclaimed singer-songwriter whose debut album broke into the *Billboard* top-one-hundred only a few months after its release, Vega has become a popular concert attraction in both the United States and Euorpe. Her delicate imagery and confessional songwriting style have made her both a critics' favorite and a popular act with both folk and rock fans. Her cool image, striking looks, and haunting songs have made her the acoustic star of the eighties.

THE VIOLENT FEMMES: Victor DeLorenzo, Gordon Gano, and Brian Ritchie form one of the most popular acoustic-oriented rock bands of the time. This new-wave band from Milwaukee records for Warner Brothers and is considered a top college attraction in an era when the college radio stations are the deciding force in a rock band's popularity. Their most recent record was produced by Jerry Harrison of the Talking Heads.

LOUDON WAINWRIGHT: One of the major acts to be signed out of the Village in the seventies. His plaintive, bittersweet songs attracted a large cult audience, and his song "Dead Skunk in the Middle of the Road" was a commercial success. Wainwright also embarked on an acting career which included a stint on TV's *M*A*S*H*. He was married to singer Kate McGarrigle, who along with her sister Anna, recorded a few of his songs.

SAMMY WALKER: Phil Ochs's protégé, and an accomplished singer-songwriter who has recorded for Folkways and Warner Brothers Records.

JIM WANN: Creator and star of the Tony-nominated Broadway hit *Pump Boys and Dinettes*.

ILENE WEISS: Singer-songwriter from Philadelphia whose songs have been recorded by Robin Flower, the Song Project, and Deidre McCalla. Her song "This Part of the World" was nominated as Best Song for the 1985 New York Music Awards. She is an extremely popular performer on the current Village music scene.

ERIC WEISSBERG: The highly respected instrumentalist who was a former member of the Greenbriar Boys. He is probably best known for his performance on "Dueling Banjos." He currently records as a sideman for many top artists.

HEDY WEST: Southern traditional folk singer, musicologist, banjoist, and guitarist. She wrote the classic folk song "Five Hundred Miles."

WENDY WINSTED: A booking agent during the seventies, Winsted is now completing her medical internship.

JIM WYNBRANDT: With his brother, Tom, Jim co-produced the Wednesday Night rock series at Folk City. Initiating a series of similar events, the Wynbrandts produced the first rock and folk benefit for New York City's homeless at CBGB's. Jim is now writing a book about the rock band U-2.

DOUG YEAGER: Agent and producer based in New York. His clients include Ramblin' Jack Elliott, Eric Andersen, and Tom Paxton.

PETER YARROW: As a member of Peter, Paul, and Mary, Yarrow enjoys a hectic, successful touring schedule. He also remains active as a solo artist and is constantly involved in political and social issues, speaking for causes and donating his time for benefits. He has written many songs, including "Puff the Magic Dragon," and "Torn Between Two Lovers."

IZZY YOUNG: Founder of the Folklore Center and the Fifth Peg. He is also a concert producer and folklorist. He currently runs the Folklore Center in Stockholm, Sweden.

JESSE COLIN YOUNG: First performing as a solo, Young soon formed the band the Youngbloods, which was considered to be in the vanguard of the folk-rock movement. Their song "Let's Get Together" became a hippie anthem in the sixties. He is currently performing with a regrouped Youngbloods and as a solo.

SUSIE YOUNG: Jesse Colin Young's wife, who was also a part of the folk-rock scene in the late sixties.

ABOUT THE AUTHOR

Robbie Woliver is the co-owner of Gerdes Folk City. He is also a journalist who has published widely in such periodicals as *Rolling Stone*, the *Village Voice*, and *Newsday*, and has taught writing at SUNY. He lives in Manhattan's Greenwich Village.

FOLK CITY
PERFORMER ROSTER
1960-1985

ALIVE! ★ MOSE ALLISON ★ DAVE ALVIN ★ PHIL ALVIN ★ AMERICAN STEEL ★ ERIC ANDERSEN ★ CASEY ANDERSON ★ LILI ANEL ★ PEGGY ATWOOD ★ HOYT AXTON ★ AZTEC TWO-STEP ★ JOAN BAEZ ★ MAUREEN BARRETT ★ BATTLEFIELD BAND ★ BEAT RODEO ★ BEERS FAMILY ★ JIM BELUSHI ★ STEVE BEN-ISRAEL ★ PAT BENATAR ★ GAIL BENSON ★ BERMUDA TRIANGLE ★ JAMIE BERNSTEIN ★ THEODORE BIKEL ★ TONY BIRD ★ STEPHEN BISHOP ★ OTIS BLACKWELL ★ RONEE BLAKLEY ★ SCOTT BLAKEMAN ★ DAVID BLUE ★ ED BLUESTONE ★ ERIC BOGLE ★ ERIC BOGOSIAN ★ MARK BOONE, JR. ★ BOYS OF THE LOUGH ★ OSCAR BRAND ★ ANDY BRECKMAN ★ SHARON BRESLAU ★ MARSHALL BRICKMAN ★ JAIME BROCKETT ★ DAVID BROMBERG ★ STANKY BROWN ★ JANE BRUCKER ★ SANDY BULL ★ CINDY BULLENS ★ KAREN BUNIN ★ BUNKY & JAKE ★ T-BONE BURNETT ★ RANDY BURNS ★ STEVE BUSCEMI ★ BUSKIN & BATTEAU ★ CHRIS BUTLER ★ PAUL BUTTERFIELD ★ JOE CAMPIOLO ★ TOM CARROZZA ★ MARTIN CARTHY ★ JOHNNY CASH ★ CASSELBERRY & DUPREE ★ JUDY CASTELLI ★ CELTIC THUNDER ★ LEN CHANDLER ★ HARRY CHAPIN ★ TOM CHAPIN ★ BLONDIE CHAPLIN ★ VALERIE CHARLES ★ DOMINICK CHIANESE ★ CHICAGO CITY LIMITS ★ CHARLIE CHIN ★ *CHORDS OF FAME* ★ FRANK CHRISTIAN ★ MEG CHRISTIAN ★ *CIRCLE OF FRIENDS* ★ TOMMY MAKEM & THE CLANCY BROTHERS ★ PAUL CLAYTON ★ MYRON COHEN ★ JUDY COLLINS ★ KENTUCKY COLONELS ★ SHAWN COLVIN ★ BERNADETTE CONTRERAS ★ ERNIE CONTRI ★ MICHAEL COONEY ★ LARRY CORYELL ★ ELVIS COSTELLO ★ ELIZABETH COTTEN ★ RHONDA COULLET ★ MARSHALL CRENSHAW ★ DAVID CROSBY ★ DAN DALEY ★ BARBARA DANE ★ RINK DANKO ★ RON DARIAN ★ ERIK DARLING ★ GUY DAVIS ★ MICHAEL DAVIS ★ REV. GARY DAVIS ★ JIM DAWSON ★ DEADLY NIGHTSHADE ★ RICH DEANS ★ DEL-LORDS ★ DEL FUEGOS ★ JOHN DENVER ★ GERRY DEVINE ★ THE DILLARDS ★ ALIX DOBKIN ★ BONNIE DOBSON ★ DREAM SYNDICATE ★ JUDY DUNLEVAY ★ BOB DYLAN ★ SALLY EATON ★ JIM EAVES ★ CLIFF EBERHARDT ★ THERESE EDELL ★ JONATHAN EDWARDS ★ ELEPHANT'S MEMORY ★ RON ELLIRON ★ CASS ELLIOT ★ RAMBLIN' JACK ELLIOTT ★ LOGAN ENGLISH ★ ESQUERITA ★ JOHN FAHEY ★ BILLY FAIER ★ MIMI FARINA ★ RICHARD FARINA ★ RACHEL FARO ★ JOSE FELICIANO ★ FERRON ★ FIONA ★ GREGORY FLEEMAN ★ HUGO FLESCH ★ THE FLESHTONES ★ THE FLOOR MODELS ★ ELLEN FOLEY ★ STEVE FORBERT ★ MICHAEL FRACASSO ★ ERIK FRANDSEN ★ DEAN FRIEDMAN ★ KINKY FRIEDMAN ★ JESSE FULLER ★ MAX GAIL ★ GALE GARNETT ★ TERRY GARTHWAITE ★ JIMMY GAVIN ★ GEORGE GERDES ★ PAUL GEREMIA ★ TOM GHENT ★ BOB GIBSON ★ STEVE GILLETTE ★ MARY ELLEN GILLESPIE ★ ALLEN GINSBERG ★ JEFF GOLD ★ LYNN GOLD ★ ANNIE GOLDEN ★ CYNTHIA GOODING ★ STEVE GOODMAN ★ JUDY GORMAN-JACOBS ★ KAREN LYNN GORNEY ★ LOU GOSSETT, JR. ★ BEVERLY GRANT & THE HUMAN CONDITION ★ NICK GRAVENITES ★ GREENBRIAR BOYS ★ NANCI GRIFFITH ★ DAVE GRISMAN ★ HENRY GROSS ★ MARJORIE GROSS ★ STEFAN GROSSMAN ★ ARLO GUTHRIE ★ JOHN HAMMOND ★ THE HARMONIC CHOIR ★ TIM HARDIN ★ JACK HARDY ★ THE HARP BAND ★ EMMYLOU HARRIS ★ JOHN HARTFORD ★ RICHIE HAVENS ★ ALAN HAVEY ★ BOBBIE LOUISE HAWKINS ★ SCREAMIN' JAY HAWKINS ★ RICHARD HELL ★ LEVON HELM ★ JIMI HENDRIX ★ CAROLYN HESTER ★ DAN HICKS ★ MARTHA P. HOGAN ★ LORETTA HOLLAND ★ JAKE HOLMES ★ PETER HOLSAPPLE ★ LUCY HOLSTEDT ★ HOLY MODAL ROUNDERS ★ HELEN HOOKE ★ JOHN LEE HOOKER ★ BOB HORAN ★ CISCO HOUSTON ★ MICHAEL HURLEY ★ MISSISSIPPI JOHN HURT ★ HUSKER DU ★ JANIS IAN ★ QUEEN IDA ★ TOM INTONDI ★ THE IRISH RAMBLERS ★ THE IRISH TRADITION ★ *THE JAZZ SINGER* ★ JIM & JEAN ★ GARLAND JEFFREYS ★ JOHN JESURUN ★ DAVID JOHANSEN ★ DR. JOHN ★ LONNIE JOHNSON ★ MARK JOHNSON

★ BILLY JONES ★ ELVIN JONES ★ JANIS JOPLIN ★ THE JOURNEYMEN ★ CITIZEN KAFKA ★ DANNY KALB ★ GABRIEL KAPLAN ★ LUCY KAPLANSKI ★ ANN KASHICKEY ★ ANDY KAUFMAN ★ RYO KAWASAKI & ALANA ★ LENNY KAYE ★ ERIC KAZ ★ DOLORES KEANE ★ BARBARA KEITH ★ LIONEL KILBERG ★ LISA KINDRED ★ CHARLIE KING ★ BRUCE KIRKMAN ★ ROBERT KLEIN ★ THE KNITTERS ★ SPIDER JOHN KOERNER ★ AL KOOPER ★ BARRY KORNFELD ★ JOSIE KUHN ★ PETER LA FARGE ★ DAVID LANDERS ★ BRUCE LANGHORNE ★ THE LAST ROUNDUP ★ CHRISTINE LAVIN ★ CAROL LEIFER ★ MICHAEL LESSER ★ LET'S ACTIVE ★ RICHARD LEWIS ★ BOB LIND ★ BUZZY LINHART ★ THE LITTLE SISTERS ★ RICHARD LLOYD ★ PAULA LOCKHEART ★ DAVE LOGGINS ★ LOUISIANA RED ★ LUCINDA ★ JOHN LURIE ★ PHYLLIS LYND ★ JOHN MacANDOE ★ EWAN MacCOLL ★ COUNTRY JOE MacDONALD ★ ROD MacDONALD ★ RAUN MacKINNON ★ ANN MAGNUSON ★ TAJ MAHAL ★ MELISSA MAN-CHESTER ★ STEVE MANDELL ★ MANHATTAN TRANSFER ★ RICHARD MANUEL ★ DIANA MARCOVITZ ★ BUFFY STE. MARIE ★ DAVE MARRASH ★ VINCE MARTIN ★ PAT MARTINO ★ CAROLYN MAS ★ DAVID MASSENGILL ★ FRANK MAYA ★ DEIDRE McCALLA ★ DANNY McCARTHY ★ MARY McCASLIN ★ HUGH McCRACKEN ★ ED McCURDY ★ GENE McDANIELS ★ MISSISSIPPI FRED McDOWELL ★ THE McGARRIGLES ★ ROGER McGUINN ★ ELLEN McILWAINE ★ SCOTT McKENZIE ★ ROD McKUEN ★ DAISANN McLAINE ★ BILL McLAUGHLIN ★ JACQUI McSHEE ★ VAUGHN MEADER ★ MELANIE ★ JAN MELCHIOR ★ LYNN MESSINGER ★ BEVERLY MICKENS ★ MICROSCOPIC SEPTET ★ BETTE MIDLER ★ JUNE & JEAN MILLINGTON ★ THE MINUTEMEN ★ MIRABAI ★ JONI MITCHELL ★ ESRA MOHAWK ★ ELISE MORRIS ★ JIM MORRIS ★ MT. AIRY ★ ROLAND MOUSAA ★ GEOFF MULDAUR ★ MARIA MULDAUR ★ MARTIN MULL ★ ELLIOT MURPHY ★ PHIL NEE ★ FRED NEIL ★ BOB NELSON ★ TRACY NELSON ★ BOB NEUWIRTH ★ NEW LOST CITY RAMBLERS ★ NEW WORLD SINGERS ★ WILLIE NILE ★ WILLIE NININGER ★ BILLY NOVICK ★ NRBQ ★ DANNY O'KEEFE ★ PHIL OCHS ★ SONNY OCHS ★ EARL OKIN ★ ODETTA ★ ONE TRICK PONY ★ OREGON ★ SUSAN OSBORN ★ TOM PACHECO ★ ROBERT PALMER ★ FELIX PAPPILARDI ★ TOM PASLE ★ TOM PALEY ★ JACO PASTORIOUS ★ TOM PAXTON ★ PETER, PAUL & MARY ★ JOHN PHILLIPS ★ UTAH PHILLIPS ★ PIANOSAURUS ★ JOE PISCOPO ★ MARY KAY PLACE ★ POEZ ★ JIM POST ★ HUGH PRESTWOOD ★ PUMP BOYS AND DINETTES ★ QUICKSILVER MESSENGER SERVICE ★ WILL RAMBEAUX ★ VICKY RANDLE ★ JEAN REDPATH ★ RENALDO & CLARA ★ JOHN RENBOURN ★ THE REPLACEMENTS ★ JIM RINGER ★ JEAN RITCHIE ★ GIL ROBBINS ★ EARL ROBINSON ★ DAVID ROCHE ★ THE ROCHES ★ JUDY RODERICK ★ JIMMIE RODGERS ★ GAMBLE ROGERS ★ STAN ROGERS ★ ROLLING THUNDER REVUE ★ LINDA RONSTADT ★ BIFF ROSE ★ MICHELE ROSEWOMAN ★ ROSIE ★ DICK ROSMINI ★ ROBERT ROSS ★ CHRIS RUSH ★ TOM RUSH ★ PATTY SCALFA ★ CLAUDIA SCHMIDT ★ JOHN SEBASTIAN ★ SECOND CHANCE ★ MIKE SEEGER ★ PEGGY SEEGER ★ PETE SEEGER ★ BROTHER JOHN SELLARS ★ MIKE SETTLE ★ NANCY SHAYNE ★ ANITA SHEER ★ SAM SHEPARD ★ RONDELL SHERIDAN ★ SUSAN SCHNEIDER ★ TRAVIS SHOOK ★ PAUL SEIBEL ★ JANIS SEIGEL ★ SILLY WIZARD ★ SHEL SILVERSTEIN ★ SIMON & GARFUNKEL ★ CARLY SIMON ★ LUCY SIMON ★ PAT SKY ★ LARRY SLOMAN ★ CARRIE SMITH ★ MARGARET SMITH ★ ORRIAL SMITH ★ PATTI SMITH ★ CHRIS SMITHER ★ THE SMITHEREENS ★ PATTY SMYTH ★ PHOEBE SNOW ★ BERT SOMMERS ★ THE SONG PROJECT ★ ROSALIE SORRELS ★ PETER SPENCER ★ DAVID SPINOZZA ★ VICTORIA SPIVEY ★ MARK SPOELSTRA ★ SALLY SPRING ★ ROGER SPRUNG ★ CHRIS STAMEY ★ PETER STAMPFEL ★ THE STAPLE SINGERS ★ STEELY DAN ★ B.W. STEVENSON ★ STEPHEN STILLS ★ ROB STONER ★ STORIES ★ SYD STRAW ★ STREET THE BEAT ★ MAXINE SULLIVAN ★ PIERRE BEN SUSAN ★ KEITH SYKES ★ ROOSEVELT SYKES ★ SYLVAIN SYLVAIN ★ IAN & SYLVIA ★ NORMA TANEGA ★ THE TARRIERS ★ CECIL TAYLOR ★ LIVINGSTON TAYLOR ★ THE 10,000 MANIACS ★ SONNY TERRY & BROWNIE McGHEE ★ TETES NOIRES ★ RICHARD THOMPSON ★ BIG MAMA THORNTON ★ THE 3 O'CLOCK ★ DAVID VAN TIEGHEM ★ LINDA TILLERY ★ LIBBY TITUS ★ PETER TORK ★ TOUCHSTONE ★ HAPPY & ARTIE TRAUM ★ GREG TROOPER ★ TAD TRUESDALE ★ TERESA TRULL ★ BIG JOE TURNER ★ GIL TURNER ★ DINO VALENTI ★ GUY VAN DUSER ★ DAVE VAN RONK ★ TOWNES VAN ZANDT ★ BEN VAUGHN COMBO ★ SUZANNE VEGA ★ THE VIOLENT FEMMES ★ VINCENT T. VOK ★ LOUDON WAINWRIGHT ★ FRANK WAKEFIELD ★ ANN WALDMAN ★ JERRY JEFF WALKER ★ JIMMY "J.J." WALKER ★ SAMMY WALKER ★ THE WANDERERS ★ JACKIE WASHINGTON ★ THE WASHINGTON SQUARES ★ MUDDY WATERS ★ THE WATERSONS ★ DOC WATSON ★ CARL WAXMAN ★ THE WEAVERS ★ ILENE WEISS ★ ERIC WEISSBERG ★ DICK WEISSMAN ★ HEDY WEST ★ HELEN WHEELS ★ BEVERLY WHITE ★ GARY WHITE ★ JOSH WHITE ★ JOSH WHITE, JR. ★ MAJOR WILEY ★ BIG JOE WILLIAMS ★ ROBIN WILLIAMS ★ ROBIN WILLIAMSON ★ JESSE WINCHESTER ★ PETER WOLF ★ JOHN DOE & EXENE OF X ★ THE YOUNGBLOODS ★ JOHN ZORN ★

INDEX

Italicized page numbers indicate interviews; **boldface** page numbers indicate photographs.